SAP® Service and Support

SAP PRESS is issued by
Bernhard Hochlehnert, SAP AG

SAP PRESS is a joint initiative of SAP and Galileo Press. The know-how offered by SAP specialists combined with the expertise of the publishing house Galileo Press offers the reader expert books in the field. SAP PRESS features first-hand information and expert advice, and provides useful skills for professional decision-making.

SAP PRESS offers a variety of books on technical and business related topics for the SAP user. For further information, please visit our website: *www.sap-press.com*.

Marc O. Schäfer, Matthias Melich
SAP Solution Manager
2006, approx. 500 pp., ISBN 1–59229–091–4

Forndron, Liebermann, Thurner, Widmayer
mySAP ERP Roadmap
Business Processes, Capabilities, and Complete Upgrade Strategy
2006, 293 pp., ISBN 1–59229–071-X

Sabine Schöler, Liane Will
SAP IT Service & Application Management
The ITIL Guide for SAP Operations
2006, approx. 96 pp., ISBN 1–59229–094–9

Mario Linkies, Frank Off
SAP Security and Authorizations
2006, approx. 500 pp., ISBN 1–592229–062–0

Gerhard Oswald

SAP® Service and Support

Focusing on Continuous Customer
Satisfaction

 PRESS

Contents

5 Generating Value Through Support 111

6 From Professionals for Professionals—SAP Services in Practice 127

7 SAP Service and Support Infrastructure 213

8 Cost Transparency with SAP TCO Framework   251

A Quick Links for SAP Service Marketplace and the Portals   263

B Glossary   267

C The Publisher   281

D Acknowledgements   283

Index   287

Preface to Third Edition

This book is not just a revised and updated version of the *SAP Service and Support* book; rather, it is a completely new and unique portrayal of SAP's entire service portfolio. With numerous additions dealing with contemporary issues, it provides an excellent overview of the services from the areas of support, consulting, education, custom development, and managed services, and shows how they interact in terms of customer requirements and solution orientation.

Based on the phases in the lifecycle of an SAP solution and on the level of SAP's engagement, the book outlines the entire offering. Individual scenarios reflect the challenges confronting today's businesses—from implementing an SAP solution through operating, optimizing, and upgrading—and furthermore, we show you how your IT projects can be enhanced by SAP's integrated approach spanning all service areas.

This complete view of the portfolio would not have been possible without the efforts of numerous experts from the respective business departments. I would like to take this opportunity to thank them all for their contributions. Their hard work will certainly have been worthwhile if, as we hope, this book inspires you in your daily work to find ways of leveraging SAP solutions in your organization to reduce expenditure and create room for innovation.

Gerhard Oswald
Walldorf, St. Leon-Rot, April 2006

Introduction

In which situation does which SAP service provide optimal support for a customer? This is the question that this book strives to answer. The most suitable time to use a service depends partly on the lifecycle phase of an SAP solution. Company circumstances—size, IT resources and budget, IT-related experience and know-how—also govern which services are appropriate, as do customer requirements, which are dictated by the company's business strategy, and might include whether the customer intends to outsource specific tasks to external service providers.

The purpose of this book is to show you how, by using effective services at the right time, you can leverage IT for your company and meet your business objectives. The book's primary concern lies with strategic considerations and carrying out IT projects, and *not* with providing detailed technical instructions on how a service should be delivered.

The book consists of three main parts:

Book structure

▶ Introductory chapters (Chapters 1 to 3)

▶ A description of the service and support offering both in theory and in practice, including maintenance services, which comprises the heart of the book (Chapters 4 to 6)

▶ Basic details of SAP's service and support infrastructure and TCO Framework, which reduces the total cost of ownership (TCO) for SAP customers (Chapters 7 and 8)

More specifically, the individual chapters deal with the following issues:

Chapter 1 briefly explains how the role of IT in business has changed in recent years, and how this affects CIOs and corporate IT strategies.

Chapter 2 examines SAP's service philosophy and the guidelines SAP follows when developing and delivering services.

SAP's focus is always on the recipients of the services, namely SAP customers. SAP customers are embedded in the SAP Ecosystem, which is presented in **Chapter 3**. Besides customers, SAP and its partners are also part of this community. The SAP Ecosystem allows its members to share their knowledge and exchange information, which ultimately enables the service offering to be improved on an ongoing basis.

Following these introductory sections, **Chapter 4** turns to the heart of the book, SAP's service offering itself. A matrix has been used to structure the information, with one axis showing the three phases in a product's lifecycle, and the other axis showing the five levels of engagement that customers can request from SAP. The service offerings come from the areas of support, consulting, education, managed services, and custom development, including system landscape optimization. This chapter illustrates those situations in which the service packages should be used and how they benefit a company.

For SAP customers, software support is a key element of SAP's service and support offering. **Chapter 5** is therefore dedicated to SAP Standard Support, SAP Premium Support—a new support offering with enhanced services—and SAP MaxAttention. It also describes SAP's maintenance strategy and the three maintenance phases—mainstream, extended, and customer-specific maintenance.

From theory to practice, **Chapter 6** describes different tasks—such as implementing or upgrading an SAP solution—as typically encountered by forward-looking companies today. You may even recognize some of the challenges from your own experience at work. The project descriptions show which services have proven themselves in different situations and how companies can profit from these services. We should also stress that all SAP services are interrelated, regardless of the department in which they were developed.

These customer scenarios provide answers to widespread contemporary questions, such as:

▶ How can we implement, run, and continually optimize our SAP solution efficiently and cost effectively?

▶ How can we consolidate our system landscape, or boost the effectiveness of our support organization?

▶ How can we upgrade smoothly—with minimal downtime and within the available time and budget?

These goals aren't achieved overnight. Careful preparation is required, all those involved must cooperate effectively, and experienced specialists must actively support the entire process. The resulting benefits speak for themselves. As the project descriptions show, the offerings in SAP's service and support portfolio are tailored to the customer's individual requirements and complement one another.

To cooperate optimally, customers, SAP, and their partners need a high-performance service and support infrastructure, which is described in

Chapter 7. With its portals for specific target groups, SAP Service Market-place provides a reliable platform for communication, and together with SAP Solution Manager—SAP's service and support platform—enables the intensive exchange of information and effective collaboration throughout the SAP Ecosystem.

The theoretical descriptions in Chapters 4 and 7 are supplemented by a series of reports from enterprises that have used SAP's service and support offerings, or currently use SAP Solution Manager. In these reports, customers assess how their company has benefited from the services and from SAP's service and support infrastructure. One thing that is made very apparent in the reports, SAP's service and support portfolio does not only exist in theory; customers are actively using the services and products offered.

Chapter 8 introduces the SAP TCO Framework and the way in which SAP helps its customers to minimize the TCO for their software and accelerate return on investment (ROI).

The **Appendices** contain a glossary, which briefly explains the key terms used in the SAP world. They also include a list of quick links, which give you immediate access to the most up-to-date information on service and support-relevant topics regarding SAP Service Marketplace.

Whether you decide to read the book from beginning to end or are interested in only specific chapters, it provides you with useful information and valuable food for thought. You will often draw parallels to your daily working environment and begin to question how the issues described would actually be handled in your own company. How do we deal with that? Couldn't we also make substantial improvements in this area? Couldn't we also reduce our SAP costs by using SAP services? To this end, the book provides you with ideas and suggestions that you can discuss in your company. If you have any further questions, you can contact SAP directly anytime at *support@sap.com*.

1   IT-Powered Business Innovation— The Changing Role of IT

In the future, company success will lie in flexible, innovative business processes. All too often, today's IT is subject to increased complexities and cost constraints. With the Enterprise Services Architecture (ESA), SAP is pointing the way toward an "IT-powered business innovation."

Which companies will be ahead of the pack in the years to come? There is no definitive answer to this question for every industry and market sector, although certain general trends are discernible:

▶ The coming years will see further consolidation transform the competitive arena in many market sectors, much to the advantage of a handful of large players.

▶ Adaptive business strategies and models will increasingly be regarded as critical success factors.

▶ Companies are focusing on innovation velocity and maintaining customer relationships to secure sustainable value and success.

▶ Information technology is regarded more and more as a competitive advantage.

Following several years of intense cost cutting, the demands on business IT are now phenomenal. The business strategy calls for consolidation— better business processes and optimized IT—while IT demands that systems be able to adapt flexibly and quickly, and are capable of integrating other companies at short notice, for instance, or allowing business models to be aligned with changed market conditions.

Consolidation and flexibility

Increasingly, product innovation is seen as depending on two factors that can constitute decisive competitive advantages: the ability to handle business processes across company boundaries in an integrated manner, and real-time transparency. Consider this example: A well-known PC manufacturer's competitor requested lists of remaining stock from the manufacturer's suppliers. The competitor used the information in the lists to draw up structural designs for products, initially taking them no further than the drawing board. Next, they were auctioned on the Internet successfully. On the basis of the buyers' orders, the relevant parts were ordered automatically from the PC manufacturer's suppliers. On receipt of the deliveries, the company was able to begin manufacturing the products at a relatively low price. This procedure significantly reduced costs and the well-known PC manufacturer even suffered revenue losses of around 10 percent, because its competitor was able to offer much cheaper products. The decisive competitive advantage lay in the new business model with its more flexible, swift business processes, made possible only by IT.

Protection of investment

While IT may have regained its strategic importance, most IT budgets have not seen a significant increase. IT is expected to become more flexible, while at the same time protecting a company's investment in its current IT solution. Maintaining the existing system landscape eats up the majority of the IT budget, leaving only a considerably smaller portion for innovation. With insufficient funding and time for redesigning IT, companies often opt for quick fixes, which eventually add to the landscape's complexity and maintenance costs.

Many companies see IT as the driving force for process innovation, differentiation from the competition, and greater flexibility. This is precisely the kind of support afforded by SAP through its platform strategy and the Enterprise Services Architecture (ESA). But the role of the CIO is also set to change.

1.1 SAP's Strategy

Core processes

What are we dealing with when a company demands differentiation and flexibility? It's a question of how the company responds to customer requirements, how it collaborates with suppliers and partners, and how it adapts its business models at short notice (if necessary) to get ahead of its competitors. Depending on the company's focus, these core processes can affect production, supply chains, sales pitch, or specific services, but they all have one thing in common: These processes are mission-critical and extremely dynamic. Companies that cannot adapt such differentiating processes flexibly and quickly soon find themselves trailing behind.

Context processes

In addition, every enterprise has business processes that are not mission-critical. Such processes are known as context processes. They usually include accounting, human resources, asset management, and warehouse management, although the latter does not apply to the retail market, whereas warehouse management is indisputably a core process. Context processes must be designed more efficiently and cost effectively, and therefore require standard IT solutions.

The two process categories have always been closely related. All new, innovative business processes become context processes (consolidation) once they have been in use for a certain period of time and cease to be mission-critical. How can a company use productive processes of this kind and transform them into differentiating processes? Ideally, existing process steps would be used to compose new core processes. In such cases, there is no need to develop new applications, which would be both expensive and time-consuming. Once a service has been created, say, to create an order, it can be used repeatedly in different business processes. It isn't necessary to keep reprogramming interfaces or entire applications.

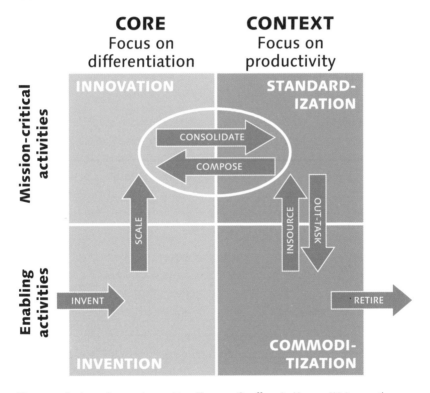

Figure 1.1 Business Process Innovation (Source: Geoffrey A. Moore: "Living on the Fault Line", HarperCollins Publishers 2002)

To enable a company's core and context processes to interact as far as possible, SAP forges close links between the IT infrastructure and business and industry-specific functions. Each company is then expected to define its own processes clearly, and thereby create a basis for planning how these processes will be realized in the software. This is the first step toward an ESA.

Enterprise Services Architecture

ESA essentially works on the same principle as service-oriented architecture (SOA) and uses both system resources and individual application functions as Web services. This kind of software architecture allows applications to be designed quickly and modified as required. Application functions that are available as Web services can be combined to create usable business functions quickly and without the need for programming.

The ESA is therefore much more advanced than the SOA concept, because it comprises not only Web services, but also the logic for business processes. In other words, the ESA always provides a plan for combining individual process components to create new functions. SAP supplies many of these functions ready-made in the form of enterprise services, which could also be described as Web services enhanced with business logic. They contain application functions, as well as complete or partial processes.

SAP NetWeaver

As the underlying platform of the ESA, SAP NetWeaver provides access to the ready-to-use enterprise services. It also provides increasing numbers of flexibly configurable business objects and components, along with pre-configured processes that will be accessible as enterprise services. SAP NetWeaver is therefore the conceptual basis for flexible system landscapes that allow enterprises to adapt their business processes quickly in response to market and business changes.

"Enterprise Services-Ready" solutions will be developed in collaboration with leading technology providers from across the IT sector, and together with Web services will provide enhanced flexibility and performance with lower costs and risks.

Development tools and runtime environments

Partners in the ESA network receive comprehensive development tools and runtime environments, for example, from the SAP Ecosystem, for developing, testing, and certifying such solutions. Developing enterprise services jointly across different technologies ensures that solutions will be compatible and simple to implement, and also reduces the risks and costs involved for the customer. In addition, collaboration among different technology providers ensures solutions that combine application logic and technical basics and that are process-oriented.

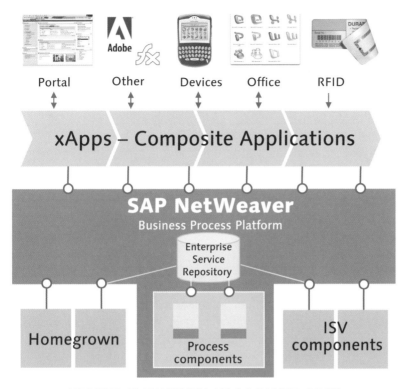

xApps – Composite Applications

SAP NetWeaver
Business Process Platform

Enterprise
Service
Repository

Homegrown

Process
components

ISV
components

HIGHER FLEXIBILITY AT A LOWER COST

Figure 1.2 Flexibility and Scope for Innovation with ESA

The ESA is the basis for all future SAP solutions. However, SAP will be just one of many software vendors producing applications in line with the ESA. Other software providers will also use the ESA to create application programs and composite applications. SAP also intends to provide a variety of services—ranging from software development to test procedures to customer support. We can assume that as the number of partners, who are using SAP NetWeaver to create their own solutions, increases, so will the number of users and production installations.

Composite
applications

To master these challenges, SAP is making huge investments in development, in the ongoing expansion of the partner network (see Chapter 3), and in its service infrastructure. In the coming years, all SAP solutions, including all industry solutions, will be based on services. Customers will benefit from lower costs and enhanced flexibility for the ongoing, innovative adjustment of processes to changing requirements.

This will essentially empower companies to differentiate themselves more from their competitors and thus boost their sales revenues while reducing the TCO.

1.2 The Chief Information Officer (CIO) as Chief Process Innovation Officer

The emergence of integrated Enterprise Resource Planning (ERP) systems placed tougher economic and technical requirements on IT. As projects and teams grew, so did budgets and responsibility. This finally gave rise to the position of Chief Information Officer (CIO). In companies with high technology requirements, the CIO's job has become so complex as to warrant the creation of an additional role, that of the Chief Technology Officer (CTO).

Shrinking budgets versus dynamic markets

Today's CIO not only has to cope with shrinking internal project budgets, but also faces external challenges from rapidly changing market conditions and tougher competition. Top management now has greater than ever expectations of the company's chief IT officer. Operationally, it demands a suitable, reliable, and economical infrastructure, as well as IT systems that support the business strategy. In addition to supporting current business, say by providing information to aid with decision-making, CIOs are increasingly expected to generate new business from innovative IT, as mentioned earlier. The CIO must be a business manager with solid IT knowledge and experience on the one hand, and an IT officer with strategic management skills on the other. The title CIO could just as well stand for Chief Process Innovation Officer (CPIO) in the future.

In the long term, the traditional CIO will gradually become less important if seen primarily as a source of expense. Ideally, the role of the CPIO should be that of a mediator, who understands business language and business needs, and can translate them into scalable solutions. At the same time, the CPIO should be capable of explaining the value of an IT investment to the business departments.

2   SAP's Service Philosophy

SAP Services, SAP's service organization, helps customers in all phases of the software lifecycle to ensure that they can use their SAP solution optimally and tap into its full potential. With this goal in mind, SAP works continually at enhancing its services.

SAP Services offers a rich selection of services covering support, consulting, education, customer developments, and managed services. It strives to provide customers and partners with first-rate support as they plan, implement, run, or enhance their IT solutions, and to help them leverage their SAP products at a minimal total cost of ownership (TCO). SAP has designed services that focus on different aspects for the individual phases of the software lifecycle.

▶ **Planning—Helps you to harness the "IT-powered business innovation" concealed in SAP products**
Lets you draw on SAP's industry expertise to develop a flexible, future-proof solution landscape

▶ **Implementation—Safeguards your project success**
Tools, content, and methods to accelerate implementation; SAP's quality-assurance expertise lets you proactively minimize risk and ensure that your solution goes live in budget and fulfills your business requirements

▶ **Operations and continuous improvement—Transform IT into "best-run IT"**
Optimization services and SAP Best Practices for operations enhance the service quality and efficiency of your IT

Lifecycle phases

With approximately 16,000 employees around the globe, SAP Services supports more than 32,000 customers and in excess of 100,000 installations. The following guidelines are integral to SAP's service philosophy:

▶ Holistic SAP service offering

▶ Systematic knowledge management and service productization

▶ Integrated service infrastructure to boost efficiency

▶ Constantly evolving service offering to keep pace with changing customer requirements

Guidelines

Comprehensive service offering

Customers choose when and how to use SAP Services, which boasts an extensive offering covering the entire product lifecycle. To give customers as much flexibility as possible when it comes to deciding which tasks to keep in-house and which to outsource to SAP partners or SAP Services, SAP has designed a differentiated offering that lets customers choose the amount of support they receive from SAP.

SAP's engagement In addition to maintenance and educational services, SAP offers a range of quality management services, aimed at ensuring successful implementation projects, or at proactively detecting and eliminating issues in live systems. The expert guidance services—such as assessment and benchmarking services—let customers draw on SAP's understanding of business processes and products in order to target specific problems.

SAP Services can also deliver a complete service solution—it could handle an implementation project from start to finish, or run a company's SAP solution.

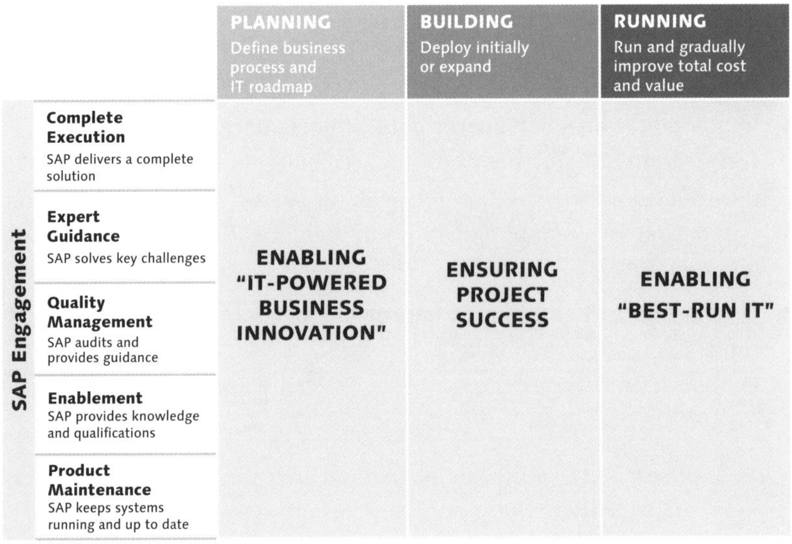

SAP Engagement		PLANNING Define business process and IT roadmap	BUILDING Deploy initially or expand	RUNNING Run and gradually improve total cost and value
	Complete Execution SAP delivers a complete solution	ENABLING "IT-POWERED BUSINESS INNOVATION"	ENSURING PROJECT SUCCESS	ENABLING "BEST-RUN IT"
	Expert Guidance SAP solves key challenges			
	Quality Management SAP audits and provides guidance			
	Enablement SAP provides knowledge and qualifications			
	Product Maintenance SAP keeps systems running and up to date			

Figure 2.1 Holistic Service Offering for the Entire Product Lifecycle

Systematic knowledge management and service productization

SAP has gained more than thirty years of experience in the IT industry and enjoys successful partnerships with some of the world's leading enterprises. Knowledge transfer and collaboration between customers, partners, and SAP have always played a crucial part in this success. This "knowledge asset," comprising industry know-how, IT best practices, methods, and tools, is embedded in service procedures and SAP solutions.

Productization

Figure 2.2 outlines the process of knowledge management and productization, which involves SAP, customers, and partners. The need for a new service, perhaps because a new product has been launched, can be met initially only by experts. SAP systematically gathers their know-how and makes it available internally for customers and partners. In the first phase, the experts can advise only a relatively small number of customers; by the scaling phase, their expertise is more widely available. The service is standardized further in the next phase. Service procedures and a selection of ready-made content and best practices provide broad access to the required information and ensure top-quality services. In this phase, SAP's attention turns to quality assurance, as it continues to adapt and enhance the service.

It goes without saying that this know-how flows into the next product release so that the service can be made even more efficient in the future.

Example: SAP EarlyWatch Alert

The SAP EarlyWatch Alert service aptly illustrates the different phases of productization. In the mid 90s, SAP offered a service that proactively analyzed the performance of SAP systems. It built on its experiences to develop a remote service called SAP EarlyWatch Alert. An SAP service engineer would connect to the customer system remotely and check the system using a standardized service procedure. The service became much more widely available as a result. By 1998, it was offered to all customers twice a year as part of the standard support package. Further productization saw the service become automated. Today, most customer systems send performance data to SAP on a weekly or monthly basis in order to obtain a service report.

In short, customers, partners, and SAP gain the following benefits from service productization:

▶ Fast and efficient knowledge transfer

▶ Lower costs for services that can be standardized

▶ Extra resources for customer-specific services that contribute greatly to differentiation

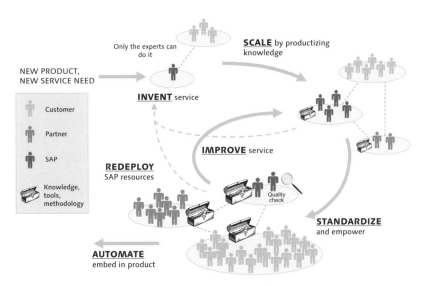

Figure 2.2 Service Development and Knowledge Transfer

Integrated service infrastructure to boost efficiency

Faced with the challenge of combining efficient collaborative service processes for customers, partners, and SAP with a basic tool for distributing methods, best practices, and productized services, SAP came up with a comprehensive, integrated service infrastructure. For a detailed description of its components, see Chapter 7.

SAP Solution Manager is the collaboration platform for the SAP service infrastructure. Its task is to provide SAP customers with optimum support during the implementation, go-live, and operational phases, as well as when tailoring their solutions to meet new requirements, and to proactively deliver high-quality, timely services that fulfill customers' needs.

SAP Solution Manager

The active use of SAP Solution Manager in all SAP and customer service departments gives rise to a new form of collaboration.

The information documented in SAP Solution Manager provides a common source of knowledge that helps customers run their solutions effectively. SAP Solution Manager delivers transparent technical information about the systems and allocates problem messages to the relevant persons at SAP. This reduces the time required to obtain additional information from the customer, as well as the time necessary to resolve the actual problem.

Automated system analyses such as SAP EarlyWatch Alert give timely warning when stable solution operations are at risk, and enable problems to be eliminated before they cause serious damage. Business process monitoring is therefore an essential part of the SAP Solution Manager communication and collaboration platform. The purpose of gathering and storing information in SAP Solution Manager is to equip the SAP support team with the necessary tools to analyze issues quickly and to provide customer-specific information.

SAP Service Marketplace is another key element of the SAP service infrastructure. The different portals bundle a wealth of information about the SAP world. For members of the SAP Ecosystem (see Chapter 3)—customers, partners, and SAP—this communal Internet platform is the gateway to SAP's online collection of information, services for SAP solutions, and support applications. For example, notifications containing information and links to other places on SAP Service Marketplace are "pushed" to users.

SAP Service Marketplace

The combination of SAP Solution Manager as frontend and SAP Service Marketplace as portal is indispensable for the SAP Ecosystem. The two platforms allow customers, partners, and SAP to exchange information and collaborate efficiently across enterprise boundaries.

Constantly evolving service offerings to keep pace with changing customer requirements

Business requirements for IT services are in a constant state of flux. In response, SAP frequently enhances its services as part of a process of continuous improvement.

It conducts customer surveys so that customers can propose improvements. The surveys are always conducted after every service; say, after a consulting project, or when a support issue has been closed. SAP also carries out quarterly customer surveys to monitor how decision-makers rate the quality of its services.

Customer surveys

Another means of continuously improving SAP Services is through collaboration with SAP user groups, such as the Deutschsprachige SAP-Anwendergruppe (DSAG) e.V. (German-speaking SAP User Group, registered association), the Americas' SAP Users' Group (ASUG), and the international SAP Customer Competence Center (SAP CCC) Community. Working groups bring together ideas and concepts for improving SAP services, which are later put into practice by SAP. Examples include the procedure for message processing that was optimized in collaboration with the SAP CCC Community, and the TCO analyses conducted jointly with the DSAG in order to compile best practices.

User groups

3 SAP Ecosystem

"Knowledge is the only instrument of production that is not subject to diminishing returns."
John Maurice Clark (1884–1963), American National Economist

As the pace of market change continues to accelerate, enterprises must be ready to act and react at all times. All enterprises face the challenge of supporting their strategy by selecting and implementing a suitable software solution and running it efficiently. Bearing this in mind, it is sometimes prudent for companies to look beyond the competencies and expertise of their own employees. Continually exchanging knowledge with other companies enables a better understanding of products, accelerates decision-making, stimulates innovation, and is becoming increasingly more critical to success.

Continuous knowledge exchange

Making contact with other companies via the Internet is often very time-consuming, the quality of the information offered is unknown, and there is no guarantee that the contact between the respective companies is sustainable. Consequently, the success of all involved is also dependent on a solution provider bringing together customers, partners, and its own employees in durable communities. Ongoing knowledge transfer, convincing innovative capabilities, and inter-enterprise collaboration characterize such communities. Therefore, as a solution provider, SAP has decided to invest in setting up and expanding the global SAP Ecosystem, composed of customers, partners, and its own employees. Powerful platforms provide the basis for their partnerships.

Its primary objective is to support the ongoing exchange of expertise and knowledge in an organized and structured manner between SAP and its customers and partners. SAP harnesses the potential this offers to align its products and services with market requirements, and returns it to its customers and partners in the form of solutions. Every member of the SAP Ecosystem has tailored access to information and can share expertise and collaborate with other members. The type of support offered in terms of information, communication, and processes depends on whether a member of the SAP Ecosystem is a partner, customer, or SAP employee. For instance, the primary concern of most customers is to get as much information as possible about the services and support available from SAP and

Knowledge transfer

its partners. For partners, on the other hand, the SAP Ecosystem is primarily a means of offering their services to customers via SAP Service Marketplace, and a way to broaden their knowledge of SAP solutions so they can sharpen their competitive edge. The SAP Ecosystem also provides customers and partners with up-to-date information about best practices and standard developments to help them implement IT strategies and projects effectively.

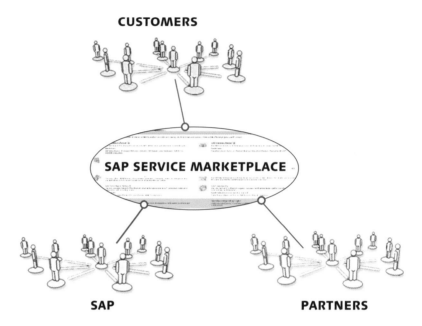

Figure 3.1 SAP Ecosystem

To locate the right partner in every situation, SAP has defined a range of partner categories, such as channel partner, service partner, and software partner. Every partner category has binding quality standards, and the partners' compliance to these standards is checked regularly. SAP also runs partner initiatives to enable partners to become qualified in contemporary issues.

SAP's partner program

SAP's partner program is the result of extensive cooperation with its partners, as well as many years of experience of its partners' and customers' best practices. The program makes it easier for partners to conduct their own business in partnership with SAP. From SAP's perspective, it provides a basis for meeting the needs for solutions and services, both of major customers and of growing numbers of small and midsize businesses. SAP's objective is to deliver first-rate solutions and services, either directly or through its partners. For this reason, it has established programs for monitoring the quality of services. SAP customers can rest assured that the selected SAP partners who support their business demonstrate consistently high levels of professionalism, technical expertise, and an understanding of customers' specific requirements. They profit from this program, because it ensures that all partners strive to bring satisfaction and success to their customers.

For customers and partners alike, the main benefits of the SAP Ecosystem are the intensive exchange of knowledge, continual quality improvement, and efficient collaboration. By sharing their knowledge in this way, customers, partners, and SAP quickly detect market trends, which SAP can convert into innovative solutions, either independently or with partners in joint development projects.

Another plus is that well organized teamwork throughout the SAP Ecosystem ensures the technical and functional quality of SAP products and leads to the definition of standards. The result is a high level of quality, testified by the trouble-free way in which SAP solutions are planned, implemented, and run, and by the findings of customer satisfaction surveys. All these factors make SAP a reliable partner for setting up and running its customers' core business processes.

Quality assurance

4 SAP's Service Offering

Regardless of which requirements customers may have over the lifecycle of their SAP solutions, SAP can offer a suitable service. This chapter outlines SAP's comprehensive service offering.

SAP has compiled a range of useful services to ensure its customers the best possible support during IT projects, as well as to safeguard and optimize the way they run their SAP solutions. SAP constantly extends and enhances this offering to reflect changes in market requirements. The matrix below provides a good overview of the services and classifies them according to two main criteria:

▶ The lifecycle phases of an IT solution in which the service is used

▶ The level of engagement that the customer requires from SAP

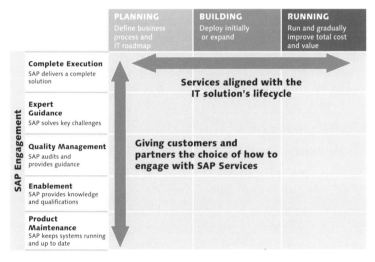

Figure 4.1 Levels of SAP Engagement and Lifecycle Phases as Classification Criteria

The lifecycle of an IT solution comprises three phases: planning, building, and running. Specific services can be allocated to each of these phases:

Phases in the lifecycle of an IT solution

▶ **Planning—Define business process and IT roadmap**
The services assigned to the planning phase are carried out before an SAP solution is implemented. The main challenges in this phase include the business and IT strategies, business process design, and the design of the system and application architecture.

- ▶ **Building—Deploy initially or expand**
  All the services necessary for implementing a customer's technical requirements in the software solution are assigned to the building phase. Examples include services for interfaces, migration, and support, which provide assistance during the transition to production operation.

- ▶ **Running—Run and gradually improve total cost and value**
  With the majority of customers running live SAP solutions, this is a particularly important phase. This is where the standard support services come into play, alongside services for optimizing and managing the technical infrastructure and the SAP solution.

The services in the planning and building phases are not just designed for new SAP customers; existing customers implementing a new SAP solution, or updating one they already have, go through all the lifecycle phases of an IT solution time and again.

Level of SAP engagement Most enterprises have their own network of resources—composed of business and IT departments and various external service providers—to deliver the appropriate expertise as required. In practice, customers often turn to SAP for support during IT projects to ensure that their projects are successful. SAP therefore lets its customers decide on the scope of service they require. Each customer can decide on how much support it needs from SAP. SAP's service offering contains five categories of customer engagement. They range from product maintenance to quality management to the complete handling of partial or entire projects:

- ▶ **Product Maintenance—We keep systems running and up to date**
  SAP Standard Support includes many services that go much further than merely safeguarding operations (see Section 5.1.1).

- ▶ **Enablement—We provide knowledge and qualifications**
  An SAP solution cannot be used effectively unless users understand its structure, its features, and how it works. SAP offers many courses and separate certification options to transfer this knowledge.

- ▶ **Quality Management—We audit and provide guidance**
  SAP provides valuable quality-assurance services to ensure that IT projects are completed on time and within budget, or to assess existing SAP solutions and recommend measures to optimize or extend them.

- ▶ **Expert Guidance—We solve key challenges**
  SAP has the right expert for every problem, who is equipped to work "hands-on" with the customer in order to solve demanding tasks directly in the SAP system.

▶ **Complete Execution—We deliver a complete solution**
In cases where SAP assumes full responsibility for tailoring SAP software to customer requirements, it can provide all the services from one source—from project management to technical implementation to running the SAP solution. Furthermore, SAP will implement large parts of an IT project if required.

The following sections outline services from all areas of the SAP offering, which are important to most customers. A detailed description of each service exceeds the scope of this book.[1]

Nonetheless, we have included customer experiences to demonstrate the benefits of SAP services. In Chapter 6 we use customer scenarios to illustrate specific services.

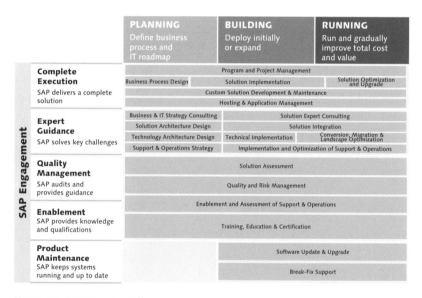

Figure 4.2 SAP's Service Offering

4.1 Team and User Training: Knowledge Transfer

Planning, implementing, operating, and using SAP solutions effectively require adequate knowledge and skills relating to business, IT, SAP software, and project methodology. This is why SAP offers a range of services for knowledge transfer and training, which are described in more detail below.

---

1 The main services are introduced in this chapter and described briefly in the glossary in Appendix B.

Knowledge transfer is a key concern for every company, regardless of size or industry sector. Recent studies identify deficits in the systematic transfer of knowledge as the main reason for employee dissatisfaction, low productivity, and mistakes.

SAP solutions form the backbone of many enterprise control systems. It is therefore strategically vital that all employees who use the software are equipped to use it proficiently. This applies to managers as well as members of project teams, internal consultants, and technical staff, and including what is perhaps the largest and most varied target group—those who use SAP applications in the business departments. According to leading industry analysts, SAP solutions currently support over 10 million people in their professional work. For that reason, SAP and its partners need to develop products and services that ensure knowledge is transferred continuously and in a controlled manner to all these target groups.

4.1.1 Knowledge Transfer Methods and Programs

SAP's product innovation lifecycle (PIL) is the framework for all process and product standards that are relevant to the development of SAP solutions. High-quality, standardized knowledge transfer products reduce the time enterprises need to implement new SAP solutions, consequently lowering the TCO. With regard to knowledge transfer, the PIL supports the development of a consistent and comprehensive training portfolio and complementary services such as best practices and certification.

The methods SAP applies to transfer knowledge can be grouped in three areas:

Knowledge
transfer methods

▶ **Documentation**
Product documentation is an integral part of SAP products. It describes features, as well as installation and implementation methods, and contains the end-user documentation. It is available on the SAP Help Portal, the central platform for SAP documentation, at *http://help.sap.com* (see Section 7.2). By bundling this information, SAP helps its customers to optimize the way they use their SAP software and consequently to attain a higher business value.

▶ **SAP Ramp-Up Knowledge Transfer**
When new SAP solutions are in the Ramp-Up phase of being launched, SAP Ramp-Up Knowledge Transfer provides initial know-how for all the groups involved, whether they be customers, partners, or SAP

employees. The comprehensive knowledge transfer model is based on a holistic, role-specific didactic approach of "learning, doing, and supporting," with a strong focus on scalable, online learning methods.

▶ **SAP Education Portfolio**
The knowledge required during an SAP implementation depends on the software component as well as the target group. SAP Education tackles various requirements and provides a training program for each current software component and each target group (consultants, key users, decision-makers, and users).

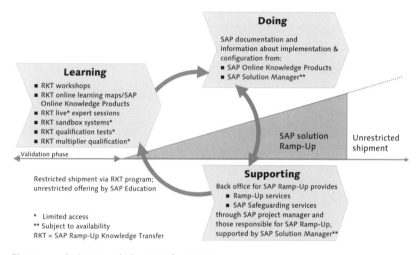

Figure 4.3 SAP's Knowledge Transfer Model

These methods are put into practice during knowledge transfer programs:

Knowledge transfer programs

▶ **SAP Ramp-Up Knowledge Transfer program**
In this training program, knowledge is transferred via various channels: Users can acquire knowledge synchronously—from workshops and live expert sessions—or asynchronously—using SAP Online Knowledge Products (OKPs).

The program prepares individual groups from the SAP Ecosystem, such as partners or SAP employees from Sales, Consulting, and Support, for the mainstream rollout of new products. The know-how gained from this program is passed on to SAP Education, where it is used to prepare the global master curriculum and certification.

▶ **SAP Empowering workshops**
SAP Empowering workshops (see Section 4.2.3) complement SAP Education's standard training program. They aim to enable customers

to solve complex tasks relating to SAP IT Service & Application Management (see Section 4.2.1). They focus on analyzing customer-specific problems—where possible, directly in the customer system—and providing solutions and troubleshooting methodologies.

▶ **SAP Education courses**
SAP's training program covers knowledge transfer for all current software components. In addition, differentiation by target group means that comprehensive, role-specific, and practical information can be offered for all current SAP solutions.

SAP Solution Manager SAP Solution Manager (see Section 7.1) integrates knowledge content, tools, and methods that benefit SAP customers throughout the implementation, support, operating, and monitoring phases of their SAP solutions.

4.1.2 The Education Portfolio

A picture says more than a thousand words, which is why SAP has drawn up a map showing the key dimensions and content of its educational offering. The individual dimensions (rows in the matrix) are combined independently to afford a high degree of variation and flexibility in the learning solutions. For a basic understanding of SAP's educational offering, the four main categories will suffice:

Four main categories ▶ **Instructor-led training (public or company-specific)**
The education process is marked by a strong social aspect. Interaction with the instructor and other students helps the course participants to absorb information and deepen their understanding, which is why conventional classroom sessions will continue to hold their appeal. SAP offers public courses for all current software components in its training centers around the world. Customers can also order tailored, on-site courses.

▶ **Self-learning materials (e-learning, computer-based training, documentation)**
An instructor is not always available when you need fast, succinct information. Self-learning materials are available for such situations—ranging from simple system documentation to sophisticated e-learning courses. For instance, the Online Knowledge Products (OKPs) help experienced SAP consultants gain first-hand condensed information for the implementation and operation of new SAP solutions or releases.

► **Learning tools and systems (simulations, application help)**

The best way to get to know a software system is on the job—by systematically trying things out. Beginners frequently need more support than is provided by conventional help functions. Learning tools such as SAP Tutor and RWD InfoPak provide further assistance in the form of online documentation and simulations to illustrate processes more clearly. SAP Learning Solution, integrated in mySAP ERP Human Capital Management (mySAP ERP HCM), provides extensive functions for managing enterprisewide education.

► **Complementary services (consulting, certification)**

Before implementing enterprisewide training measures, we advise you to determine what employees already know and what they need to learn. Major organizational or strategic changes call for knowledge about change management, for example. Learners are keen to show their command of the material and strive to gain certification where possible.

4.1.3 The Portfolio Map

Figure 4.4 illustrates all aspects of SAP education.

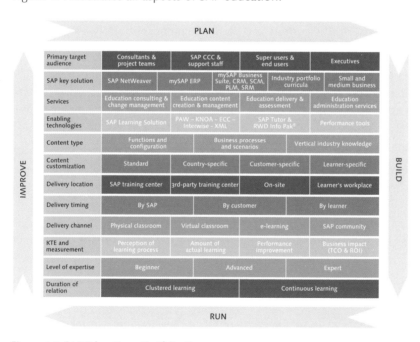

Figure 4.4 SAP Education—Portfolio Map

Target groups SAP's educational offering is aimed at anyone whose professional work brings them into contact with SAP solutions. This primarily involves members of implementation project teams, consultants, and the technical support team, but also includes users and managers. The training measures are scaled in accordance with the level of knowledge they require, and use the different learning methods and tools described earlier. Users in particular, due to their large numbers and multitude of roles, have to learn directly on their system at their workplace, that is, "on-the-job" training.

SAP solutions and associated educational offerings The basic principle is no SAP solution without adequate training. At an early stage in the SAP's product innovation lifecycle (PIL), the SAP Ramp-Up Knowledge Transfer provides specialists with expertise in the form of Online Knowledge Products (OKPs). Training for the other target groups, such as the project team or users, is provided as public or company-specific courses. The offering currently comprises around 250 different seminars, along with variants that have been tailored to customer needs.

Types of learning content SAP courses are often based on software functions and configurations, especially for developing technical expertise for implementation and upgrade projects. Users and managers, on the other hand, have different priorities, namely the business processes and scenarios being mapped by the software. The current SAP portfolio comprises both types of courses, as well as a growing number of industry-specific seminars.

Tailoring to specific requirements In addition to the many standard, public courses, SAP offers training tailored to the needs of specific countries (language, culture, legislation) and customers (corporate design, internal practices, and terminology). The latest generation of e-learning products can even be tailored to meet individual needs.

SAP training measures and products are flexible across three dimensions:

▶ In terms of location, they can be held in SAP training centers, hotels, on the customer's premises, or even at the learner's workplace.

▶ The time may be fixed (public seminars), arranged (on-site courses), or completely flexible (self-learning units).

▶ The methods used vary from traditional instructor-led training to virtual classroom sessions through to prepared e-learning programs.

Measuring success Consultants and users needing proof of their training can take certification tests offered by SAP. Forty test centers worldwide and the option of certification using an Internet-assisted application ensure comprehensive availability. For companies seeking to measure the economic benefits of investments in education, SAP is currently developing a return on investment (ROI) method, which is used in a case study.

In practice: INVISTA Resins&Fibers GmbH

INVISTA Resins&Fibers GmbH is part of the international INVISTA Group, the integrated polymer, intermediates, and fibers business. The globally active chemicals manufacturer and distributor successfully conducted an upgrade to mySAP ERP with the support of SAP Consulting. To ensure a smooth transition in dynamic operation, the company commissioned SAP to conduct a carefully prepared transfer of expert knowledge to the INVISTA Resins&Fibers GmbH organization. Therefore, it was necessary to train 500 SAP software users at company sites—Germany and the Netherlands—within a short time frame.

With these requirements, SAP Education specialists designed a training program that was tailor-made to the specific needs of INVISTA Resins&Fibers GmbH. The customer identified "super" users, who went through a train-the-trainer program to become "knowledge multipliers." They built up the skills necessary to train staff in the company's departments, in part, on their own. In addition to the training program for end users, the team used the SAP Tutor tool to develop numerous tutorials for INVISTA Resins&Fibers GmbH. Lothar Hafner, Lead Project Manager at INVISTA Resins&Fibers GmbH, says: "Using SAP Tutor, our key users recorded each mouse click and each step in each application, thereby generating training material, and published it in our intranet to help our SAP [software] users. These tutorials are both an online reference of our work and an excellent source of information, especially for new members of the staff."

In total, 67 days were invested in training key users and end users. Hafner summarizes: "We accomplished the training goals we set for ourselves. The train-the-trainer workshop for our key users was a real highlight. It achieved its purpose so effectively that we have decided to extend this very successful program. Eventually, our key users will be able to teach other employees to work with our SAP system."

4.2 Enabling Support and Operations

An ongoing challenge facing every enterprise is that of keeping IT-supported business processes in tune with market conditions while driving excellent performance. In response, SAP has compiled a wide range of programs, services, methodologies, and tools that actively support the organizations responsible for continuously improving SAP-centric solutions and ensuring they run smoothly.

4.2.1 SAP Customer Competence Center Program

The SAP Customer Competence Center (SAP CCC) program—an initiative intended to allow customers to exploit the SAP Ecosystem to an even greater extent, in order to benefit from better knowledge transfer and closer partnerships with other members—was conceived in 1994. This program is intended for specific target groups and addresses the customers' own support organizations, which are integral to the welfare of the enterprises that they support, because they have the necessary skills, knowledge, and decision-making powers when it comes to SAP-centric solutions. Only such successful support organizations can ensure that the SAP-centric solutions are running smoothly, while safeguarding the company's competitiveness through continuous improvement.

In SAP terms, a successful support organization is known as an SAP CCC. Comprehensive support continually enhances and fine-tunes existing solutions to better serve the needs of users, enabling them to become more productive. Therefore, the yardstick for measuring the success of a support organization is the satisfaction and efficiency of the users.

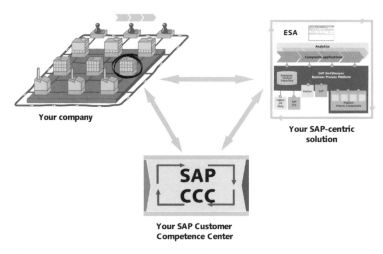

Figure 4.5 SAP CCC—Competencies within Your Company

Tasks of SAP CCCs

Knowledge of processes

To achieve optimal user support, support organizations must have in-depth knowledge of the performance features of the particular software solutions deployed, know exactly how the business processes are mapped in the software, and understand their technical impact on the IT infrastructure. Therefore, these support organizations act as a central link between pure IT operations and the business areas concerned. By collaborating closely with the relevant business areas, support organizations ensure that their knowledge of the company's business processes is current and consistent, and that any demands from business areas that are required to enhance business processes also lead to the optimization of the implemented software solution. Such knowledge transfer and mutual coordination is vital for the smooth operation and enhancement of the deployed solution, which, ultimately, boosts the efficiency of the business areas.

The main objectives of an SAP CCC are listed below:

▶ Safeguarding the stable operation of the solution according to the Service Level Agreements (SLAs)

Main objectives

▶ Optimizing the deployed solutions continually to enhance the efficiency and performance of users

▶ Minimizing operating costs

▶ Safeguarding the required solution performance or throughput

▶ Safeguarding data consistency

▶ Ensuring fast and effective problem resolution

▶ Defining the requirements for hardware and infrastructure operation

▶ Ensuring continuous change management—from the business process to the software technology and vice versa

Figure 4.6 The Typical Functions of an SAP CCC

Strategic positioning of SAP CCCs

The skills and basic functions examined and evaluated during SAP CCC certification help SAP CCCs attain their goals. Depending on the focus, fields of activity, and the results expected from the company, a distinction is made between two main SAP CCC objectives:

1. Safeguarding the stable operation of the SAP solution
2. Supporting innovation and continuous improvement of the SAP solution

SAP calls CCCs that fulfill only the first objective "product CCCs" and those meeting both "solution CCCs."

Safeguarding stable operation SAP CCCs, whose main focus is to safeguard the stability of the solution, are generally hard hit by the current cost-cutting programs implemented by companies. The work involved in running the existing solution is taken for granted, and since they don't generate any direct profit, support organizations are often merely regarded as cost factors. Consequently, many companies are opting to offshore or outsource these activities instead of performing them in-house. Therefore, it is important to clarify exactly what is understood by SAP solutions and which activities are required to safeguard a stable operation.

Examples of SAP solutions are mySAP Enterprise Resource Planning (mySAP ERP), mySAP Customer Relationship Management (mySAP CRM), or mySAP Supply Chain Management (mySAP SCM). Often, the software solutions deployed by SAP customers comprise SAP products and solutions that are interfaced or networked with products from other vendors. Such solutions are called "SAP-centric," and, where overall operations are concerned, have to be viewed as a whole. Processes and errors can be analyzed only in contemporary software and system landscapes if the entire end-to-end process is examined holistically, including all the systems and software components involved in the process.

The activities required to ensure stable operation are described in the SAP IT Service Management methodology, which is explained in the next section. There are no hard and fast rules when deciding what activities to outsource. Ultimately, it depends on the organizational and process structure of the company concerned. Nonetheless, responsibility for business processes, especially the core business processes, should remain an internal task, since this forms the basis for continual improvement and optimization.

To generate true value added for the company, SAP CCCs must assume responsibilities that go beyond their basic tasks. By supporting innovations that are important for the company and are based on new and existing technologies, platforms, and solutions, SAP CCCs are integrated into the companies' business areas. Even though innovations don't always stem from IT, the support of IT or the SAP CCCs is always required to analyze, select, and implement them.

Innovation and continuous improvement

Many SAP customers exploit the bundled knowledge available in the SAP CCCs to optimize existing solutions. Here, existing solutions refer to those that are already in use or are, at least, included in the customer's license model. Often the utilization rate of SAP software that has already been purchased is relatively low. This does not refer to the number of users or the engines used, but to the functions that are available and installed but not implemented.

This is precisely where measures for continuous improvement come into play. More specifically, the business processes are improved by using existing solutions. In the course of delivering services such as the SAP Solution Management Assessment (SMA), it became clear, in many cases, that efficient use of existing solutions or individual functions, such as workflows, best practices, or entire modules, meant that business processes could be supported better, which, in turn, leads to reduced costs and enhanced user satisfaction.

By ensuring a stable operation, SAP CCCs merely fulfill the basic requirements expected of them. It is only by continuously improving processes and supporting innovations that are critical to gaining a competitive edge, that SAP CCCs generate value added for businesses, helping to consolidate and extend their position within the companies.

The functions and processes in an SAP CCC

SAP helps CCCs to achieve their main objectives by providing SAP IT Service & Application Management, which is based on the service support and service delivery processes described in the IT Infrastructure Library (ITIL) and is complemented with SAP-specific details. SAP deploys these processes, because they are regarded by the market as the de facto standard and are used for general IT processes; however, running an SAP solution calls for specific processes and procedures that are not available in the ITIL. Therefore, SAP has included these in process and model descriptions focusing on the operation of SAP solutions. SAP IT Service Manage-

SAP IT Service & Application Management

ment comprises the basic activities of a product CCC, whose emphasis is on ensuring stable operation.

SAP Application Management essentially pertains to the lifecycle of solutions and applications. Its activities range from planning to replacing the system with a new one, if required, or implementing a new generation of software applications. SAP CCCs play a key role in implementation projects of this kind. Their main responsibilities include assessing the technical feasibility of the solution, integrating it with existing solutions, and ensuring a smooth transition from the implementation phase to the operating phase. Ineffective handover from the former to the latter phase can delay the value generated from the solution and drive up costs, especially in the initial phase of operation.

SAP NetWeaver Management You cannot simply combine SAP Application Management with the processes of SAP IT Service Management. Attempting to link both areas is like trying to merge a company's business areas with its IT department. SAP has therefore defined a group of appropriate integration processes, called SAP NetWeaver Management, within SAP IT Service & Application Management. These processes enable you to combine the two areas to take a holistic view of IT services and applications.

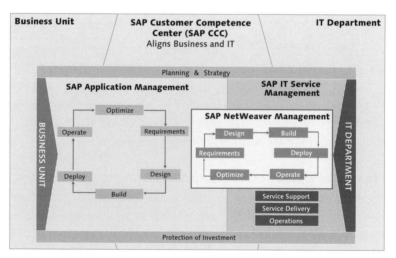

Figure 4.7 SAP IT Service & Application Management

Based on this description, an SAP CCC implements processes to attain the following objectives and, in turn, greatly enhances corporate success:

▶ Safeguard the stable operation of the SAP solution
▶ Reduce TCO

- ▶ Protect investments by lowering integration and upgrade costs
- ▶ Reduce implementation costs, thereby achieving a faster ROI
- ▶ Support continuous improvement and tailor the SAP solution to dynamic business processes

These goals must align with both the IT and the company's overall strategy.

Advantages of SAP CCCs

The excellent support available to users of SAP systems and the opportunity to collaborate closely with SAP are the main advantages companies derive from CCCs. The SAP CCC is the central point of contact for users who experience problems with their SAP system or require up-to-date information. Expertise and knowledge are managed centrally and are available to all group units. In addition, the SAP CCC safeguards the implementation of business processes in the group units since, before an SAP solution is implemented, existing business processes undergo a comprehensive analysis and are then optimized.

Companies build up the required expertise and SAP knowledge necessary to run SAP solutions on their own by training SAP CCC employees and learning from the experience they acquire in day-to-day activities. Consequently, companies can adapt faster, more flexibly, and cost-effectively to changes without having to rely on outside help. Thanks to the in-depth, company-specific knowledge that SAP CCC employees possess—and the fact that they are employed within the company—users are ensured timely and individual support. As a result, the specialist knowledge acquired by SAP CCC employees and their close collaboration with SAP ultimately cuts costs and minimizes the risks of implementing projects while the system is in operation.

The SAP CCC program

As already discussed, the maximum value added by a solution cannot be leveraged fully unless the solution is tailored optimally to the company's business processes and run effectively by the support organization. Support organizations deploy a multitude of different processes and functions for running complex SAP solutions. SAP, as the vendor of the solution to be supported, advises customers on how to operate it.

The original objective of the SAP CCC program was to establish a central point of contact within a customer's organization to deal with SAP-related queries and issues: the SAP CCC. Companies were quick to recog-

Central point of contact

Development of SAP CCCs

nize the advantages of SAP CCCs, namely, constant and intensive collaboration and knowledge transfer with SAP. Therefore, SAP continually expanded the SAP CCC program to support the CCCs taking on new tasks. Soon the SAP CCC's role grew from being the point of contact for issues relating solely to SAP to being the organizational unit responsible for coordinating and implementing the processes and functions required for running a complete SAP-centric solution. Now, the SAP CCC's area of responsibility encompasses much more than the technical operation of the solution; in fact, it implements, manages, monitors, and optimizes all the processes that are required for optimally running an SAP-centric solution. As the role of CCCs has evolved, SAP has regularly adapted the scope of the services, options, and contents of its CCC program to ensure that support organizations receive the best possible assistance.

SAP CCC certification

SAP CCC certification is a vital element of the SAP CCC program. Certain basic functions provide the key to efficient CCCs. These essential functions are described below and form an integral part of SAP CCC certification. This is useful for both the customer and SAP to ensure that the basic requirements are met to run an SAP-centric solution with stability. Certification essentially confirms that the SAP CCC fulfills the basic requirements of a support organization and has been set up successfully. Moreover, by having SAP certify their CCC, customers demonstrate that they are committed to working closely with SAP, within the framework of the SAP CCC program.

Basic functions of an SAP CCC

SAP defines a CCC's scope of duties via four basic functions—support desk, contract management, development request coordination, and information management—as well as three additional functions—business support, technical support, and service planning. Furthermore, these functions have several subordinate areas of responsibility; for example, the support desk function comprises the subfunctions help desk, application hotline, Basis hotline, escalation management, monitoring of CCC customers, and SAP Service Marketplace management.

A detailed description of the basic functions is as follows:

1. **Support desk**
   A support desk is set up and operated during the location's usual business hours (at least eight hours a day, five days a week) and is staffed by

an appropriate number of qualified support staff for Basis and the relevant applications. The SAP CCC and SAP ascertain and check the customer's support procedure and capability.

2. **Contract management**
SAP helps CCCs with contract and license processing. This entails license auditing, maintenance billing, release order processing, and the management of user master data and installation data.

3. **Development request coordination**
Development requests are collected in the company and are mostly presented to SAP by various user groups.

4. **Information management**
SAP CCCs communicate all important information to the company by organizing events and internal presentations especially for this purpose.

SAP CCC certification audit

Audit

As already mentioned, certification proves that an SAP CCC meets the basic requirements of a support organization. It is also indicative that a close collaboration with SAP exists. It entails a certification audit, which involves holding interviews to establish via a checklist, whether the functions have been implemented and work correctly. The certificate is valid for two years; then, a re-certification is necessary. Certification is carried out at the customer site. But, if the processes and functions have not changed when SAP CCCs seek to renew certification, re-certification can be conducted remotely.

How the SAP CCC program supports SAP CCCs

Besides SAP CCC certification, which is the basis for operating SAP solutions optimally, SAP has extended its CCC support to include other areas. In its CCC program, SAP, together with international and national user groups, identified the areas that would benefit most from collaboration between CCCs and SAP:

▶ Planning and definition processes in SAP service and support

▶ Information and knowledge transfer

▶ Problem-handling process

Planning and definition processes

For service and support within SAP, it is imperative that information relating to a new product, solution, or service development is communicated promptly. To ensure this, certified SAP CCCs are integrated into the planning and development phases at an early stage. Therefore, they can test products while they are still being enhanced, instead of having to wait until the products are finished. Past experience has emphasized the importance of information gained from workshops with SAP CCCs in leveraging the services and solutions discussed and adapting them to market requirements. Both parties benefit from incorporating SAP CCCs in the planning and development process. Indeed, the partnership can be described as a "win-win situation."

Information and knowledge transfer In addition to sending CCCs newsletters containing exclusive information, SAP organizes a number of events especially for them, which are held directly after main SAP events. Participants in the SAP CCC info forums are informed of topics relevant to CCCs and receive news from previous events, such as SAPPHIRE.

To promote innovation within a company, it is often necessary to know about new products. Such knowledge is available exclusively in the SAP Ramp-Up Knowledge Transfer program. Certified SAP CCCs can access relevant knowledge products, even if they are not involved in the particular Ramp-Up. Consequently, they can evaluate solutions early on and build up the knowledge required.

Furthermore, certified SAP CCCs can benefit from special knowledge transfer sessions among experts. For this purpose, SAP organizes special online events, such as WebEx™ sessions on selected topics, during which it shares all its specialist knowledge with the certified CCCs.

Problem-handling process Collaboration between the CCCs and SAP in the problem-handling process means that incoming customer messages from certified CCCs are automatically identified as such at SAP. Consequently, the SAP employees processing the messages know immediately that these messages have, for the most part, already been clarified and that communication should involve customer and SAP experts. Furthermore, if the messages are sent to SAP using SAP Solution Manager (Service Desk function in SAP Solution Manager), they are given a higher ranking in SAP's message queue and are, therefore, processed faster.

Collaboration with SAP CCC Communities

User groups Collaboration between SAP and the various SAP CCCs is on an individual basis and is usually initiated by setting up and certifying CCCs. Frequent communication with user groups is also an integral part of the SAP CCC program. This level of communication helps to optimize collaboration between CCCs and SAP on issues relevant to more than one customer. In many countries, national user groups have their own subgroups to deal with issues relating to SAP CCCs. In Germany, for instance, Deutsch-sprachige SAP-Anwendergruppe (DSAG) e.V. (German-speaking SAP User Group, registered association) comprises the work group CCC/Service & Support. In other countries, subgroups of national user groups are known as "focus groups" or "communities of interests," as is the case with the U.S. user association, the Americas' SAP Users' Group (ASUG). The relevant SAP international subsidiary collaborates and communicates with these special interest groups. Such activities are controlled by global SAP CCC program management.

Communication and meetings between user groups and SAP take place at various levels. For some issues, such as improving the certification process or defining roles and responsibilities in user groups, work is organized in the form of workshops. In other cases, user group representatives meet with SAP service and support managers.

Advisory councils are held to determine the strategic direction of products, solutions, and services. Representatives of customers who have a special interest in a particular topic meet SAP to discuss the future strategy for that area. Often, both parties sign a confidentiality agreement prior to discussions.

Advisory councils

Furthermore, SAP recently intensified collaboration with ASUG. For instance, enhancements to SAP's CCC program were incorporated in an ASUG Influence Council, which works on further development of the program.

Notably, collaboration with the International SAP CCC Community, established at the beginning of 2003 to represent the interests of the representatives of CCC user groups, has since led to groundbreaking developments in the SAP CCC program. Today, this community comprises mainly European countries; however, one of its immediate goals is to increase the number of representatives from American and Asian regions.

4.2.2 The Organization of an SAP CCC

An efficient support organization needs to reflect the company's organizational structure and philosophy. Therefore, there is no universally preferred structure; each one is designed to suit the requirements of the particular company. SAP does not stipulate any fixed criteria for the organizational structure of SAP CCCs. They can be run by a department within a corporate group, a group subsidiary, or an external service provider. Companies also have different types of support organizations. They can have one central organization or several local ones. Local organizations are often separated into regions, enabling round-the-clock support at usual business hours in a particular region in line with the "follow-the-sun" principle. Moreover, separation according to business areas, functions, or other company principles is conceivable. Besides differences in organizational structure, the approach of support organizations can also vary. For example, some companies prefer a virtual approach, involving employees from various departments in the support processes. Companies frequently deploy several different software solutions from various vendors. Consequently, they must decide whether these solutions are to be run in a cross-application support organization, or one that specializes in SAP solutions.

The SAP CCC organization is always company-specific.

 One central SAP CCC

 Several SAP CCCs are responsible for particular:

- Regions/time zones (such as Europe, America, Asia)
- Company divisions (such as textiles, chemicals, services)
- Functions (such as production, retail, financials)
- Mixed structures (such as financials worldwide, textiles Europe)

 Virtual structure

 External service provider (outsourcing)

Figure 4.8 SAP CCC Structures

While there may not be a universal, ready-made support organization, guidance is available to help companies build a new support organization or optimize an existing one. Companies can refer to best practices from the SAP CCC Community, and SAP offers a range of consulting and support services, the most relevant being the SAP Empowering services.

4.2.3   SAP Empowering

SAP Empowering comprises a range of services and training courses targeted at the support organizations and CCCs belonging to SAP customers (see also Section 6.10). Software solutions often play a key role in the success of companies today. Consequently, it is all the more important to be able to rely on a good support organization with efficient processes and excellently trained staff.

SAP Operations Competence Assessment

SAP Empowering aims to help the customer optimize the way it runs and supports its SAP solutions. The first step of the program usually entails an SAP Operations Competence Assessment, which analyzes your current situation, and identifies what you need to do to optimize how you operate and support your SAP solution. The information is used to draw up an action plan with detailed sets of tasks. The customer will be able to complete some of the tasks independently, based on recommendations from SAP. For other, more complex issues, the SAP Empowering program offers support-specific training courses and workshops to prepare you to be able to complete the tasks. Note that the assessment is by no means a prerequisite for the courses and workshops.

Benefits

Companies that use SAP Empowering can expect the following benefits:

▶ Peace of mind in the knowledge that end-to-end solution support is available to safeguard cross-functional business processes

▶ Processes that become more stable and reliable thanks to clearly defined procedures, roles, and responsibilities

▶ Consistent change management processes as a result of change requests and their impact on business scenarios and IT solutions being documented successively

▶ A gentler learning curve, with best practices to help you acquire and share knowledge effectively and steer clear of stumbling blocks

▶ Greater efficiency by using SAP's collective expertise to increase the level of know-how and hone problem-solving skills within the company

▶ The ability to build up a knowledge bank, thus reducing the company's dependence on external consultants, and thereby costs

SAP NetWeaver Empowering

The new challenges associated with operating and supporting an IT landscape based on SAP NetWeaver often call for a company to review its existing skills and processes. Any SAP NetWeaver-based solution demands a highly trained support team capable of analyzing and resolving problems quickly and efficiently, while at the same time safeguarding the operation, availability, and performance of the solution. To help your support organization obtain the skills it needs, SAP offers specially designed services as well as certification as part of SAP NetWeaver Empowering. The goal is to empower companies to leverage their investments in SAP solutions, so they can keep users satisfied and still keep operating costs at an acceptable level.

The emphasis is on analyzing the support processes that are already in place for SAP NetWeaver, with a focus on identifying all the tasks needed to run the solutions—based on SAP NetWeaver—efficiently and successfully. Certification is the next step, which comprises two mandatory elements and one optional element:

▶ Skill assessment for individual roles

▶ Skill assessment for operations

▶ Efficiency assessment (optional)

Certification Certification for SAP NetWeaver operations demonstrates the capabilities of the entire support organization and how well they comply with SAP standards; and not just how well particular individuals support the solution. The efficiency assessment reviews operations in terms of stability and reliability, and results in a professional development plan for the support team.

Certification for SAP NetWeaver operations begins with SAP experts visiting your company for one or two days. They assess your support team's skills and the effectiveness of your processes and procedures. The specialists determine, in advance, what kind of staff your support organization needs. They provide you with a detailed service report, describing how well equipped the support organization is to operate and support the SAP NetWeaver landscape. They also explain the steps you should take to improve your processes and procedures and increase your staff's skill level. Lastly, SAP offers Empowering workshops, which are based mainly on SAP standards and can be split into two categories:

▶ Generic SAP NetWeaver administration; duration approximately three to four days

▶ Component-specific SAP NetWeaver administration, for instance, SAP NetWeaver Portal, SAP NetWeaver Exchange Infrastructure (SAP NetWeaver XI), or SAP NetWeaver Business Intelligence (SAP NetWeaver BI); duration approximately two to three days per component

The actual duration of a workshop depends on the customer's requirements.

In addition to the services for solutions based on SAP NetWeaver, SAP continues to offer "conventional" Empowering services, such as SAP Operations Competence Assessment and SAP Empowering workshops that focus on:

► Support strategy for managers
► SAP Solution Manager
► Support Desk—message processing
► Application and technology
► System and solution optimization

In practice: Sony Electronics Inc.

Sony Electronics Inc., a global leader in the consumer electronics industry, used SAP Empowering to better understand how it could most effectively leverage its SAP resources and expertise. "The better you can use your business solutions, the better your results will be," says Jim Milde, Senior Vice President and CIO for Sony Electronics Inc. "SAP Empowering helped us spotlight our strengths and weaknesses and enhance the value of our SAP solutions."

SAP and Sony worked together to optimize the Sony support operations by combining processes, streamlining operations, and reorganizing the support groups. Once all of the agreed-upon tasks were completed, SAP assessed Sony's progress. At the end of the engagement, SAP awarded Sony an SAP Customer Competence Center (SAP CCC) certification. "Through SAP Empowering, we discovered that we had a greater level of competence in our SAP solutions than we thought," says Carlton Greene, Vice President of the SAP Competency Center. "With guidance from SAP, we were able to build on that. Our success with the process, the positive reaction from our employees, and the measurable improvements in our practices all validated that we were driving in the right direction."

The certification also delivered financial benefits. Sony not only reduced its SAP maintenance and support costs, but also generated savings by merging two production support environments into one and reducing redundancies. "We've seen significant operational cost reductions," explains Milde and continues: "Being certified as an SAP Customer Competence Center helps us to continue to build our organizational capabilities, boost Sony's efficiency on a regional and global basis, and enhance our collaboration capabilities with other units of Sony. This kind of innovation and partnership with SAP is key to Sony's ongoing efforts to increase our market share and serve the customer."

4.3 Quality and Risk Management (Considering SAP Safeguarding as an Example)

SAP offers a range of quality assurance services designed to minimize the risks associated with IT and to ensure that deadlines and budgets are observed in IT projects, as well as when SAP solutions are in use. SAP Safeguarding is described below to illustrate the support SAP provides during the phases in the lifecycle of an SAP solution.

Core business processes are usually distributed over several systems. While complex software solutions optimally support these business processes, they involve risk in terms of manageability, availability, and performance. The goal of SAP Safeguarding is to identify risks while a system is being implemented and operated, and to create an action plan to minimize these risks.

For optimal results, you should use the SAP Safeguarding checks as early as possible in the project. The earlier you use them, the more likely you are to reduce the number of technical and operational problems and their associated costs. You can use the different checks for implementations and upgrades, as well as for continuously optimizing and monitoring your software solution. SAP Safeguarding significantly reduces operating costs, and thus the TCO, while minimizing the risk of system failures by:

Benefits
▶ Accelerating your SAP project—such as an implementation or upgrade—which means you need fewer resources

▶ Providing technical guidelines to help you avoid unnecessary work and complications

▶ Ensuring that your SAP solution runs with optimum performance, availability, and maintainability

▶ Identifying areas that could benefit from optimization

Based on the experience gained from thousands of installations, the SAP Safeguarding checks help you to avoid complications from the outset. SAP Safeguarding is invaluable for your mission-critical business processes, because you incur substantial costs if your projects fail.

You would use SAP Safeguarding for Implementation, for example, to safeguard complex implementation projects. In cases where a system has already gone live, we recommend SAP Solution Management Assessment, which focuses on the technical optimization of business processes and of the operation of the SAP solution.

An individual risk management plan and service plan are created based on the results of these checks. The risk management plan defines a common procedure for you, SAP, and SAP partners to follow in order to manage the risk of your particular solution. The service plan matches advanced services to your specific needs regarding the performance and availability of core business processes.

Individual service plan

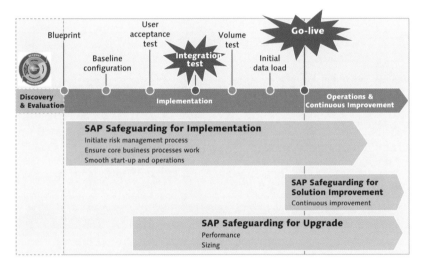

Figure 4.9 Elements of SAP Safeguarding

The program comprises the following service packages, which are described below:

Customer Intentions	Safeguarding Offerings
Implementation	SAP Safeguarding for Implementation
Continuous Optimization of the SAP Solution	SAP Safeguarding for Solution Improvement
Upgrade	SAP Safeguarding for Upgrade

Table 4.1 Safeguarding Offerings for the Software Lifecycle

SAP Safeguarding for Implementation

We recommend that you use *SAP Safeguarding for Implementation* to safeguard large, mission-critical implementation projects. *SAP GoingLive Check* is sufficient for simple implementation projects, which means you don't need the complete service package. The scope of services delivered with *SAP Safeguarding for Implementation* is tailored to meet the needs of your project with the goal of minimizing risk right from the beginning. The services determine whether the functions you want to implement are functionally and technically feasible within your current software solution. They proactively optimize the configuration of the systems you want to implement, thereby reducing your hardware costs.

SAP Safeguarding for Implementation comprises the following services:

▶ SAP Safeguarding Planning

▶ SAP Feasibility Check

▶ SAP Technical Integration Check

▶ SAP Operations Readiness Assessment

▶ SAP GoingLive Check

▶ On-Site GoingLive Support

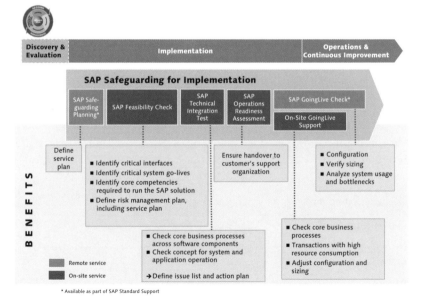

Figure 4.10 Functional Scope of SAP Safeguarding for Implementation

In practice: Porsche AG

Porsche, a global leader in the automotive industry, implemented SAP Advanced Planning & Optimization (SAP APO), a central component in mySAP Supply Chain Management (mySAP SCM), to handle its global spare-parts business. SAP Safeguarding SCM helped the implementation project stay within its planned time frame and budget, and played a part in preventing problems at an early stage.

"Implementing SAP APO in 2000 was our first step toward achieving worldwide coverage of our entire supply chain process in one system. Besides sequential planning for Porsche AG and imports, over the last two years we have also integrated over 300 dealers into the supply chain in a VMI scenario," explains Sascha Neurohr, responsible for SAP APO at the Stuttgart sports car manufacturer. Due to the very large amounts of data involved in the various stages of this process, SAP recommended that Porsche use services from the SAP Solution Management Optimization program. SAP employees performed an in-depth analysis of the hardware and software and quickly identified areas in which Porsche could make improvements. SAP Active Global Support cut the time required for mass processing large datasets by a factor of 2.5. This was achieved by technical improvements and optimizing planning runs for forecasting, procurement, and replenishment planning in line with processes and resources.

"Thanks to SAP Solution Management Optimization services, it has become much quicker and simpler for us to plan and monitor our processes," says Neurohr. System resources are now used much more efficiently. The improved system performance means there is less demand on the CPU and previous plans to upgrade hardware have been put on hold.

SAP Safeguarding for Solution Improvement

SAP offers two services for identifying weak points in system operation and providing recommendations for optimization. SAP Solution Management Assessment (SMA) focuses on analyzing the core business processes and often forms the basis for targeted optimization services. SAP OS/DB Migration Check is conducted when an operating system or database is upgraded.

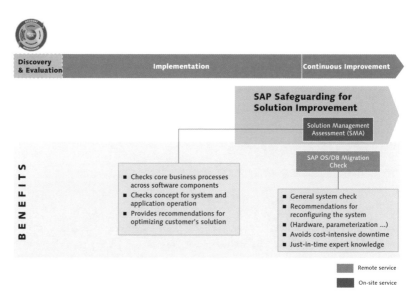

Figure 4.11 Elements of SAP Safeguarding for Solution Improvement

SAP Safeguarding for Upgrade

The ever-increasing demands placed on enterprise software mean the functions provided by your SAP solution have to be upgraded continuously. When you upgrade to a new release, you can use the latest functions immediately. As soon as you have decided to upgrade, you can draft a project plan and determine the central cost drivers and risk factors involved. Experience shows the following factors to be the main cost drivers:

Cost drivers

▶ Project planning for upgrade

▶ IT infrastructure setup

▶ Technical upgrade and downtime

▶ Customer-specific developments

▶ Tests

▶ User training

SAP GoingLive Functional Upgrade Check

We recommend SAP Safeguarding for Upgrade to ensure that the upgrade is completed as quickly, smoothly, efficiently, and cost-effectively as possible (see also Section 6.8). SAP GoingLive Functional Upgrade Check, the main element of SAP Safeguarding for Upgrade, is a remote service that provides important project information. It checks the software compatibility, sizing, and technical configuration, and analyzes bottlenecks. It also identifies ways to reduce costs.

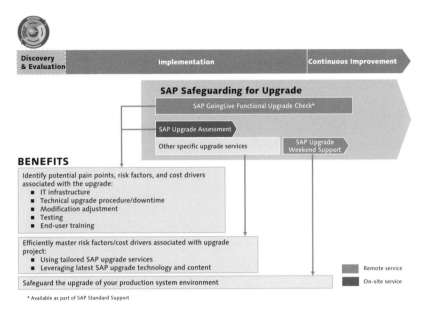

Figure 4.12 SAP Safeguarding for Upgrade Service Portfolio

In addition to this service, which is provided free of charge with SAP Standard Support (see also Section 5.1.1), SAP offers numerous fee-based services to provide you with even more comprehensive support. In the first session of the SAP GoingLive Functional Upgrade Check, we recommend using upgrade services that are particularly suited to your project.

Specially Adapted SAP Safeguarding Services

In addition to the Safeguarding services available for the individual phases of the product lifecycle, SAP offers specially adapted services for minimizing technical risks. They focus on mySAP Supply Chain Management (mySAP SCM), and specific industries such as banking, insurance, utilities, and telecommunications:

▶ SAP Safeguarding SCM

▶ SAP Safeguarding for SAP Bank Analyzer

▶ SAP Safeguarding for Contract Accounting (FI-CA)

4.4 Business and IT Strategy Consulting

The Business and IT Strategy Consulting services help you to use information technology to increase business value through more efficient business processes, to transform established business, and to create new business. They provide the guidance necessary to develop business plans and IT infrastructure, and accurately assess the value of new solutions and processes.

SAP consultants work hand-in-hand with you to:

▶ Review your enterprise's strategy to make the most of state-of-the-art SAP software

▶ Identify and quantify the business value of proposed and existing IT investments

▶ Determine the TCO of your solutions, and find ways of reducing that cost

▶ Pinpoint and reduce the technical and business risk associated with your processes

▶ Create a portfolio of prioritized projects, with a business case and a clearly defined, long-term roadmap for business success

Scope of Business and IT Strategy Consulting Business and IT Strategy Consulting encompasses the following global services:

▶ SAP Business Strategy

▶ SAP Business and Value Assessment

▶ SAP TCO Analysis

▶ SAP Risk Assessment

▶ SAP IT Strategy

▶ SAP Strategic Organizational Alignment

In practice: Siemens Communications

With a workforce of around 60,000, Siemens Communications (Com) is a market leader in the global telecommunications industry. Much of the company's business is handled by outsourced SAP solutions. In line with Siemens' overall strategy, Siemens Com is committed to continuously monitoring and streamlining its spending.

Against this background, Siemens Com decided to analyze the TCO of the SAP software it deployed for Sales in Germany, focusing on its solutions for sales and distribution, materials management, controlling, and financial accounting. The goal was to pinpoint cost drivers and identify opportunities for savings.

In addition, the IT managers in Munich wanted facts and figures to help them decide whether to upgrade or to stay with their current release. Siemens Com called in a team from SAP Consulting to deliver the TCO analysis. "We chose SAP consultants, not only on account of their close links with SAP, but also because of their comprehensive product and technology expertise and extensive experience," says Hans-Peter Vogel, head of IT, CRM Direct Channel, Siemens Communications.

The team took a long, hard look at operating costs. It analyzed the way outsourced systems were operated, focusing particularly on application management. Data was collected using questionnaires and face-to-face interviews with on-site managers. On the basis of this information, operating expenditures were assigned to individual cost components. SAP TCO Model clearly highlighted the main cost drivers. In this case, it revealed that 90 % of application management spending was generated by six TCO components.

The use of SAP reference data enables the TCO analysis to provide more visibility into the assessment of costs and cost structures. The TCO specialists from SAP's Business Consulting group used their own reference data, as well as their experience of SAP's development, consulting, and support environments. In Siemens Com's case, they compiled the reference data from a group of seven companies. "Benchmarking of this kind forms the basis for delta analyses, enabling us to demonstrate where there is potential for improvement and how to achieve it," explains Gerhard Claus from SAP Consulting.

The TCO analysis established a transparent basis for implementing improvements and cutting costs. This includes concrete figures in the form of monetary quantifications (in this case, 13 % potential savings), as well as initiatives to realize the identified potential. The new visibility into spending also provided insight into the cost of IT support for specific business departments. "This enabled us to identify tasks that are not, strictly speaking, part of application maintenance, but that are currently performed on behalf of user departments," says Vogel of this benefit of the TCO analysis.

4.5 Technology Architecture Design

These consulting services help you align complex system architecture with project-specific technical requirements. Explicit recommendations are provided to ensure that you have a workable IT environment that is stable and extensible.

With these services, you benefit from:

▶ Sound advice on global implementation strategies that involve multiple languages, currencies, and sites

▶ Strategic assessments to identify how your infrastructure can be made more efficient and cost-effective

▶ Close collaboration on the planning of an integrated enterprise architecture, comprising all your SAP and non-SAP solutions

▶ Expert support to design a flexible platform that can grow with your business needs

Scope of Technology Architecture Design Technology Architecture Design comprises the following services:

▶ SAP IT Assessment

▶ SAP IT Planning

▶ SAP System Architecture Planning

▶ SAP Globalization and Language Consulting

4.6 Solution and Architecture Design

For Solution and Architecture Design, SAP offers services that bring technology in line with application and business strategies. Services that directly target the infrastructure are complemented by the Enterprise Services Architecture Adoption Program, which has been designed to help you create a long-term solution blueprint based on SAP's Enterprise Services Architecture (ESA) concept.

4.6.1 Solution and Architecture Design

These consulting services influence the application landscape and align technology and application strategy with business needs. Business solutions are integrated into an overall enterprise architecture, ensuring that the infrastructure optimally supports your business strategies.

SAP consultants provide the assistance you need to:

- Establish effective and efficient processes designed for achieving your organization's specific objectives

▶ Design an enterprisewide landscape for your applications

▶ Pilot SAP software in your production landscape, paving the way for a fast, cost-effective implementation

▶ Determine the right approach, scope, costs, and timelines for your projects

▶ Identify the risks and benefits of your implementation at an early stage

Solution and Architecture Design offers the following services:

▶ SAP Solution Prototyping

▶ SAP Feasibility Study

Scope of Solution and Architecture Design

4.6.2 Enterprise Services Architecture Adoption Program

To keep pace with today's rapidly changing markets, you have to be able to adapt quickly and effectively to new business imperatives and opportunities, without impacting ongoing operations. But traditional approaches to creating innovative processes—across heterogeneous IT systems and enterprise boundaries—have proven too costly, too inefficient, and too rigid.

SAP's answer is Enterprise Services Architecture (ESA). Enabled by the SAP NetWeaver platform, ESA leverages the benefits of open Web services to bridge the gap between business and IT and to deliver on the promise of a flexible, service-oriented architecture (SOA). With ESA, your organization has a blueprint for composing new applications on the basis of existing systems—increasing agility and efficiency, and making process innovation affordable.

Service-oriented architecture

But introducing a service-oriented approach is not something you can do overnight. Careful planning is required to determine where best to begin, what services to implement, and in what order. Moreover, you need to consider which systems to retain, which to offload, and how to integrate the old with the new. And before moving to ESA, you want to be sure it will deliver the desired results.

To help you find the answers to these questions, SAP has developed the ESA Adoption Program. This flexible methodology enables you to tackle your transition to ESA (see also Section 6.1) in a clearly structured series of logical steps—reducing complexity and costs, accelerating change, and mitigating associated risk.

ESA Adoption Program

Because no two paths to ESA adoption are likely to be the same, the program has been designed to accommodate a wide range of requirements, budgets, resources, and objectives. So, whether you're looking to rethink your entire IT strategy, or planning more modest ESA projects to meet specific needs, you can be certain of getting effective advice and assistance, plus proven tools and services.

Four Steps to ESA Adoption

ESA Adoption Program comprises four interrelated phases (see Figure 4.13), each with its own compact portfolio of tried-and-tested support services. These include dedicated tools, templates, and workshops designed to smooth the way to ESA adoption. Depending on your specific needs, you can select one or two of these services at each stage of the process.

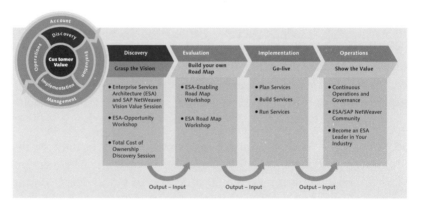

Figure 4.13 Four Steps to ESA Adoption

▶ Discovery

During this phase, the emphasis is on acquiring a firm grasp of the ESA vision and of its implications for your company in terms of costs and business value. Tools deployed include opportunity workshops, which provide initial insight into how ESA can enhance your business processes. During these sessions, your organization's IT and business leaders work hand-in-hand to discover how and where service-oriented architecture (SOA) could best drive innovation and efficiency.

▶ Evaluation

Drawing on the results of the preceding step, the evaluation phase focuses on creating a tailored roadmap for your company's ESA. Dedicated workshops define the scope of your ESA project, determine the

business process best suited to a service-oriented approach, and identify the IT projects most likely to increase your organization's competitiveness and responsiveness.

▶ Implementation
Leveraging the roadmap created during the evaluation phase, the third
step of the program helps you convert the ESA blueprint into practice.
Key tasks include choosing the right plan, build, and run services from
SAP's comprehensive portfolio for ESA. By carefully matching these
services to your specific needs, you can ensure fast, effective implementation, while minimizing risk and costs.

▶ Operations
In the fourth phase, SAP provides a range of offerings that help you
manage your applications and maintain a consistent business and IT
strategy over the coming years. Particular attention is given to ROI, and
SAP can deliver dedicated tools that enable you to measure results,
quantify the benefits derived from ESA and the SAP NetWeaver platform, and compare them with your original expectations. Insight is also
provided into opportunities for generating additional value, which can
be addressed in a further, fifth phase.

With the adoption program, you and your business can take the steps
needed to achieve greater flexibility, competitiveness, and business value.

In practice: LHI Leasing GmbH

LHI Leasing is a financial services and property leasing company based
in Munich, Germany. To support standard as well as non-standard
leasing agreements, LHI needed to make its IT infrastructure and processes more flexible. When the company set about restructuring, it
decided to adopt ESA, a concept based on SAP's Web services platform SAP NetWeaver.

Drawing up an ESA roadmap demands in-depth knowledge of a company's business processes, IT environment, and strategic goals—a challenging undertaking that calls for accurate research and analysis. Furthermore, those involved must have a thorough understanding of how
the business processes are structured and how they are supported by
IT. LHI commissioned SAP Consulting to create the roadmap. "The SAP
consultants understood the new business processes and IT services
that we needed for this company," says Thomas Büsch, Managing
Director and head of IT at LHI.

Over a period of several weeks, the SAP consultants trained LHI's in-house experts and introduced them to the benefits of SAP NetWeaver and ESA.

This was also a chance for the SAP consultants to familiarize themselves with LHI's business processes, particularly those for reporting, employee and manager self services, and knowledge management. "During these workshops, SAP Consulting actually adapted their agenda to our needs," says Büsch. "They understood that midmarket companies have special needs and addressed them on a technical, process, and organizational level."

Together, they came up with a 24-month roadmap for implementing ESA with mySAP ERP. The map also included potential risks, a management summary, and a three-to-five-year timeline for major project milestones. The timeline addressed the creation of portals for self services and external services, including personalized customer reports and integrated ad-hoc workflows for creating new projects. "The roadmap process helped me understand ESA more deeply, and then apply it to a sequence of steps that achieve business flexibility by transforming both business processes and IT architecture," says Büsch.

LHI is deploying SAP NetWeaver and its portal components to provide employee and manager self services: This allows employees to request leave electronically, change their own data, and use knowledge management applications. In addition, managers can review leave requests and see salary details, as well as cost center overviews.

Certain elements of the roadmap will be implemented at a later stage, and will include services for personalized interaction between LHI and its customers. The portal will also be used in a pilot program to give customers direct access to more information and, in some cases, allow them to update data themselves. Eventually, LHI will be able to create modular contracts that combine subcomponents from old contracts.

By upgrading to mySAP ERP—based on ESA—LHI will not only become more flexible and faster, but will also save money. LHI's infrastructure will be made up of a set of reusable services. Designing an implementation concept for SAP NetWeaver across LHI's intranet and extranet will make it easier for the company to combine existing products and incorporate new functions. "We will be able to deliver business services that are more flexible, faster, and cheaper," summarizes Büsch.

4.7   Solution Integration

Solution Integration services focus on detailed design, implementation, and management with the goal of linking applications to one other, or to an established or planned IT infrastructure.

SAP's integration experts can achieve the following for you:

▶ Help you to integrate company-specific solutions with both SAP and non-SAP solutions

▶ Assist you in aligning your IT landscape with organizational change quickly and cost-effectively

▶ Optimize the architecture and interfaces of heterogeneous system landscapes

▶ Provide effective strategies for data conversion

▶ Archive data across your entire SAP environment, while ensuring compliance with statutory requirements

▶ Integrate new functions, new releases, and custom applications

The global Solution Integration offering comprises the following services:

Scope of Solution Integration

▶ SAP Application Integration

▶ SAP Technical Feasibility Check

▶ SAP Technical Integration Check

▶ SAP Solution Management Assessment

▶ SAP Interface Management

4.8   System Landscape Optimization

The System Landscape Optimization (SLO) services are SAP's answer to the increasing need to implement major changes in production for SAP solutions. They are designed to ease and fully leverage customers' business-driven change by effectively aligning system landscapes

The SLO services suite (see also Section 6.9) was built to ensure and support adaptivity along the lifecycle of SAP solutions. There is a whole set of well-known cases of business-driven change:

Reasons for system changes

▶ Mergers, acquisitions, and divestitures

▶ Restructuring of business organization

▶ Alignment with best-of-industry business processes and IT strategies

▶ Reduction of IT complexity

In the face of such challenges, the SLO services aim to:

▶ Enable improved business processes to be implemented

▶ Reduce the TCO

▶ Optimize a global, heterogeneous system landscape

▶ Harmonize enterprise data, interfaces, and data exchange

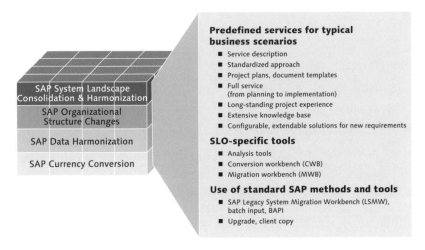

Figure 4.14 SLO Service Portfolio

SLO service areas SLO is composed of four key service areas:

▶ **SAP System Landscape Consolidation & Harmonization**
During the life cycle of an enterprise IT solution, major changes often have to be made to the underlying system landscape. Such changes are generally made in response to new or modified business strategies or if an environment becomes excessively complex.

▶ **SAP Organizational Structure Changes**
These services help you to implement changes affecting the definition and usage of organizational units within your SAP software. In this context, organizational units can be company codes, controlling areas, business areas, plants, and so forth.

▶ **SAP Data Harmonization**
These services help you to modify large amounts of data quickly and cost-effectively, while ensuring data consistency. Changes are made to all business objects—such as open items and historical data—regardless of their business status.

▶ **SAP Currency Conversion**
These services help you change your current currency to the target currency, guaranteeing audit-proof financial statements and ensuring that all currency-specific entities are aligned throughout your solutions.

SLO has a proven track record of identifying missing and conflicting data in existing systems and finding fast, efficient, and transparent solutions to overcome the technical complexities involved in separating and merging data. **SLO expert packages**

SLO provides and enhances expert packages that contain specific services and tools for projects involving data harmonization, system landscape optimization, and organizational change. All expert packages follow a generic and standardized approach to ensure that all data is transferred quickly and reliably. One clear benefit is the use of existing conversion programs—with predefined business content—which operate directly at database level and ensure high-performance conversions.

Not only does SLO offer customers a large service portfolio, it also works constantly to enrich its toolkit. The Migration Workbench (MWB) helps customers migrate data at object or table level from the source to the target system. The Conversion Workbench (CWB), on the other hand, converts data within one system. Other tools can analyze complete ERP systems, or change the organizational/business structure of the whole system. All services can be applied to the full range of mySAP Business Suite. **SLO tools**

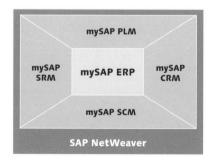

Harmonization of structures and processes
- **More transparency, fewer redundancies**
  - ◆ Unified master data – customers, vendors, materials
  - ◆ Unified controlling structures
  - ◆ Unified chart of accounts
- **Improved communication and integration**
  - ◆ More efficient information exchange through unified structures
- **Facilitates cross-system processes**
  - ◆ Master Data Management (MDM)
  - ◆ Cross-system planning
  - ◆ Central purchasing
  - ◆ Central/cross-system reporting

Company reorganization
- **Merger or divestiture of companies or parts of companies**

System setup
- **Initial load, for MDM server, for instance**

Figure 4.15 SLO Supports the Implementation and Operation of mySAP Business Suite

The benefits of SLO services include:

▶ **Protection of your investment**
Ensuring your solutions can adapt to changing requirements is key to extending their life.

▶ **Greater system flexibility**
To deploy your enterprise applications for maximum benefit, you need to ensure that the system landscape can support your business processes and can be adapted to changing requirements.

▶ **Lower cost of ownership**
Your dual challenges are to minimize IT costs and to capitalize on new developments in the dynamic IT market. SLO services help you to identify and take full advantage of potential improvements and efficiencies.

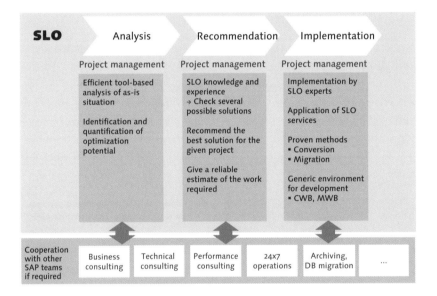

Figure 4.16 Typical Procedure for SLO Projects

In practice: Marubeni Corporation

When Marubeni Corporation, a global Japanese trading firm, consolidated and upgraded its SAP systems, it benefited immensely from expert assistance from SAP Consulting, SAP Active Global Support, and SAP Custom Development.

It faced and mastered a number of major challenges: consolidating 10 SAP R/3 systems into one target system, and simultaneously upgrading from Release 3.1H to SAP R/3 Enterprise; transferring one existing company code—distributed across nine existing systems—to a single system/server; and merging the purchasing organization (distributed across four systems and used in sales and distribution, as well as materials management operations) into a single client/system.

Marubeni's overall project objective was to consolidate multiple systems that used SAP R/3 software into a single, upgraded system, with a focus on reducing IT infrastructure and TCO at the same time. SAP Japan led the successful project, which reflected high levels of multicultural teamwork, effective planning, and technical expertise. "The cooperation between Marubeni Corporation, MJS, the SLO group, SAP Japan, and SAP Services was extremely efficient," says Fumihiko Nishita, Customer Engagement Manager at SAP Japan. "It helped the consolidation project to become an overall success."

The SLO group and its products and services, as well as their expert tools MWB and CWB, helped the customer to come through the project with flying colors. SAP services and technology enabled Marubeni, a long-time customer with positive experience using SAP solutions, to preserve existing data and successfully transfer all Marubeni-specific developments to the new target system. After consolidating its systems and reducing the number of clients, the Marubeni Corporation can now get a quicker overview of its financial data. The same is true of the consolidated purchasing organization; the company can now make better use of its financial and sales data to strengthen its market position. Above all, the initiative has helped the company to lower its operating costs for IT.

Furthermore, users now have the advantage of being able to access information more easily, and to analyze data using the management information system. "The fact that the data can be found in one client within one system has improved our reporting capability and helps us manage our applications in a much more effective way. It is also much easier to meet management requirements," says the Deputy General Manager at Marubeni Corporation, Jutaro Shiraishi.

Koji Shibagaki, General Manager of the Information Strategy department, Marubeni Corporation, sums up the project as follows: "The system consolidation is regarded as an overall success, because it helped us to reduce IT costs and to enhance the management decision-making process."

4.9 Technical Quality Assurance for Implementations, Operations, and Upgrades

When implementing, running, or upgrading complex solutions, you may need special support to meet your business requirements. Therefore, SAP Active Global Support has designed additional offerings to ensure that your solutions go live smoothly and run efficiently. For mission-critical solutions, SAP offers first-rate support with SAP MaxAttention, which provides the best technical quality management and support services tailored to your needs. Additionally, you may require SAP Expertise on Demand to ensure that you have the right expert, at the right time, for your project or operations.

4.9.1 SAP MaxAttention

The potential for optimizing existing IT landscapes can often be considerable, especially in large companies with complex business scenarios and a global presence. The primary objective is to protect existing investments and create a wide scope for innovation. This calls for a solution support model of the highest quality, which, in turn, requires a holistic approach to the IT solution and a thorough understanding of the following areas and the relationships between them:

▶ Business processes

▶ System landscape

▶ Automation

▶ Investment protection

Analysis of processes Core business processes have to be regarded systematically and consistently. Besides data consistency, you will need to consider such aspects as the performance of customer developments. It is also important to assess performance in business terms, on the basis of a price calculation or at month-end closing, for instance. Other key concerns include error handling and business process monitoring. The objective is to establish transparent, reliable business processes and increase their efficiency.

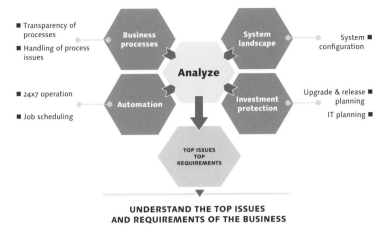

Figure 4.17 Essential Areas of Continuous Improvement

The purpose of analyzing the system landscape is to safeguard the scalability and stability of the technical infrastructure and optimize the use of available resources. The entire system landscape (SAP and non-SAP systems), including the network, is considered. The analysis also covers system and database settings, performance bottlenecks, and possible reasons for data inconsistencies.

Analysis of the system landscape

Automation can enable your business processes to run continuously. Aspects covered in the analysis include job scheduling (sequential and parallel processing of jobs, restart and recovery procedures), data volume, and the criteria for 24/7 operation.

Automation

When it comes to investment protection, SAP analyzes your upgrade and release planning, your rollout planning, and the way you use global templates. The assessment considers the overall IT strategy, technical upgrades, system consolidation, and aspects such as customer-specific maintenance options. It helps to ensure that investments in SAP software remain safe and future proof.

Protection of investment

SAP knows that short-term support in these areas does not produce the desired results. What is needed is long-term support exploiting the full potential of SAP's experience. This need is met by a special offering called SAP MaxAttention (see also Section 6.6). SAP MaxAttention is tailored to each customer's needs and is designed to optimize the SAP solutions that are in place, consolidate the know-how present in in-house support organizations, safeguard software implementation projects, and reduce risks—always with a high degree of cooperation between the customer and SAP experts.

Elements of SAP MaxAttention

SAP MaxAttention comprises two essential elements: a management component and an extensive portfolio of expert services.

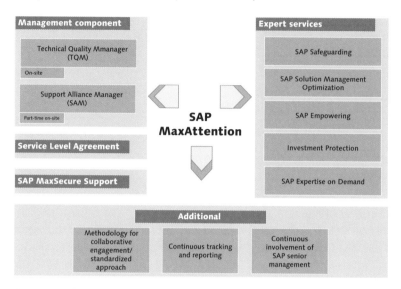

Figure 4.18 The Elements of SAP MaxAttention

Technical Quality Manager

The management component covers the stages involved in preparing, planning, and establishing mutual relationships between the customer and SAP. SAP designates a Technical Quality Manager (TQM)—or several, according to the customer's requirements—to work on-site with the customer and oversee the jointly defined project. The TQM can call on solution, technology, and development experts, service and support specialists, and consultants, who may also help out on-site if required.

Support Alliance Manager

For particularly complex situations, SAP also appoints a Support Alliance Manager (SAM), who works regularly with customer counterparts. Regular meetings are held with the customer's executives, keeping both parties up to date on the status of completed and current actions and providing an opportunity for agreeing future activities.

Expert services

The expert services included with SAP MaxAttention cover a vast range of offerings from SAP Safeguarding (see Section 4.3), SAP Solution Management Optimization (see Section 4.10.2), SAP Empowering (see Section 4.2.3), and SAP Expertise on Demand (see Section 4.9.2). An on-site analysis evaluates your situation and the potential for solution optimization, taking into account your strategic planning. The analysis results determine which expert services are deployed from the aforementioned programs. SAP constantly monitors success and informs you of any changes initiated as a result of the services.

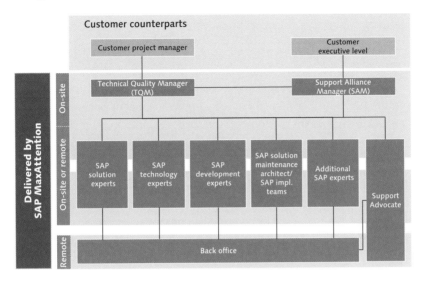

Figure 4.19 Sample Structure for Professional On-Site Support

A standardized method supports the components within SAP MaxAttention. Balanced Scorecards (BSCs) are used to monitor individual points. In addition, jointly defined key performance indicators (KPIs) form the basis for reports. SAP's Executive Board and senior management are also kept apprised of how the project is progressing.

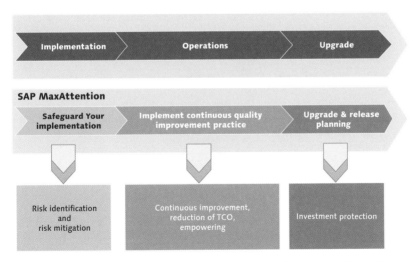

Figure 4.20 SAP MaxAttention Focuses on Implementing, Running, and Upgrading SAP Solutions

Quality management and continuous improvement

The different variants of SAP MaxAttention focus on quality management and continually improving SAP solutions in the main phases of their lifecycle. When software is being implemented, the main objective is to avoid and minimize risks and prepare for effective, cost-efficient operations.

SAP solutions that are already running are analyzed and fine-tuned to reduce costs. Ways of achieving this include minimizing maintenance requirements and continually enhancing both system performance and the capabilities of the customer's support organization. A customer-specific Service Level Agreement (SLA) accelerates message processing with SAP MaxAttention.

SAP MaxSecure

To support customers who may have special security and confidentiality constraints, SAP MaxAttention includes an additional component—SAP MaxSecure. SAP MaxSecure Support is composed of three broad areas: empowering, remote support, and on-site support. You can choose the services that best suit your requirements from these three areas.

The empowering services are designed to build up your support capabilities through workshops and mentoring, so that your company is able to resolve common problems independently, without disclosing company information to third parties. Remote support enables you to take advantage of special "safe rooms" with separate access control, additional encryption when transferring data, session watching and session recording, as well as logically or physically isolated connections to the SAP network. Even with these security precautions, you may still have systems or clients that you cannot release for remote support. In such cases, SAP can provide on-site support.

Continual Quality Management with SAP MaxAttention

It is essential to set down the roles and responsibilities of all partners involved in the program and project: customer, partner, and SAP. SAP's role can range from that of software vendor to provider of expertise in defined SAP product areas to software partner.

Technical Quality Manager

The TQM constantly checks and assesses the risks associated with the SAP solution. On the basis of the analysis results, action plans are compiled stipulating roles, responsibilities, and deadlines to mitigate any identified risks effectively. Preventive measures can be taken because the actual activities, as well as their impact on risks, are under constant observation. Monthly reports reveal to what extent proposals implemented for reducing identified risks have been successful. Another element ensuring that your projects receive optimum support is the service plan, which is updated periodically and tailored to your specific requirements.

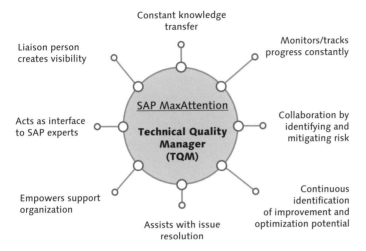

Figure 4.21 The Role of the TQM

When drawing up this plan, the whole range of SAP support programs is considered. The TQM collaborates closely with the customer and, where appropriate, partners with the customer to put the steps stipulated in the plan into practice. In order to safeguard the technical feasibility and operation of a customer solution, SAP, as the service provider, must be actively involved.

The procedure comprises four key phases, as depicted in Figure 4.22.

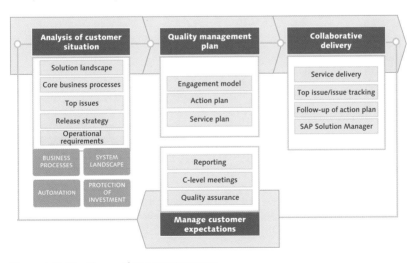

Figure 4.22 The Phases of SAP MaxAttention

▶ **Analysis of customer situation**
During the evaluation phase, SAP assesses and prioritizes risks and potential problem areas. First, the TQM interviews the relevant SAP employees from the account, consulting, and support teams.

▶ **Quality management plan**
This results in a consolidated, evaluated overview of risks and problem areas and an action plan for the areas that need addressing. It also includes a proposal for integrating SAP into the process. The findings of the evaluation phase are cleared with the customer and, where appropriate, with the partners as well.

▶ **Collaborative delivery**
SAP, the customer, and partners work hand-in-hand to implement the plan.

▶ **Continuous monitoring**
While the individual measures are being implemented, SAP tracks the status and coordinates the other measures at project level. In addition, activities are coordinated at C-level, which involves monitoring the status of ongoing activities as well as managing strategic aspects.

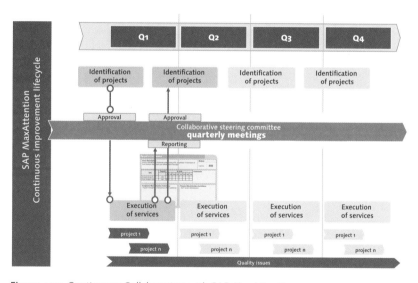

Figure 4.23 Continuous Collaboration with SAP MaxAttention

SAP experts collaborate closely with the project partners to create a monthly status report and action plan. The monthly-consolidated documents are presented and signed off at a project steering committee. At the customer's site, a TQM from SAP is responsible for coordinating the services that SAP is to deliver. The TQM can call on a global team of experts from SAP.

Front- and Back-Office Support

As a top-rate service, SAP MaxAttention is tailored entirely to customer needs and must therefore be extremely flexible. One of the program's main advantages is that it provides access to a network of highly specialized resources. The TQM sets up and runs a front office at the customer's site to integrate the customer in this network. The front office is always connected with the back office at SAP.

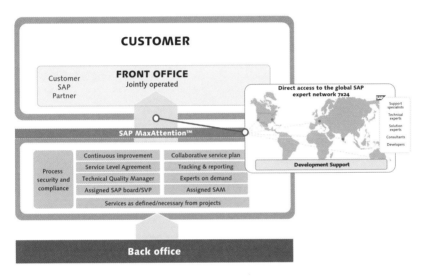

Figure 4.24 Front and Back Office with SAP MaxAttention

The front office's main task is to deliver the services as defined in the action plan. The permanent connection to the back office ensures that any resources involved always have up-to-date information that flows into all services. What's more, this channel makes it possible for consultants and application and Basis programmers to be called in temporarily and provide support at short notice.

SAP MaxAttention in an Outsourcing Context

Unfortunately, our experience has shown that outsourcing IT to external providers often entails a loss of competence. SAP MaxAttention, however, can reconcile the two areas and enables the requirements arising from business processes to be converted to requirements for the underlying technology. With SAP MaxAttention, customers can preserve the IT

Preserve competence

skills they have built up within their company. The program allows the customer, outsourcing provider, and SAP to work together to identify and proactively avoid risks and to continually optimize the solution.

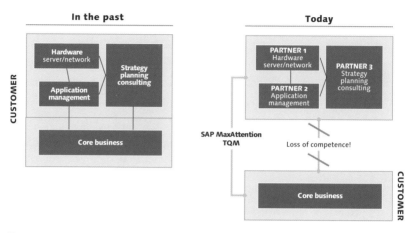

Figure 4.25 SAP MaxAttention in an Outsourcing Context

Quick Check: Is SAP MaxAttention Suitable for Your Company?

While SAP Standard Support (see Section 5.1.1) is intended for all SAP customers, SAP MaxAttention is primarily intended for large companies. This top support package can make IT solutions considerably more secure and reliable. If large companies fulfill the following criteria, they should take a closer look at what SAP MaxAttention has to offer:

Criteria for SAP MaxAttention

▶ The company operates in a sensitive industry sector in which the performance and availability of the IT solution are extremely important.

▶ The company has a number of complex, mission-critical projects on its agenda that require a substantial budget.

▶ The company has Service Level Agreements (SLAs) with customers or users.

▶ The company would like to set up its own support organization, or, if it already has such an organization, to optimize it and benefit greatly from having SAP experts on-site.

In practice: Postbank AG

SAP has been working with Postbank, the largest retail bank in Germany, to develop the most up-to-date core banking software.

A business as sensitive as financial transactions also requires a special kind of support. This, too, was new territory for Postbank, so they integrated a special support product—SAP MaxAttention.

"For our bank, smooth system operation is essential. A downtime of even a few hours could prove critical," explains Dr. Thomas Mangel, IT director at Postbank Systems AG. "This downtime would not only be a legal and financial disaster; it would also seriously damage the bank's public image."

To ensure smooth system operation, Postbank chose SAP MaxAttention, a first-rate product that supports SAP applications with additional services not covered by the standard support offering.

"When we designed the system, it was clear to us that a special kind of support from the provider would be needed for the complex architecture," says Mangel. "Postbank requires support that is fast, customized, and completely reliable, and SAP MaxAttention meets these criteria." For Mangel, one of the most important aspects is development support, because it gives Postbank access to SAP developers when problems have to be resolved quickly.

Five SAP employees work on-site at Postbank in an "SAP front office." They are the first line of support for messages and have direct contact to other SAP experts in the support and development departments at SAP. SAP front-office employees work in shifts and are on call 24 hours a day. The advantages of the SAP front office are clear to Mangel: "The employees have a direct view of the system and can effectuate many improvements there."

4.9.2 SAP Expertise on Demand

With SAP Expertise on Demand, you can call on SAP experts to resolve your problems on a short- to medium-term basis. This kind of temporary engagement is intended for technically demanding or unusual problems that cannot be resolved by your own staff. The service is designed to put you in touch with experts who understand the technical and functional challenges that you need to overcome to optimize your company's business processes.

Any problems that occur are documented in SAP Solution Manager, either by one of your experts or by SAP. If a remote or on-site service is being delivered using SAP Solution Manager and a problem is identified, it is recorded automatically in the issue list. SAP Expertise on Demand is the ideal service to deal with problems that are not caused by software errors and that demand specialized SAP expertise. You can send your request directly to SAP at the push of a button; information about the problem and the business context is included automatically. SAP can use this information to select suitably experienced experts quickly and in directly to resolve your problem. Depending on the type of request, the SAP specialists will work remotely or on-site. The entire process is documented in the issue list in SAP Solution Manager, which you can view at any time.

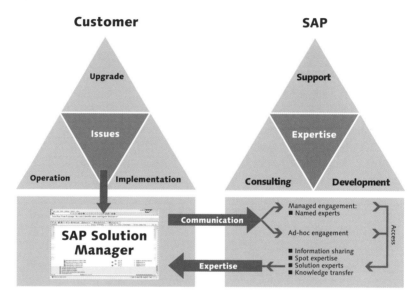

Figure 4.26 SAP Expertise on Demand

Prerequisites You need to meet the following conditions in order to take advantage of SAP Expertise on Demand:

▶ You use SAP Solution Manager (Release 3.2, Support Package 9 or above) as the platform for communication and collaboration with SAP.

▶ Your solutions and business processes have been defined in SAP Solution Manager.

▶ You have configured SAP Solution Manager to transfer requests to SAP.

▶ In SAP Solution Manager, any problems that occur are documented in the issue list.

You can expect the following benefits from SAP Expertise on Demand:

▶ Immediate access to the knowledge and experience of SAP experts, whose collective expertise spans a wide range of subjects and who are familiar with thousands of customer situations and the solutions to a multitude of varied problems

▶ Uncomplicated, direct communication with SAP specialists to get your problems fixed faster

▶ The chance to learn from SAP experts so that you can build up your in-house skills and knowledge

▶ No other service provider has as much technical SAP know-how as SAP itself. You will be assigned a suitably qualified SAP expert to ensure that you get the best results.

To summarize, SAP Expertise on Demand empowers you to optimize your business processes, get the best possible performance from your system, equip your in-house SAP team with extensive knowledge and best practices, and consequently cut your operating costs and TCO.

4.10 Implementing and Optimizing Support and Operations

As we explained earlier, SAP strives to help its customers go live smoothly with new IT solutions. While Section 4.2 focuses on helping organizations to help themselves, customers can also elect to have SAP optimize their SAP solutions for them. Examples of such services include the Best-Run IT and SAP Solution Management Optimization service programs.

4.10.1 Best-Run IT

This multi-phase program aims to help SAP's customers and partners to plan, implement, and run an SAP-centric solution efficiently. Best-Run IT provides customers with SAP's lifecycle framework to measure and improve the performance of IT organizations. Performance is assessed on the basis of four factors:

▶ Financial benefit

▶ Total cost

▶ Technical quality

▶ Customer satisfaction

The program provides an opportunity for customers to acquire the expertise they require for application management and IT service management. Best practices and de facto standards such as the IT Infrastructure Library (ITIL) help them to convert their knowledge into effective processes within their company.

Best-Run IT comprises six separate components, which are described in detail below.

Figure 4.27 The Components of the Best-Run IT Program

Components

▶ **SAP's lifecycle framework**
When it comes to the best way of running SAP solutions, SAP Support has a wealth of expertise that it incorporates in existing and new service components. This knowledge is made available to partners and customers in a structured and optimized form. Both sides profit from SAP's many years of experience in this area.

▶ **Education and certification**
SAP is creating a new, profile-based training program that builds on existing courses and is being extended to include know-how from SAP's lifecycle framework. These measures empower customers and partners to standardize the use of new SOA technologies and ESA-based methods in SAP-centric environments. To verify that users have a sufficient level of knowledge, SAP will round off its profile-based training program with the option of certification.

▶ **SAP Ecosystem/partner program**
Using its lifecycle framework, SAP will also prepare standardized IT processes in the form of SAP-specific operating methods based on ITIL. A qualification program will be introduced and embedded in the

present partner program to check whether IT organizations are observing the operating methods. The benefits for partners will range from reduced operating costs to simplified tasks, in that they will no longer need to define their own proprietary standards. Communication with both SAP and customers should become much easier, and customers will be able to differentiate competitors better as qualifications provide a yardstick for quality.

▶ **Services**
SAP intends to turn its services into products to empower partners to deliver cost-effective, standardized services. It will begin by addressing the services that affect the running phase of SAP solutions. Partners will be able to license productized services from SAP and integrate them in their own service offering. This will make it easier for customers to assess both the services and the providers.

▶ **Discussion group in SAP Developer Network (SDN)**
A separate discussion group is being set up in the SDN (see Section 7.2) for partners who have gained the profile-based training certification. It will provide a forum for exchanging expertise and communicating with SAP. It is intended to be the first step toward continually improving the entire program and optimizing communication throughout the SAP Ecosystem.

▶ **Tools and infrastructure**
To automate and simplify the processes of defining services, licensing services, and quality assurance, SAP Solution Manager will come into play and gradually be enhanced with specialized functions.

Best-Run IT comprises four consecutive steps: **Four steps**

1. **Review and evaluation of present situation**
The findings from this step can be divided into three areas:

   ▷ **IT organization, processes, and tools**
   Areas of focus include required roles and responsibilities, processes, skill profiles, and support tools. The objective is to ascertain how customers can realize the processes required for application management and IT service management and determine which tools would be useful.

   ▷ **SAP Application Management**
   The emphasis is on application change management and maintenance management, integration expertise, as well as performance and available capacity. Implementing the defined processes calls for analytical expertise.

> ▶ **IT Service Management**
>
> This area centers on managing systems and business processes, as well as protecting systems and data. It deals primarily with the technical knowledge that is required to map the processes in the IT service management area.
>
> The review of the present situation results in an action plan detailing the recommended improvements. Customers whose organizational and staffing circumstances prevent them from implementing the improvements with their own resources receive a personalized enabling plan from SAP.

2. **Enablement**

   If the customer's support staff lacks specific skills, specially tailored training programs can be designed to close gaps in the team's knowledge. SAP employees also hold workshops with the customer to identify the scope for improvement within the support organization and ways of fulfilling its potential.

3. **Realization**

   In this phase, the customer puts the recommendations into practice. SAP experts are on hand, should the customer have any queries while implementing the improvements. In most cases, these specialists will be the same people who reviewed the customer's initial situation and accompanied him or her through the enabling phase.

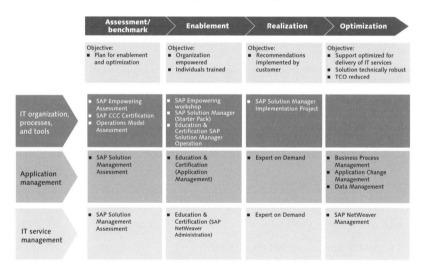

Figure 4.28 Roadmap for Best-Run IT in the Operating Phase

4. **Optimization**

Even once the recommendations have been implemented, experts are called in to deal with specific issues in order to optimize the current SAP solution.

4.10.2 SAP Solution Management Optimization

SAP Solution Management Optimization (see also Section 6.6) consists of various services that ensure that your SAP solution attains its full potential throughout its entire lifecycle. Application and system performance is optimized so that your core business processes always deliver the best possible performance and allow you to reap the benefits of your investment in SAP software.

The services focus on optimizing your complete solution—from the efficiency of your core business processes and the integration of applications in a heterogeneous system landscape to system administration and managing datasets effectively. This reduces the risk of inconsistent data and system downtime while leveraging existing hardware resources.

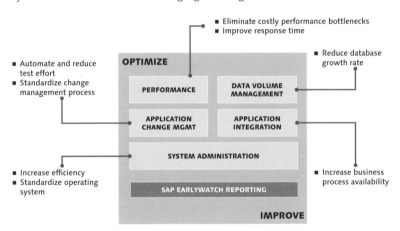

Figure 4.29 SAP Solution Management Optimization Goals

These services enable you to eliminate existing performance issues. You can also use them proactively to stop such problems from arising in the first place. To determine which areas of your company could benefit most from the SAP Solution Management Optimization services, SAP recommends running an SAP Safeguarding check, such as SAP Solution Management Assessment. SAP uses the results from this check to compile a detailed list of all the optimization services best suited to meet your individual requirements.

SAP Solution Management Optimization is aimed at fine-tuning the following areas of your SAP solution: performance, application integration, data volume, tests, system administration, and reporting. For you as a customer, this means:

▶ Your core business processes are supported, safeguarding the process flow and consistent data within your company and avoiding unnecessary and costly system downtime.

▶ You eliminate costly performance bottlenecks, shortening response times and increasing data throughput in your SAP solution.

▶ You minimize or defer future hardware investments by optimizing your existing resources.

▶ Your users become more productive as the stability, speed, and availability of their business processes improve.

▶ You spend less time on system maintenance and on upgrading, recovery, and making backup copies.

▶ The services transfer knowledge about your core business processes and their impact on system operation, enhancing the stability of your solution.

▶ With automated reporting, you can recognize and avoid risks early on and control the success of optimization services.

SAP offers the following SAP Solution Management Optimization services:

Optimization Area	Service
Performance	SAP Business Process Performance Optimization
	SAP Storage Subsystem Optimization
	SAP Remote Performance Optimization
Application Integration	SAP Interface Management
	SAP Business Process Management
Data Volume	SAP Data Volume Management
Tests	SAP Volume Test Optimization
	SAP Test Management Optimization
System Administration	SAP System Administration
	SAP Security Optimization

Table 4.2 SAP Solution Management Optimization Services

Optimization Area	Service
Automated Optimization Reporting	SAP EarlyWatch Alert
	SAP EarlyWatch Check

Table 4.2 SAP Solution Management Optimization Services (cont.)

In practice: Fresenius AG

Fresenius AG, a global healthcare company, used SAP Solution Management Optimization services to enhance the performance of its IT solution.

Faced with high numbers of transactions—in addition to database problems caused by performance bottlenecks, and the enormous increase in the volume of data after new functions were implemented—the company turned to SAP for help. SAP first performed an SAP Solution Management Assessment to identify areas in which the solution could be optimized, and recommended the following SAP Solution Management Optimization services:

▶ SAP Data Volume Management to improve database maintenance and archiving

▶ SAP Business Process Performance Optimization to optimize core business processes and reduce expensive SQL statements

▶ SAP Storage Subsystem Optimization to enhance storage subsystem configuration and data distribution

Dr. Holger Teutsch, head of Operations at Fresenius Netcare GmbH, reports on the results: "The project was completed in just two to three months, and has achieved lasting improvements with response times. We were able to reduce infrastructure-related costs, because we no longer needed to extend the database server and could do without two of the application servers. Increasing the bandwidth in the WAN, and the costs this entails, was also avoided."

The average response time for dialog processes was reduced from 1.5 seconds to 1 second, while the average response time for order entry fell from 2.5 to 1.5 seconds. Month-end closing used to take a whole week; now it takes just two or three days. Sales order throughput has become more efficient. At the same time, employees have had to work less overtime. Ultimately, considerable savings were made due to optimized system performance.

"We really got value for money," says Holger Teutsch. "To put it in a nutshell, optimizing the system has saved us around Euro 300,000 (or USD 371,000) in hardware and has increased performance by approximately 15 percent."

4.11 Program and Project Management

These consulting services ensure the success of every aspect of your implementation, from initial planning through to continuous improvement of a production system.

Program and Project Management services deliver the expertise you need to:

▶ Master the challenge of organizational change and maximize the benefits of your SAP solutions

▶ Identify risks proactively, helping you to achieve your business goals while avoiding cost overruns

▶ Manage and run projects and programs with maximum efficiency

▶ Optimize resources, maintain quality, and stay on time and within budget

Program and Project Management services

The following services are available worldwide for Program and Project Management:

▶ SAP Project Organizational Change

▶ SAP Program Management

▶ SAP Project Management

▶ SAP Technical Program and Project Management

▶ SAP IT Risk Management

4.12 Business Process Design

The Business Process Design services focus on optimizing business processes and the associated systems and organizational structures to achieve a dramatic improvement in business performance.

SAP's business process specialists work with you to:

▶ Examine your business strategy, technology, and organization so you can identify where change could generate improvement

- Analyze your current processes to pinpoint opportunities for creating value
- Standardize and manage your all important master data
- Gain valuable insight into the costs and benefits of your IT investments

The following individual services are available:

Scope of Business Process Design

- SAP Business Process Optimization
- SAP Master Data and Content Management Consulting
- SAP Value Measurement
- SAP Business Process Improvement

4.13 Application Implementation

These consulting services utilize powerful tools, methodologies, process models, and best practices to support the implementation and roll out of new applications. They provide valuable recommendations on how to use the SAP solution features to support your business requirements.

SAP consultants help you to master a wide range of tasks, including:

- Technical analysis and design
- Installation
- Configuration and Customizing
- System and data migration
- Development of project-specific enhancements
- Design and implementation of security concepts
- Analyses and reviews

Application Implementation comprises a wide range of separate services:

Scope of Application Implementation

- SAP Technical Analysis and Design
- SAP Technical Installation
- SAP Technical Migration
- SAP Security Concepts and Implementation
- SAP Solution Implementation Consulting
- SAP Configuration
- SAP Solution Expert Consulting
- SAP Development Consulting

- ▶ SAP Solution Testing

- ▶ SAP Technical Upgrade Consulting

- ▶ SAP Business Applications Upgrade Consulting

- ▶ SAP Project Review

- ▶ SAP Solution Review

- ▶ SAP Technical Review

- ▶ SAP Development Review

In practice: Adubos Trevo SA

Adubos Trevo SA is a leading Brazilian fertilizer manufacturer with manufacturing facilities across the country. Norway's multinational corporation and one of the world's largest fertilizer makers, Yara International ASA/Norsk Hydro ASA, acquired Adubos Trevo in 2000. The $400 million company has 860 employees and more than 10,000 customers.

Adubos Trevo's new management had high expectations for the company's ability to compete in the Brazilian market. The subsidiary's outdated IT infrastructure, however, hindered its competitive efforts. Reliance on batch processing to update orders, for example, caused lengthy delays in integrating sales-performance data with Adubos Trevo's production planning system.

Maintaining current stocks of raw materials is a challenge because the company buys raw materials globally, has manufacturing facilities across Brazil, and customers can place orders at any time. An additional hurdle involves the time lag—up to 60 days—between placing an order and delivery of raw materials, as well as several more days to transport the raw materials to the appropriate plant. Fluid pricing depends on currency exchange rates, which may cause customers to wait until rates change to place large orders. Orders themselves may change from month to month and must meet customers' specific demands.

To remain competitive, Adubos Trevo had to overhaul its IT infrastructure, meet new demands, improve the speed of business processes, and prepare for growth. A revamped IT system would help the company gain full control of operations, automate processes, and eliminate employees' routine processes.

It would also enable a better flow of strategic data and ensure consistency between information and corporate goals. At the same time, legal and fiscal demands increased. The Brazilian government, for example, required constant import and export documentation of raw materials, and investment banks demanded real-time visibility into the firm's financial operations.

To meet all of its challenges, Adubos Trevo chose SAP R/3 Enterprise software (functions now found in mySAP ERP), which it deployed in nine months. Because the company also had to train employees from 11 countries with 11 different cultures, Adubos Trevo enlisted SAP Consulting as the prime contractor. SAP Consulting managed local consultants and used a project-management methodology that covered the entire project—including planning, requirements definition, quality assurance, and administrative closure. Consultants helped different nationalities communicate with each other and offered guidance throughout the project.

"SAP Consulting helped enormously in bringing together all the different cultures and interests of our project team and in ensuring that local training was successful," says Biagio Caetano, Adubos Trevo's CIO.

Since deploying SAP software to some 300 users, Adubos Trevo has improved all key business processes, from raw materials forecasting, to customer pricing, and financial visibility. The company has also enjoyed substantial growth, including a 16% increase in sales volume in 2004 and a 36% return on investment (ROI). The company exceeded its overall financial goals by 62%. Adubos Trevo also reduced its planning time and can respond with greater accuracy to market demands.

"SAP helped us perform the technological update and set our forward-looking vision, and allowed our corporation to meet its bottom line," says Caetano.

4.14 Developing and Maintaining Custom SAP Solutions

High quality projects to develop custom software, coupled with ongoing support from SAP Custom Development, provide SAP customers with tailor-made software solutions that continue to strengthen their competitive position over the long term and that are also aligned with SAP's overall release strategy.

4.14.1 SAP Development Services

The SAP Development Services offering is typically requested by organizations that want to stay ahead of their competitors and are looking for ways to leverage existing software investments in order to support their unique, innovative, and competitive business processes.

Response to dynamic markets The objective of the service is to help organizations develop custom solutions to address their specific and competitive business requirements. The service helps organizations adapt flexibly, quickly, and securely to rapidly changing business and market conditions while leveraging existing investments.

Whether an organization wants to extend and complement existing SAP solutions or build completely new and original business solutions, SAP Development Services can help. It offers several possibilities, including the development of enhancements, composite applications, service-oriented applications, and mobile applications.

Using established SAP development methodologies and standards, the SAP Development Services offering delivers custom solutions to reflect the business needs of individual organizations. SAP developers and project managers guide customers through each phase of the custom development project. This entails an in-depth analysis of requirements, scope definition, functional and technical specifications, design, development, quality assurance, acceptance testing, production, and project closeout.

Protection of investment This offering is delivered by SAP Custom Development, part of SAP Services, and enables customers to realize more SAP value—by leveraging the latest SAP technologies in custom solutions—and protect their investments in SAP software by:

▶ Following the SAP standards and development methodology to ensure the quality and upgradeability of the custom developments

▶ Synchronizing solutions with SAP's release strategy to ensure that custom developments have the right focus and to mitigate future business risk

▶ Offering maintenance options to support custom solutions over time

When organizations decide to build custom solutions, they can take advantage of their existing investments in software, hardware, and talent. Whether they're replacing a legacy solution or building an entirely new one from scratch, this custom solution will have a positive impact on the

TCO. By delivering this service worldwide from nine development centers, SAP Custom Development is able to assemble a well-balanced project team comprising both on-site and remote members. This helps to ensure service flexibility while reducing delivery costs.

BEAT COMPETITION	Offers services to address unique, competitive, and changing business requirements
BE INNOVATIVE	Facilitates ability to adapt flexibly, quickly, and securely to changing business needs
LEVERAGE INVESTMENT	Helps to leverage existing investment in software, hardware, and people
FLEXIBILITY AND COST	Ensures service flexibility and reduced delivery costs through optimal access to global resources
PROTECT INVESTMENT	Assures peace of mind with custom maintenance options to best protect customers' IT investments
QUALITY AND UPGRADEABILITY	Follows SAP development methodology and standards to ensure quality and upgradeability
BUSINESS RISK	Mitigates business risk by synchronizing solutions with the SAP release strategy
ACCESS TO KNOWLEDGE	Able to leverage a vast global partner services network

➡ **THE ULTIMATE RESULT: LOWER TOTAL COST OF OWNERSHIP**

Figure 4.30 The Value of SAP Development Services

In addition, SAP Custom Development leverages other SAP development units and a vast, global network of partners to ensure that the best experts are engaged in specifying, designing, and developing custom solutions.

4.14.2 SAP Development Maintenance Services

SAP Maintenance Services are typically requested by companies who have implemented custom-developed solutions and want to be certain that these solutions will not be outmaneuvered by SAP release upgrades, system enhancements, or changing business imperatives. These solutions may have been developed with SAP Custom Development, or they may have already been part of the customer's SAP landscape. This offering can be tailored to meet the maintenance needs of individual organizations.

▶ **Problem resolution**
This service is offered to organizations that want to have SAP continue supporting their custom solution after they have gone through the formal acceptance process and the solution has been delivered. Problem resolution is offered in a similar manner to traditional maintenance. Once an organization has entered into a maintenance agreement with

Maintenance options

SAP Custom Development and they encounter a problem with their custom solution, they report the problem using SAP's standard problem-reporting infrastructure. Regardless of the problem, behind the scenes there is a team that monitors the appropriate message queue according to the established Service Level Agreements (SLAs). The team dispatches the problem to the right person, who delivers a solution. Once an issue has been resolved, it goes through regression testing; then, the solution is documented, and the organization formally signs off on the correction.

▶ **Upgrade support**
This service is offered to organizations that are applying Support Packages or upgrading to a newer release and want to ensure that their custom solutions will run smoothly after the upgrade.

▶ **Continuous improvement**
This service is offered to organizations that have gone live with their custom solution and now want to enhance their original development; typically, this is due to changing business processes. The service is offered on a project basis.

The custom development maintenance offering is constructed so that each organization decides what it needs, when it needs it by, and for how long. If a custom solution is the underpinning for a mission-critical business process, an organization may opt for 24/7 support. If less critical processes are involved, 8-to-5 local-business-hour support will suffice.

SAP Development Maintenance Services are typically delivered remotely; however, on-site support can be incorporated, based on the individual support needs of each organization.

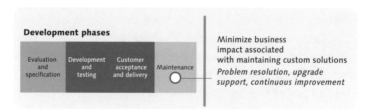

With SAP Custom Development Maintenance, you can:

■ MINIMIZE your risk during upgrades
■ SYNCHRONIZE with SAP's future release strategy
■ ACCESS the original SAP development team
■ REDUCE costs with a well-balanced mix of remote and on-site members
■ FREE UP employees to work on more strategic tasks
■ LEVERAGE SAP's proven maintenance and support procedures

Figure 4.31 The Benefits of SAP Development Maintenance Services

When organizations implement custom-developed SAP solutions, they want to be sure that they will perform optimally for years to come, and won't be outmaneuvered by SAP release upgrades, system enhancements, or changing business imperatives. They also want to ensure that this is done in the most cost-effective way possible. SAP Development Maintenance Services can help customers achieve these objectives by:

▶ Aligning developments with SAP's future release strategies

▶ Maintaining access to the team that originally developed the custom solution

▶ Eliminating the need for new defect-resolution processes and employee training by leveraging the existing problem-resolution channels that exist for their standard SAP solution

▶ Delivering this service worldwide from nine development centers; SAP Custom Development can ensure a well-balanced project team comprising both on-site and remote members. This helps to ensure service flexibility while reducing delivery costs.

▶ Helping to free up in-house IT resources to work on more core, strategic tasks

In practice: Canada Post

Canada Post Corporation collects, processes, and delivers mail to the country's 31.9 million residential customers and nearly one million businesses and public institutions.

With increasingly more online communication and a growing number of competitors in fields like advertisement and distribution, competition has increasingly shaped Canada Post's strategic priorities. To defend established revenue sources, address competitive challenges, and grow in new areas, Canada Post initiated an enterprisewide business transformation program. A cornerstone of this program was providing visibility throughout its delivery network, thereby enabling new business and reduced cost via process standardization.

The company selected the new event management capabilities of mySAP Supply Chain Management (mySAP SCM) to address emerging requirements and support its efforts to achieve profitable growth.

To enhance these event management capabilities, and meet the company's unique requirements for visibility in its distribution network, Canada Post engaged SAP Consulting and SAP Custom Development. SAP Consulting helped Canada Post to analyze opportunities and SAP Custom Development coordinated the development plans. "Our partnership has worked very well," says Louis O'Brien, Senior Vice President of business transformation and sourcing management at Canada Post.

During early phases of the project, it became evident that increasing visibility and process control was essential to addressing the issues that Canada Post was facing. SAP Consulting conducted research into the new SAP Event Management application. At that time, it was in beta testing and available for limited use to SAP customers in order to manage the transport of manufactured goods.

SAP Event Management provided visibility into events such as procurement and delivery to a warehouse, as well as providing alerts and recommended actions when expected events did not take place—this was exactly the type of visibility that Canada Post needed. Canada Post envisioned that SAP Event Management could replace its track-and-trace system and support the provision of new capabilities—such as real-time parcel delivery alerts, release date control for advertising mail, direct access by customers to delivery status and performance, and management reporting tools.

As part of the project, SAP Custom Development developed an e-signature solution fitting Canada Post's unique business needs: In the past, signatures at Canada Post had been captured electronically, but they were stored in a dedicated center—separate from the track-and-trace system data. Retrieving signatures from this center was labor-intensive and time-consuming. SAP Custom Development established a process using SAP Event Management for capturing electronic signatures. The solution reduced the company's cost of managing the e-signature database and distributing signatures. It also lowered the cycle time for retrieving e-signatures from two to 15 days to one day. Finally, the e-signature process improved the compliance rate by 5.2% for retail customers and 3.2% for commercial customers. Through the new development, Canada Post was able to reduce costs, streamline its delivery process, and ensure greater customer satisfaction and profitability.

"SAP Consulting and SAP Custom Development played a significant role in this creative coupling of SAP technology and Canada Post's business requirements," summarizes O'Brien.

4.15 SAP Managed Services—Hosting and Application Management Services

All IT solutions are only as good as the quality of operations and of the support provided; however, building up and operating powerful in-house systems, support structures, and processes involves considerable financial expenditure and a sizeable investment in personnel. The process of constantly evolving and adapting the infrastructure, systems, and production applications is another key cost factor. With this in mind, it may be worth outsourcing selected aspects of system operation and application support, which would also lighten the workload of your in-house staff during particularly strenuous phases (like new implementations or rollouts).

4.15.1 SAP Hosting Services

SAP Managed Services is a portfolio of outsourcing services for SAP and SAP-related systems. The services present an attractive and professional alternative to establishing your own support organization to maintain and operate SAP solutions and technology. The scope of SAP Managed Services is broad, encompassing mySAP Business Suite and new products, as well as mySAP All-in-One solutions. This seamlessly integrated, modular service offering provides support for all aspects of hosting, from the evaluation and implementation phases right through to operating and optimizing production solutions. The services bring you closer to your business objectives by ensuring that your SAP solutions perform optimally and reliably.

Outsourcing services

Modern, high-performance data centers around the world provide a powerful infrastructure comprising the latest hardware and state-of-the-art technology for networks, communications, and data security. A globally accessible customer service center works around the clock, seven days a week, to handle requests submitted via SAP Service Marketplace, ticket, telephone, fax, email, or web portal. This is where all customer systems and processes—be they in the preparatory phase or the production phase—are monitored and recorded. Experienced system administrators and database specialists, together with SAP Basis and application consultants, draw on their extensive expertise to ensure that systems and applications afford maximum availability, stability, and performance. What's more, customers benefit immensely from a "direct line" to the SAP development team, particularly with newer solutions.

Service Level Agreements With clearly defined Service Level Agreements (SLAs) and fixed-price services that aren't bound by rigid contractual periods, customers can plan more reliably, make their costs transparent, and free up internal resources. Enterprises can focus more on strategic tasks and mapping their business processes, especially in early project phases using development, test, and implementation environments where the requirements for production operation have not yet been defined. Outsourcing basic tasks gives companies additional time and resources to prepare for production operation more effectively and quickly, regardless of whether the production system will be operated in-house or by SAP.

24/7 support Companies entrusting the long-term running of their mySAP Business Suite solutions over several years to one of SAP's high-performance data centers are ensured that they will receive 24/7 global support. SAP Managed Services sets up the systems, installs the SAP components, and works with the customer to ascertain performance requirements. With the Application Hosting service, companies experience substantially reduced infrastructure costs and improved overall cost planning. In addition, customers have their own personal contact person.

SAP expertise, proven ITIL-based processes, and high-availability solutions make the Hosting services a source of measurable benefits for customers; excellent performance provides optimal support for all areas of its customers' business, whether their focus is internal or external.

Benefits SAP Hosting services position you to:

► Boost the value of your SAP solution by aligning application and environment optimally

► Safeguard the availability and performance of your SAP systems and prevent downtime; support team available globally 24 hours a day

► Cut your own operating costs and thereby make planning easier and more transparent

► Launch new solutions faster by creating scope for innovation

► Improve the quality of your support services and thereby increase user satisfaction

► Avoid doubtful infrastructure investments, bridge bottlenecks, and adapt systems quickly and flexibly as required

▶ Reduce project durations; plan and implement upgrade and migration projects more easily

▶ Wait to specify the hardware sizing for a new solution until you know the exact requirements

▶ Allocate different tasks to your team, such as mapping and supporting business processes

SAP offers the following Hosting services:

SAP Hosting services

▶ **SAP Evaluation Hosting**
SAP Managed Services usually provides you with a suitable system environment within two weeks so that you can evaluate a new SAP solution, and manages running the environment and basic administration tasks.

▶ **SAP Development/Prototype Hosting**
SAP Managed Services develops a prototype for you within a maximum of four weeks. You then access it from your site, enabling you to test a new SAP solution with your own data, for example.

▶ **SAP Implementation Hosting**
When you implement a new SAP solution, SAP Managed Services can provide you with a tailor-made environment within 10 days and ensure a smooth system operation. That way, your project team can devote itself to optimizing and mapping your business processes.

▶ **SAP Ramp-Up Hosting**
Companies participating in the Ramp-Up program need an appropriate IT infrastructure. Relevant expertise and close ties with SAP development teams put SAP Managed Services in an excellent position to provide such an infrastructure at an early stage, leaving you free to focus on the functions central to your core business.

▶ **SAP Upgrade Hosting**
SAP Upgrade Hosting was designed to generate more reliable planning, lower risks, and shorter project durations for customers migrating to a higher release. Within a matter of weeks, SAP Managed Services provides you with a suitable infrastructure, operates the test system in one of the SAP data centers, and oversees the technical upgrade.

▶ **SAP Hosted E-Learning**
SAP Managed Services sets up and manages a technical infrastructure for e-learning applications, allowing training to be provided directly on the customer site.

▶ **SAP Application Hosting**
SAP Managed Services operates its customers' SAP systems over the long term in one of the high-performance data centers, which provide the entire infrastructure as well as 24/7 support and customized levels of service. As part of SAP Remote Application Operations, SAP can provide remote support for SAP solutions in a customer's own data center.

▶ **Strategic Outsourcing Consulting**
If customers decide not to arrange for their outsourcing with SAP directly, SAP can provide consulting services, ranging from the selection of providers through to the design of SLAs and contracts. Customers who are about to extend their outsourcing contract can take advantage of the SLA optimization check offered by SAP Managed Services.

In practice: Carl Edelmann GmbH & Co. KG

Carl Edelmann GmbH & Co. KG is a midsize company at the forefront of Europe's packaging industry, excelling in the development, manufacture, and finishing of folding cartons. Edelmann signed up to SAP's Ramp-Up program and is implementing mySAP ERP 2004 before it becomes available on general release—a step that will harmonize the solution landscape: The new SAP system will replace the current SAP solution and another ERP system.

"We signed up to the Ramp-Up program so that we could use new functions sooner. This meant we needed a suitable infrastructure at short notice, as well as personnel to set up and operate the project system," explains Rainer Hoch, SAP Project Manager at Edelmann. "For that reason, we opted for SAP Ramp-Up Hosting from SAP Managed Services." SAP Managed Services provides Edelmann with the appropriate infrastructure at a fixed price, as well as SAP experts to guarantee smooth system operations.

The advantages: Edelmann does not have to commit to hardware or sizing until the test system is running satisfactorily with original customer data. The company benefits from increased project security and accelerated implementation, not to mention lighter workloads for its internal IT staff.

Furthermore, there is a continuous flow of expertise from SAP Managed Services to Edelmann. "SAP Ramp-Up Hosting means that implementing mySAP ERP 2004 is not a huge burden for us," says Gerhard Klein, SAP administrator at Edelmann. "We'll be able to profit sooner from the new SAP solution. One area where we really expect to see clear improvements is in the electronic exchange of data with customers and suppliers." This facilitates scheduling agreement processing and accelerates order processing. And one more major advantage: The harmonized system landscape cuts the costs for maintenance and support.

"We are really pleased with the response times demonstrated by SAP Managed Services. Our only setback—a hard disk problem—was fixed in just two hours," explains Rainer Hoch. "We are now considering using SAP Application Hosting from SAP Managed Services to operate the system once it goes live."

4.15.2 SAP Application Management Services

These services focus on supporting, optimizing, and enhancing live SAP-centric IT solutions. They help SAP customers to set up and optimize their support organizations and processes and to support their applications and users, say by flexibly adapting support resources in line with business demands or by outsourcing some or all of their application management tasks. Customers also gain access to the latest product know-how and can even let SAP Managed Services provide support during the night shift. Professional support means enterprises get the maximum benefit out of their SAP applications and can therefore safeguard their investments.

SAP Application Management services are modular and comprise the following services, which can be ordered individually:

Services

▶ **Support Enabling**
Support and optimization services for your own support organization, including setup, sizing, structure, and costing

▶ **Second-level support**
Support for your users and key users for handling problems and SAP components

▶ **Continuous Maintenance**
Ongoing support for production applications

- ▶ **Continuous Improvement**
  Ongoing optimization and adjustment of your IT solution

- ▶ **Continuous Change**
  Implementation of new components and processes

- ▶ **Solution Optimization**
  Optimization of system settings

- ▶ **Business Process Management**
  Process monitoring and optimization

The services are available, irrespective of whether you run the applications in-house, or use conventional hosting to outsource this task to a qualified SAP Hosting partner or directly to SAP Managed Services. The single services are described briefly below.

Support Enabling

Should you decide to manage the applications in your SAP landscape, SAP can help you to plan and set up your support organization—from estimating the workload and designing effective support structures and processes, through selecting and implementing the right monitoring tools to keep your IT solution efficient and stable, and thus increase user satisfaction. SAP experts train your employees and assist them in establishing an efficient SAP CCC (see Section 4.2.1), right through to certification. You benefit from the expertise that SAP Managed Services has gained after setting up over 100 support organizations.

Second-Level Support

SAP Managed Services provides handling advice for your users and key users while the system is in operation. An efficient incident management scheme (problem handling) is in place to receive your messages and monitor the workflow; specialists in particular areas analyze and fix the problems and document the solutions. Should critical problems arise, they work with you to restore order and control of the situation.

Continuous Maintenance

SAP maintains and supports your applications. Our experts analyze and optimize your SAP solution while it is in use, by proactively monitoring system components, interfaces, performance, and individual business processes. SAP Solution Manager is an important tool in this process. Furthermore, they take care of periodically recurring tasks, such as importing

Notes, service packages, and patches, monitoring master data and transaction data, and batch jobs.

Continuous Improvement

The services for optimizing and adapting SAP systems help you to tailor your solutions to market conditions, say, if you decide to enter new business areas or to expand abroad. They deal with creating and enhancing programs, reports, and forms, provide support for authorization and archiving concepts, and aim to optimize processes and structures. Where necessary, we can provide training for your key users and users. Improving the stability and performance of your applications and Basis components lets you get the maximum benefit from your SAP solution.

Continuous Change

SAP employees advise you on the necessity, advantages, and feasibility of using new components, functions, and processes. They work with you to initiate implementation projects and assist you when selecting an implementation partner. Continuous Change is also designed to support functional release upgrades and migrations.

Solution Optimization

Solution Optimization services proactively analyze the system configuration in order to eliminate performance weak spots, for instance, by enhancing coding, data storage, and system parameters. This results in sustained lower operating costs, thanks to better system settings. You can order the services as part of the Continuous Maintenance services or individually.

Business Process Management

Business Process Management involves the application support team revising the service levels to guarantee the required level of process performance. SAP implements proactive business process monitoring based on SAP Solution Manager and continuously optimizes all aspects of the processes involved. The service uses standardized methods to proactively identify and eliminate process weak spots within the system.

SLA Management and Personal Support

At the customer service center, the staff works around the clock to process requests that come in via the SAP Support Portal, email, fax, or telephone. It is here that all requests are recorded and monitored centrally. You can check the status of your support requests in the SAP Support Portal at any time. You will also receive monthly service reports with detailed information on the status of your SAP solution, compliance with SLA parameters, and any necessary actions or system changes. Furthermore, we allocate for every customer his or her own personal contact person— the Customer Service Manager (CSeM). The CSeM assumes the role of project manager and oversees all aspects that relate to support for your application. This involves coordinating and monitoring all services at SAP, verifying compliance with SLAs, and compiling regular reports and recommendations to proactively boost the value of your SAP solution.

Benefits Customers benefit from SAP Managed Services in the following ways:

▶ The IT department is relieved of routine tasks.

▶ The stability and availability of the applications is guaranteed.

▶ Optimized systems ensure that applications meet their full potential.

▶ Redundant resources to cover absent support staff (due to leave, illness, or any other reason) are not necessary.

▶ Response times are assured and customers can tailor the SLAs to meet their requirements.

▶ Monthly flat rates make it possible to plan costs and keep them transparent.

▶ Support is provided for all time zones, languages, and cultural areas.

▶ Requests are handled centrally.

▶ Costs are reduced as a result of flexible, combinable resources.

In practice: BOS

The BOS Group, an international supplier for the automotive industry, develops, manufactures, and distributes systems for vehicle interiors, such as sun protection systems and luggage covers. The company has grown considerably in recent years—not least due to acquisitions— and now has 12 different software systems to operate. It wants to replace these systems with SAP for Automotive, with a goal of unifying the IT landscape, creating more organizational flexibility, and standardizing processes. BOS has chosen SAP as partner for implementation and application management.

"Our main concern is our core business, which does not include implementing, rolling out, and running or supporting an international SAP solution. That's why we're using SAP for consulting, hosting, and application management," says Franz Brunner, project manager for ERP/MIS systems in the BOS Group.

"For this project, we wanted to work with the partner that offered the greatest investment protection and that mapped most of the functions we need as standard. We also wanted everything from one source. When you work with several partners, there is always friction, and when it starts to get critical, everyone is keen to pass the buck. We haven't got time for that," says Brunner, explaining the company's decision to use SAP services and software.

SAP experts will implement the new software in 18 plants around the world by the end of 2007. "We are not afraid of losing control," says Brunner. "The consultants and Application Management services take the pressure off us during the implementation phase, as well as when the software is live. Later, we'll profit from knowledge transfer, enabling us to take on many of the support tasks again." Brunner has no intention of building up in-house implementation and rollout skills. He prefers to leave that to the specialists and let his own employees concentrate on their core business. Brunner summarizes as follows: "The automotive industry is an extremely fast-moving industry, and the manufacturers set the pace. We have no alternative but to keep up."

4.16 Business Process Outsourcing

Today's dynamic business landscape requires evermore investment and resources, leading more and more enterprises to outsource certain business processes and services to external providers. True to the motto that "The best-run businesses run SAP," SAP even provides solutions for outsourcing.

While SAP does not offer Business Process Outsourcing (BPO) services directly, it does support leading BPO providers in delivering high quality, BPO-specific process solutions—solutions that generate sustainable business value, dramatically reduce technical risks, lower costs, and improve service quality. SAP understands the intricacies of outsourcing information-intensive business processes without compromising on support and integration. SAP can also help you to evaluate and implement outsourcing options—specifically focusing on the all-important link between out-

SAP supports BPO providers

sourced and in-house processes. Monitoring your BPO contracts will also be a concern—here again, you can rely on SAP solutions.

It is no coincidence that the success of many service providers rests on SAP solutions, or that numerous internal shared service centers prefer SAP software. SAP's robust platform, its service-oriented software architecture, its support for multiple languages and country versions, and its compliance with local legal requirements make its solutions the obvious choice for centralized service delivery and BPO. SAP's clearly conceived ESA ensures that outsourced processes are kept up to date with the latest technology. Your investments in technology are also protected, because the ESA enables BPO providers to ensure continuous innovation for your business processes.

SAP continues to invest in long-term partnerships with leading outsourcing providers that deploy their services on SAP's technology platform and standard applications. We have committed substantial resources to enable our selected BPO providers to deliver high quality services using SAP solutions.

BPO Powered by SAP As part of the "BPO Powered by SAP" program, SAP's global BPO organization certifies BPO providers to ensure that they have the relevant technical knowledge and expertise to provide quality support, as well as in-depth knowledge of SAP solutions and sufficient experience to meet customer needs. Once certified, partners are recertified every two years to ensure they continue to meet SAP's high quality standards.

With "BPO Powered by SAP," customers profit from more than just the SAP software alone. The program also offers:

▶ Flexibility, continuous business process supervision, and better monitoring of BPO providers, and all with lower business process costs

▶ A comprehensive package of leading BPO-capable solutions based on SAP NetWeaver

▶ An integrated, powerful, and extensible technology platform, which is shipped with all the critical business applications

▶ A clearly defined concept for using ESA to implement a granular, service-oriented approach in business process solutions

▶ Seamless integration of outsourced and in-house processes

▶ Advice on the scope for implementing BPO in enterprises, thanks to a global support team with extensive experience of BPO and shared service centers

- Long-term partnerships with leading BPO providers to ensure "Powered by SAP" quality and superior service

- Guaranteed enhancement of BPO-specific solutions by SAP

- Sustainable and effective benefits from collaborating with SAP as a reliable and stable partner

5   Generating Value Through Support

Support is critical for every software solution. The quality of the support offered is often what convinces customers to select one solution over another. Support is what enables you to protect your business processes—and your company's success—from risk.

Enterprises today are under increasing pressure to achieve better results with fewer resources. The vital key figures are total cost of ownership (TCO) and return on investment (ROI), which is why SAP helps customers optimize costs—a factor that will remain a central issue for a long time to come. Yet, it is by no means enough to concentrate on costs alone; you want the support you receive to actually generate value for your company. Support services should not only curb expenditure, they should also add to the overall value created by your SAP solution. Consequently, SAP is designing new offerings and support concepts that enable you to use your existing solutions to steadily improve your business processes. You benefit by increasing the value generated by your existing solutions.

Value of maintenance

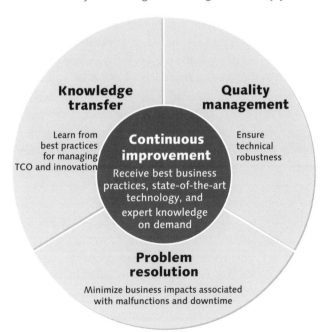

Figure 5.1 Support for the Continuous Improvement of Business Processes and Solutions

Constant change in the world of business and technology means that what is expected of customers in terms of adapting their IT solutions is also subject to a process of organic growth. Regardless of what the market demands, SAP can provide the support you need to improve your software solutions and business processes, to move one step ahead through innovation, and to continually adapt your company to your business environment—all of which reduces TCO and accelerates ROI. It is precisely because the business processes—supported by SAP's business solutions—are mission-critical that they deserve optimal support.

Easing hot spots SAP's services are designed to facilitate smooth and quick implementation and to enhance operations. They include special services for efficiently attacking *hot spots* such as performance or database growth, and for encapsulating modifications or returning them to the standard. In any integrated solution, a host of technological layers has to be considered—ranging from the storage level to databases, application servers, web catalog servers, and desktop servers to the desktop itself. While SAP has been covering this spectrum for years, it is still the only software vendor on the market that provides such an extensive range.

Support services With the standard support agreement, a diverse range of services and tools is available. To increase the effectiveness of customer solutions on an ongoing basis, SAP provides program source code and software upgrades—such as new releases and SAP Support Packages—as well as templates, roadmaps, and special tools to support software change management. It is also important to ensure that installations offer high availability and functionality. SAP does so through proactive remote services (such as the SAP EarlyWatch Check and the SAP GoingLive Checks), tools for test administration and automation, tools and methods for implementation, and monitoring tools for systems and core business processes. Access to information on SAP Service Marketplace and in the portals, as well as to Best Practices and certain functions such as those in the e-learning area of SAP Solution Manager, provides for an intensive transfer of knowledge between SAP and its customers. When it comes to efficient problem-solving, knowledge bases, tools, and corrections are invaluable. But SAP's resources don't stop there; standardized processes are also available. Experts from SAP's support organization process customer messages, depending on their priority, up to 24 hours a day, seven days a week.

Understanding the customer This support offering—outstanding in terms of scope and quality—can be attributed to SAP's excellent understanding of its customers' competitive environment, business goals, and required solution landscape, which is the result of more than 30 years of collaboration with customers from a wide range of industries. This expertise is the product of SAP's experience in challenging projects, and with the largest research and development budget in the industry, SAP is well positioned to build on this know-how in the long term. This enables SAP to engage continuously and intensively with its customers and promote their success with high-quality products, services, and tools.

5.1   Support Offerings

Support provides a basis for long-term partnerships between SAP and its customers. Like its products, SAP's support concept is designed to continually improve and optimize customers' business processes, ensuring that they are stable and future proof.

SAP offers three levels of support with different scope that are based entirely on customer needs.

Support options

▶ SAP Standard Support

▶ SAP Premium Support

▶ SAP MaxAttention

SAP Standard Support comprises proven tools for safeguarding your core business processes and continually enhancing your SAP solution. It also enables you to implement, run, and modify your solution more easily (see Section 5.1.1).

SAP Premium Support is a new support offering. It is ideal for customers who want to work more closely with SAP to ensure that their business processes offer high availability and run efficiently. With SAP Premium Support, you get a personal contact person (support advisor) and regular assessments that include planning and various Service Level Agreements (SLAs, see Section 5.1.2).

As already described, SAP MaxAttention (see Section 4.9.1) incorporates additional features that can be individually combined to meet customers' different needs. For instance, it comprises services from the SAP portfolio, SLAs, and on-site teams to ensure customers the best possible support from SAP. It therefore represents a qualitative complement to SAP Standard Support and SAP Premium Support.

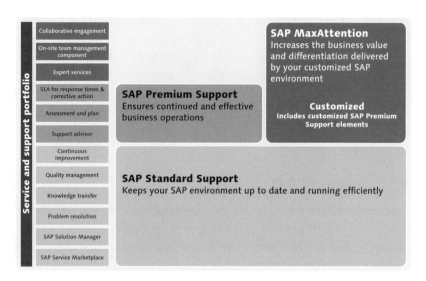

Figure 5.2 SAP Support Offerings: Value at All Levels

SAP provides maintenance in three phases (see Section 5.2.1):

▶ Mainstream maintenance

▶ Extended maintenance

▶ Customer-specific maintenance

SAP Standard Support forms the basis for every phase. SAP Premium Support and SAP MaxAttention are available in all three phases. However, the scope of the services provided with SAP Standard Support, SAP Premium Support, and SAP MaxAttention is tailored to the respective maintenance phase.

5.1.1   SAP Standard Support

SAP is always improving its support processes and looking for new ways to help you manage your solutions more efficiently and easily. For example, SAP has reduced the frequency with which Support Packages are shipped and has introduced customer-specific corrections. SAP Standard Support is committed to continually improving solutions by providing you with Best Practices and state-of-the-art technology. Its other focal points include problem resolution, quality management (to safeguard the solution's stability), and knowledge transfer from SAP to its customers.

Continuous improvement
- Available source code
- SAP software upgrades
- Software change management

Quality management
- Test administration and automation
- Monitoring for systems and core business processes
- Proactive remote services
- Implementation tools and methodologies

SAP SOLUTION MANAGER

Knowledge transfer
- Access to Best Practices
- Empowers SAP Customer Competence Centers

Problem resolution
- Global 24x7 problem resolution
- Global 24x7 escalation procedures

SAP SERVICE MARKETPLACE

Figure 5.3 Services and Tools Included with SAP Standard Support

Continuous Improvement

Upgrades

SAP never stops extending and improving its software to meet the ever more exacting requirements of its customers. Such improvements are made available to customers in the form of upgrades, which optimize programs and also ensure compatibility with new databases and operating systems. New releases are supplemented with tools and detailed process descriptions for upgrade projects. The Upgrade Assistant, for example, enables you to control and monitor the upgrade process, while the Upgrade Monitor calculates the time required to perform the upgrade.

Support Packages

Support Packages can help you to continually optimize your SAP solutions. They contain minor software corrections and improvements that can boost an IT solution's performance and stability. SAP R/3 HR Support Packages are a special case; they contain any applicable legal changes, and therefore are essential for anyone using SAP's HR component. The Support Package Manager—SAP's tool for importing Support Packages into SAP systems—implements the changes automatically.

In 2003, SAP also introduced Support Package Stacks—combinations of Support Packages for all software components in a particular release that are harmonized with one another and thus allow corrections to be implemented more efficiently. Support Package Stacks also create more transparency, which ultimately contributes to reducing costs.

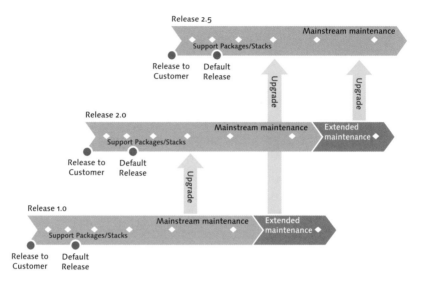

Figure 5.4 Support Packages and New Releases to Promote Continuous Improvement

Roadmaps When you change or improve your business processes, you also have to modify your software to reflect the new conditions. This might involve reconfiguring the system settings or upgrading to a more recent release that contains new or enhanced functions. The roadmaps provided by SAP can help you perform these steps efficiently and successfully. They contain a structured list of activities and references to useful tools, services, and proven procedures. The following SAP roadmaps are currently available:

▶ Implementation Roadmap for mySAP Business Suite (mySAP ERP, mySAP CRM, mySAP SCM, mySAP PLM, mySAP SRM), SAP xApps, SAP NetWeaver, and SAP Solutions for Mobile Business

▶ Implementation Roadmap for SAP NetWeaver Portal

▶ Implementation Roadmap for SAP NetWeaver Exchange Infrastructure

▶ Solution Management Roadmap

▶ Global Template Roadmap

▶ SAP Upgrade Road Map

SAP also provides numerous tools to enhance your software change management processes, such as tools for copying clients and comparing or synchronizing Customizing settings.

Tools for change management

If you want to extend or modify standard programs, SAP supports you by providing the ABAP source code for all applications, as well as a suitable development environment.

Knowledge transfer

SAP Service Marketplace is an Internet platform that gives all SAP customers access to a wide range of information, support functions, and collaborative services. The benefits of both SAP Service Marketplace (see Section 7.2) and of actively participating in the SAP Ecosystem (see Chapter 3) are outlined in this book.

SAP Solution Manager (see Section 7.1) includes detailed information about software change management and implementing, running, and monitoring SAP solutions. With tools, content, and methods designed primarily for planning and implementing such tasks, this integrative platform represents a valuable means of transferring knowledge between SAP and its customers.

Quality management

Proactive services are another key element of SAP's support offering. Their objective is to prevent problems from arising, as well as to make SAP solutions more reliable and less susceptible to downtime. Every calendar year, customers can select one of the following support services for each of their installations:

Proactive services

▶ SAP GoingLive Check

▶ SAP GoingLive Functional Upgrade Check

▶ SAP OS/DB Migration Check

In addition, if SAP EarlyWatch Alert (which should be run once a week) discovers critical warnings, customers are entitled to up to two SAP EarlyWatch Checks per year for each production installation. This ensures that critical warnings are analyzed in more detail, which increases the reliability of the solution.

The aforementioned services are performed by SAP remotely and are usually delivered via SAP Solution Manager. This platform also gives you access to various monitoring tools, which enable you to oversee your core business processes, systems, and interfaces. In this way, you know the exact state-of-play with your solution and can identify critical factors before bottlenecks occur.

Implementation tools The implementation phase is supported by tools and standardized methodologies such as SAP roadmaps and SAP Best Practices. These tools help you design, configure, and test your SAP solution. For configuration, in particular, you can use the Implementation Guide (IMG) and Business Configuration Sets, a technique for combining and reusing Customizing settings easily. The ultimate goal of all these tools is to accelerate the implementation phase and, by association, the rollout phase.

Testing Factors such as customer developments, modifications, customizing, and infrastructure make every implementation project unique. This is why the solution must be tested before it is used for the first time and after any changes have been made (for example, after Support Packages have been imported) to ensure that all the components interact well and that a high level of performance is achieved. The Extended Computer Aided Test Tool (eCATT) enables you to combine business processes and automate them as repeatable test procedures, such as process transactions and transaction chains. Remote systems can also be tested with a central test system. All relevant programs and user interfaces are supported. The Test Workbench enables you to organize the tests for your SAP systems and third-party systems efficiently, to monitor the progress of the tests, and to evaluate the test results. If you have documented your business processes in SAP Solution Manager, you can organize your test procedures all the more efficiently.

Problem resolution

SAP Notes database SAP gathers the solutions for known problems and makes them available to customers in the SAP Notes database. The SAP Notes database contains software corrections, as well as tips for optimizing performance and specialized information for selected areas. All customers can access this database on SAP Service Marketplace. A sophisticated search engine helps them find the relevant SAP Note to solve their problem. Ideally, SAP Notes should not be implemented manually, but by using the Note Assistant, an effective and user-friendly tool that hastens the procedure and provides an overview of SAP Notes that have already been implemented.

Online messages If a solution cannot be found in the SAP Notes database, customers can send an online message to the SAP support team. The experts there work to find a solution and customers can check the status of their messages at any time. Transferring information in this way between SAP and customers ensures short response times and knowledgeable replies. Because knowledge is shared within the global support organization, customers can always be certain that their problems will be handled and solved by experts.

SAP offers global support around the clock for particularly urgent problems. The global structure of SAP's support organization ensures that any of the support specialists involved can access all the customer's information at any time, in any place.

24/7 support

Defined escalation procedures ensure that, in critical cases, all the necessary activities will be coordinated smoothly within SAP Active Global Support so that the situation can be rectified to the satisfaction of all involved as quickly as possible. This may involve providing access to the required resources and, if necessary, dispatching expert teams to work on site with the customer.

5.1.2   SAP Premium Support

SAP regularly aligns its support offering with changing market requirements and technological advances. Recent customer surveys conducted by SAP show that many customers from a range of industries would like to work more closely with SAP. Customers expect their business processes to be more reliable over the long term, and their SAP solution to run more efficiently due to more intensive support. SAP Premium Support is SAP's answer to this specific customer need. In addition to the elements already available in SAP Standard Support, it includes:

▶ An SLA for support requests
▶ Regular assessments and planning for the customer's SAP solution, which is carried out by SAP experts
▶ A named contact person (support advisor)

SAP Premium Support includes an SLA for response times and corrective action, which means that SAP guarantees that customers will receive a quicker response to support requests and will be provided with corrections sooner. When a customer reports a problem, the first thing that he or she can expect is a qualified reply from an SAP expert, within a defined period of time. The same expert handles the entire problem-solving process. SAP ensures that customers with *very high* priority requests will be

SLA on response and corrective action

contacted by an SAP expert within one hour, while *high* priority requests will receive a response within four hours.

Within the first four hours, customers with very high priority problems can also expect corrective actions in the form of software corrections or appropriate workarounds. At the very least, they will receive a list of actions with a schedule for their implementation. In addition, the expert responsible will provide the customer with regular feedback about the status of the problem and any activities planned by SAP.

Regular assessment and planning With SAP Premium Support, SAP experts also assess the customer's SAP solution at regular intervals. Depending on the customer's priorities, they will focus on different aspects:

▶ Avoiding risk when implementing SAP solutions

▶ Optimizing system operation for the SAP solution

▶ Optimizing the technology behind core business processes

The purpose of these assessments is to ensure that the customer's SAP solution continues to improve in quality and reliability. Assessements are also intended to reduce costs by providing for a more efficient operation. Based on the assessments, the customer receives actual recommendations on how to avoid risks and tap into existing potential for optimization.

Support advisor Every customer is also assigned an SAP expert, or support advisor. The support advisor coordinates the regular assessments and helps the customer to implement the measures recommended. Together with the customer, the support advisor drafts a service plan that shows which services should be delivered and when they should be delivered in order for the customer's goals to be achieved. Finally, the support advisor is available to act as an additional escalation level for the customer.

5.1.3 SAP MaxAttention

Unlike the standardized offerings SAP Standard Support and SAP Premium Support, SAP MaxAttention allows customers to combine individual elements to create a form of support that is tailored to their own unique needs. The goal of SAP MaxAttention is to provide customers with as much support as possible, which is why on-site teams are a key element of this offering. Other elements might include services from SAP's portfolio and SLAs (for more details, see Section 4.9.1).

5.2 Maintenance Strategy

SAP's maintenance strategy is used to focus on individual components. But, since the beginning of 2004, SAP has applied a "5–1–2 maintenance strategy" to its solutions. This strategy applies to all solution editions based on SAP NetWeaver 2004 or above. The numbers 5–1–2 describe the duration of the individual maintenance phases:

▶ Five years of mainstream maintenance at the standard support rate

▶ One year of extended maintenance for an additional maintenance fee of two percent

▶ Two more years of extended maintenance for an additional maintenance fee of four percent

These phases are followed by customer-specific maintenance.

The scope of the different services provided with SAP Standard Support, SAP Premium Support, and SAP MaxAttention is tailored to the respective maintenance phase.

5.2.1 Maintenance Phases

Mainstream maintenance

With the 5–1–2 maintenance strategy, SAP offers maintenance services for the respective solution from the start of the SAP Ramp-Up phase. Mainstream maintenance, the first maintenance phase, usually lasts five years. During this period, customers benefit from the full range of maintenance services provided with SAP Standard Support. SAP Premium Support and SAP MaxAttention are also available during this phase.

In the past, SAP extended the mainstream maintenance phase several times for certain releases in response to its customers' requests to prolong their software's useful life. With the additional options of extended maintenance and customer-specific maintenance, SAP developed a consistent strategy to replace its previous method of deciding whether to extend the mainstream maintenance phase on a case-by-case basis. For customers, this means better protection for their investments, because each release has a longer useful life.

Moreover, being able to plan maintenance services early on gives customers greater planning security and flexibility—not every customer was able to or wanted to upgrade during the mainstream maintenance phases defined before 2004. The current strategy gives customers the independence to assess their particular circumstances and decide whether to upgrade to a more recent release or stay with their current system.

Extended maintenance

Extended maintenance is usually available for three years. A small additional fee applies; customers can decide whether or not to order extended maintenance.

Scope | During this extended maintenance period, you receive comparable services to those covered by mainstream maintenance. SAP Standard Support, SAP Premium Support, and SAP MaxAttention continue to be available.

Details about ordering, possible restrictions, and additional fees are posted in good time in the SAP Support Portal on SAP Service Marketplace.

Ordering extended maintenance couldn't be simpler: The order form is available in the SAP Support Portal, and you just have to enter the installations for which you want to order extended maintenance. The contracts department uses this information to create an addendum for your existing support contract.

All customers, not just specific customer groups, can take advantage of extended maintenance.

Customer-specific maintenance

There are three possible occasions when a release can enter into customer-specific maintenance:

▶ The mainstream maintenance period ends and no extended maintenance is offered.

▶ The mainstream maintenance period ends and the customer does not take advantage of the extended maintenance offering.

▶ The extended maintenance period ends.

Customer-specific maintenance is covered by the standard maintenance fee and has no time restriction.

Limited scope | During the customer-specific maintenance phase, you receive similar support to the support offered with mainstream and extended maintenance, but with a number of restrictions regarding the scope of SAP Standard Support. SAP no longer ensures that it will provide legal changes for existing software; the provision of Support Packages is no longer guaranteed; and current technology will not always be supported. This can mean that new SAP kernels will not be made available to support new versions of databases or operating systems, that direct upgrades to a more recent release in mainstream maintenance will no longer be offered (upgrades then have to be conducted in several steps), or that new interfaces will not be supported.

Customer problems are solved on an individual basis. The maintenance fee does not cover solutions to problems not yet known to SAP, especially if it requires modifications.

The SAP Premium Support services are also limited in the customer-specific maintenance phase. More specifically, the SLAs for response times and corrective action do not apply to installations of releases that are in customer-specific maintenance.

The following SAP Standard Support services are available during the customer-specific maintenance phase:

Scope

▶ Worldwide, 24/7 problem resolution for customer messages prioritized as "very high" (solutions for problems already known to SAP)

▶ Global, 24/7 escalation procedure

▶ Access to online information and communication channels: SAP Service Marketplace and the portals provide access to the SAP Notes database and a range of information (guidelines, documentation)

▶ New releases and upgrades for licensed software, in line with the standard support contract

▶ Test administration and automation tools

▶ Monitoring tools for systems and core business processes

▶ Proactive remote services

▶ Implementation tools and methodologies

▶ Best Practices

5.2.2   Maintenance Periods for Specific Releases

Maintenance for older releases of non-R/3 products

The 5–1–2 strategy does not apply to older releases that are not based on SAP NetWeaver 2004; specific maintenance periods are defined for such releases. Mainstream and customer-specific maintenance is available, but not extended maintenance.

Maintenance for SAP R/3, SAP R/3 Enterprise, and mySAP ERP

SAP is offering extended maintenance for SAP R/3 3.1I, 4.0B, 4.5B, and 4.6B until the end of December 2006.

Extended maintenance will also be available for SAP R/3 4.6C. This release will be covered by mainstream maintenance until the end of 2006, and from the beginning of January 2007, it will be covered by extended maintenance until the end of December 2009.

Mainstream maintenance for SAP R/3 Enterprise 47x110 and 47x200 is available until the end of March 2009. From April 2009 through March 2012, SAP will offer extended maintenance for the two SAP R/3 Enterprise releases.

A key advantage for all customers using an industry-specific add-on is that extended maintenance will also cover add-ons that are based on SAP R/3 4.6C and SAP R/3 Enterprise 47x110 and 47x200. If multiple releases of an add-on exist for the underlying SAP R/3 or SAP R/3 Enterprise release, only the highest add-on release will be supported until the end of the mainstream maintenance phase and during extended maintenance.

Extended maintenance for SAP R/3 and SAP R/3 Enterprise gives you extra leeway to switch to mySAP ERP—you can plan and carry out an upgrade without having to worry about the impending expiration of mainstream maintenance for your current release.

mySAP ERP 2004 itself will be covered by mainstream maintenance until the end of March 2010. This will be followed by a period of extended maintenance until the end of March 2013. Mainstream maintenance for mySAP ERP 2005 is due to expire by the end of March 2011, and will be followed by extended maintenance until the end of March 2014.

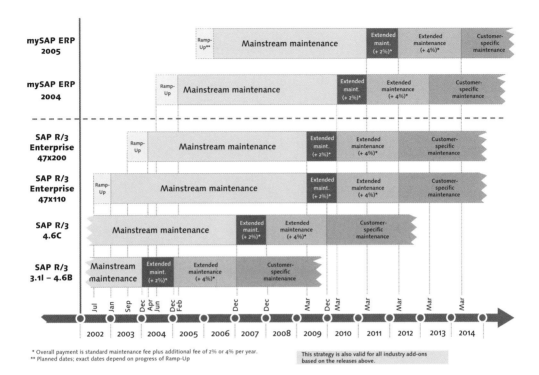

Figure 5.5 Maintenance Phases for Different Releases

6 From Professionals for Professionals—SAP Services in Practice

This chapter describes the challenges typically encountered throughout the lifecycle of an SAP solution, as well as tried-and-tested ways of mastering such challenges with the help of appropriate SAP services.

Based on the experiences of real customers (customer names have been removed), this chapter describes how SAP Services can help customers to improve the availability of their IT, cut costs, and increase business value.

The first example demonstrates how changing from business applications to Enterprise Services Architecture (ESA) allows SAP customers to strengthen their competitive position. The next scenario looks at determining the business value of IT projects to aid with decision-making when it comes to investments. Our third customer scenario deals with the implementation of an SAP solution, while the fourth scenario describes the development of customer-specific functions. The fifth example illustrates how a large corporation might roll out an SAP implementation internationally.

The individual support afforded by SAP MaxAttention for mission-critical IT solutions is outlined in the sixth customer scenario. The next example looks at implementing a new SAP solution that is part of the SAP Ramp-Up program. The eighth scenario describes how a company might upgrade various different systems—starting with the initial assessment of business value, through planning and realization. SAP also provides proven services for consolidating system landscapes, as illustrated by the subsequent case. The tenth scenario shows how SAP Empowering helps customers to standardize and optimize their support and administration processes.

The eleventh example describes how SAP can help customers if they want to analyze the costs for operations and support, or to outsource systems or specific tasks for application support that are currently performed in-house. The final scenario focuses on the Best-Run IT service program as a way of optimizing operational systems during the operating phase.

6.1 First Steps Toward an Enterprise Services Architecture

By describing a fictitious midsize media company, this first example demonstrates how SAP Consulting provides the expert advice and assistance that customers require in order to put enterprise services architecture (ESA) to work for their business. Of course, needs and challenges vary greatly—from industry to industry, and from company to company—and it is unlikely that any two ESA projects will ever be identical. This scenario simply illustrates how SAP Services can help customers take their first steps toward an ESA and from there, plan their way forward.

6.1.1 Background

The company used in this example is based in the United Kingdom and employs a staff of around 200. It designs and sells advertising space in various leading national newspapers and magazines. It also markets classified ads and banners for websites. The enterprise has been running SAP software successfully for several years. In addition to SAP R/3 for core ERP tasks, the company deploys industry-specific solutions from the SAP for Media portfolio, such as the SAP Classified Advertising Management application. The software landscape also includes a number of non-SAP systems.

The company was an early adopter of web-based solutions, launching an Internet ad-sales portal in the late 1990s. This allowed customers to enter orders via a user-friendly GUI, thereby streamlining processes and significantly reducing manual effort. The online channel proved to be very popular.

Business challenge

In 2004, the enterprise began to examine ways in which to further enhance online collaboration with customers and business partners. Because the original portal covered all the newspapers and magazines for which the company sold advertising space, users sometimes had problems locating the specific information and functions they needed. To resolve this issue, the company decided to create dedicated online channels for different publications and customer groups; however, the technology on which the legacy solution was based had reached its limits. Coupled with inflexible, hardwired processes, this made it extremely difficult to reuse established portal functions in a new context.

Against this background, the company decided to look into new ways of leveraging its existing IT investments in order to:

▶ Make its online offerings more differentiated and user friendly

▶ Increase responsiveness to changing market needs

▶ Provide innovative services quickly and cost-effectively via multiple portals in order to address different groups of customers

▶ Automate key activities

▶ Significantly reduce the development effort required to create new processes and modify existing ones

▶ Reduce administrative overhead

▶ Boost employee productivity

In addition, the company wanted to outline a new business-driven mid- to long-term IT strategy built around SAP's ESA blueprint. To help achieve these goals, it called in SAP Consulting.

6.1.2 Mapping an Evolutionary Path to ESA

As part of the *ESA Adoption Program*, SAP's business and technology consultants sat down with experts from the company to determine how the ESA blueprint could best support the customer's objectives. In a series of workshops, SAP Consulting and the customer created a roadmap charting a company-specific route to implementing ESA. From the outset, it was clear that the customer favored an evolutionary approach over a big-bang approach. This is in line with SAP's flexible ESA adoption methodology, which lets companies determine the scope and pace that suits them.

Deploying a clearly structured, standard procedure, SAP's consultants created the company's roadmap in five stages:

Roadmap in five steps

1. **Align ESA strategy with customer strategy**
   During this initial phase, SAP's consultants focused on gaining a clear understanding of the customer's overall business and IT strategy, and how ESA could support it.

2. **Gain insight into business processes, the IT landscape, and how they interrelate**
   Next, SAP Consulting and the customer's specialists examined the company's existing business processes and IT landscape. In addition, workshops were held to draw up a list of initial candidates for enterprise services.

3. **Evaluate potential for enterprise services**

   SAP's experts leveraged a proven consulting methodology to identify the most promising ESA candidates in terms of business value. On the basis of their findings, the SAP consultants created a matrix showing which enterprise services should be prioritized. This provided a foundation for a phased introduction, ensuring that the customer would reap added value with each stage.

4. **Design ESA**

   SAP Consulting and the company conducted workshops to match the candidates identified in Step three to SAP applications and SAP NetWeaver components. The SAP experts went on to plan the short-listed enterprise services and created a high-level ESA design matrix.

5. **Define ESA strategy and roadmap**

   Lastly, the results from the preceding steps were combined and consolidated to create the final roadmap. This comprised a customer-specific implementation schedule, taking into account the company's and SAP's release plans. Consideration was also given to any dependencies between IT and business projects, and it was determined what services should be implemented and when this should occur to achieve maximum business value.

Results The company's map featured:

- ▶ Major implementation milestones
- ▶ Supporting projects, such as Web design, change management, employee training from SAP Education
- ▶ Temporal and contextual dependencies, regarding business performance, for instance, strategic projects, or solution availability
- ▶ Implementation priorities
- ▶ Customer release schedule
- ▶ Timelines for realizing long-term objectives
- ▶ Impact on related areas, partners within the group, and external parties
- ▶ Required decisions
- ▶ Recommendations for further steps
- ▶ Risks to be addressed in the individual phases

The roadmap also included suggestions for the company's mid- to long-term IT strategy. On the basis of their findings, SAP's consultants advised the customer to implement the following SAP NetWeaver components step-by-step over a three-year period:

SAP NetWeaver components to implement

▶ **SAP NetWeaver Portal**
Providing rapid, role-based access to information, and streamlined collaboration between employees, customers, and partners

▶ **SAP NetWeaver Business Intelligence**
Enabling flexible reporting and analysis in line with real-world requirements

▶ **SAP NetWeaver Exchange Infrastructure**
Enabling end-to-end processes across multiple applications and systems

▶ **SAP NetWeaver Application Server**
Providing a complete environment for developing and running software based on ABAP and Java

▶ **SAP Solution Manager**
Supporting the implementation, testing, rollout, and ongoing operation of SAP software

▶ **SAP NetWeaver Master Data Management**
Ensuring that master data is accurate, non-redundant, and effectively managed

▶ **SAP Composite Application Framework**
Enabling the straightforward creation of new applications and the orchestration of legacy applications by reusing existing functions

6.1.3 Implementing Enterprise Services

As explained, instead of introducing ESA immediately across its entire IT and business landscape, the company opted to focus initially on optimizing the processes for sales of different kinds of advertisements via its portal. In the third step of creating the roadmap, SAP's specialists confirmed this was the area that promised greatest value from existing software and hardware investments.

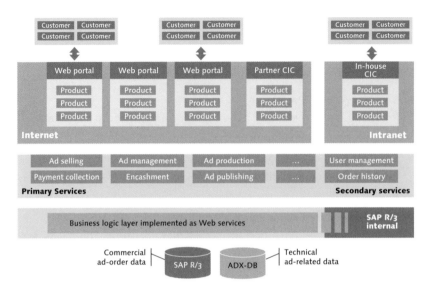

Figure 6.1 Overview of the Planned Solution

Analyzing processes

Working together with the customer, the SAP consultants analyzed the various advertising sales processes supported by the online channel, breaking them down into many distinct logical units common to all. These included:

▶ Creating new users

▶ Selecting design templates

▶ Accessing available products

▶ Providing ad content

▶ Calculating prices

▶ Creating orders

▶ Processing payments

Modeling as enterprise services

Each individual step was then modeled as a self-contained enterprise service. These modular services are stored in a dedicated repository and can be combined flexibly to create new process flows. Based on the open Web Services Description Language (WSDL) standard, each service encapsulates functions from the company's SAP software and makes them available via an intuitive web frontend.

As the company's repository grows, it will become possible to configure processes rapidly simply by plugging services together, significantly reducing development outlay, and accelerating projects. Accordingly, the company will be able to create new customer or product-specific online offerings quickly and cost-effectively in any portal environment.

With the expert support of SAP Consulting, the enterprise transformed its portal in just three months. Leveraging open enterprise services, it now operates four separate online resources, covering different publications and serving the needs of specific customer groups and partners. Each online resource provides seamlessly integrated, end-to-end self-services, enabling users to design, order, and pay for ads quickly and easily by using a series of easy-to-understand user interfaces. The initial response has been very positive, and the company anticipates a significant increase in the number of users over the coming years.

6.1.4 Business Benefits

By adopting an ESA-based approach to its portal solutions, the enterprise has reaped a host of benefits. Its enterprise services encapsulate functions and processes already available in its SAP and non-SAP systems, linking them to create fully integrated, end-to-end online offerings. This has decreased the TCO by reducing the amount of costly, time-consuming development and maintenance tasks, and by eliminating the need for new IT investment.

Thanks to the loose coupling of the interface, business logic, and back-end systems, the new portals have retained the familiar look and feel of the original online resources, while providing a wealth of additional information, such as prices and copy deadlines. This has increased user acceptance and loyalty, and reduced the number of telephone and fax inquiries to the company's customer service center, freeing up staff for other tasks.

Additional functions

The enterprise has also been able to automate the vast majority of online ad ordering tasks. For example, whenever a transaction is completed in the portal, the resulting advertisement is sent automatically to printing/production, and all relevant details are forwarded to the company's financial accounting system for invoicing—eliminating time-consuming, error-prone manual processing and increasing employee productivity. While some customers continue to use traditional channels, and not all advertising tasks can be completed online, the company's streamlined processes have halved the cost of selling advertising space.

European legislation requires public-sector requests for proposals to be published in local newspapers. To date, many organizations have placed their orders by fax. Using its new enterprise services, the company has

Next steps

created a portal specifically for this purpose. Since many of the activities involved in the process are similar to those in advertising sales, it was able to establish the new offering with very little development effort.

In line with SAP's recommendations, the enterprise now plans to implement the SAP NetWeaver platform as a basis for the phased rollout of the ESA blueprint across the entire enterprise, thus enabling the creation of more innovative offerings and the provision of enterprise services to an even wider variety of customers.

6.2 Designing and Realizing a Strategy for Growth and Efficiency

The fictitious company described in this section is a European-based automotive component supplier. It manufactures a wide variety of small plastic parts for many leading European automakers and engineering companies and has recently started moving into the U.S. and Asian markets. Founded in the late 1970s, the enterprise has grown continuously over the years. Today, it has around 8,000 employees, operates five production facilities, and has a worldwide sales network with 10 dedicated distribution centers.

6.2.1 Background

The component supplier expects to grow significantly over the next few years by developing innovative new products to enable it to win new customers and extend its business beyond the automotive industry. To support this strategy, it has plans for a major acquisition. However, because its systems have evolved piecemeal over a period of years, they included a large number of heterogeneous standalone solutions—some dating back to the company's foundation. It was therefore decided to revamp and consolidate the entire IT landscape in preparation for the proposed takeover. In 2000, the company took the first step by migrating financial accounting, human resources, and some supporting systems to the predecessor of mySAP ERP (SAP R/3), thereby considerably increasing efficiency.

Heterogeneous landscape

As well as SAP R/3, the company had some 30 IT systems, including homegrown solutions and aging legacy systems. This presented major obstacles to business—particularly in sales, production planning, and logistics. What's more, the enterprise recognized that production inefficiencies required urgent attention. Another top priority was to improve customer relationship management. This area had been fraught with problems due to the many ad-hoc business processes used to deal with the very diverse needs of customers, suppliers, production units, and maintenance departments. Poor visibility into supply and demand also impacted the efficiency of these processes, as well as the reliability of information for key performance indicators (KPIs) such as lead times, quality ratios, and process costs. Figure 6.2 provides an overview of the supply chain.

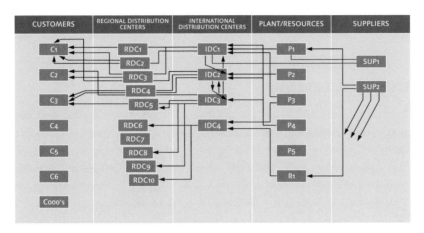

Figure 6.2 The Company's Supply Chain

6.2.2 Challenges

Issues identified

The company's senior management was aware that the organization had developed around manufacturing and that other key areas had been neglected as a result. While it had insight into some core activities, the component supplier lacked an understanding of its processes as a whole. It became readily apparent that the existing structures could not support the company's strategy and urgently needed reengineering. The following issues were identified:

▶ Inadequate understanding and documentation of procedures made optimization impossible.

▶ The company could no longer achieve the levels of flexibility and timely delivery demanded by customers.

▶ Increasing production capacity would merely exacerbate the problems.

▶ Valuable time would be lost if completely new processes and interfaces had to be defined and developed following the acquisition and integration of another enterprise.

The company was no longer able to conduct business effectively without formalized procedures. It therefore needed to optimize its processes in order to increase employee productivity, maximize capital investments, cut costs, and grow the business. In particular, its goal was to continue to expand outside its original core markets.

To overcome these problems, the enterprise's senior management recognized that it would be necessary to closely align the processes and business strategy, while developing a flexible, state-of-the-art IT landscape that was capable of meeting customers' requirements and growing with the company.

6.2.3 Initial Analysis

To get a clear picture of the overall state of affairs, the company required advice and assistance from external experts. On the basis of positive experience gained during the SAP R/3 implementation some years earlier, the company turned to SAP Consulting. Its initial goals were to identify critical business processes requiring optimization, to determine which interfaces would have to be created, and to map out the necessary change processes. Other tasks included developing a corresponding IT strategy and assessing the potential value of the investment and the proposed changes. The company's senior management—and above all, its investors—wanted a well-structured breakdown of the expected benefits of process improvements, as well as a forecast of the costs and savings. So, the enterprise engaged the Business Consulting group of SAP Consulting to conduct a six-week assessment. This assessment comprised the *SAP Business and Value Assessment* service, which analyzed the relevant production and logistics processes and targeted problems, and the *SAP IT Planning* service to define a roadmap for making the proposed improvements by implementing an SAP solution.

SAP Business and Value Assessment

Within the scope of SAP Business and Value Assessment, experienced SAP consultants leveraged proven methodologies and best practices to help identify areas for improvement. They also showed how leading edge SAP technology could be deployed to achieve the component supplier's goals. SAP Consulting helped the company to validate critical success factors and potential benefits in the run-up to the project. This provided a reliable basis for justifying future investments in terms of benefits and cost, and established a clear link between IT investments and business results.

Thanks to the service, the customer gained:

▶ Qualitative analysis of business benefits, promoting buy-in and commitment from key stakeholders

▶ Insight into how the transformation project would affect business operations

▶ Full understanding of return on investment (ROI), ensuring that IT is aligned with business goals

▶ A clear picture of how the proposed SAP solution would meet its specific needs

SAP IT Planning

The SAP IT Planning service enabled the company to develop a highly effective IT architecture, aiding with the transition from an initial IT framework to a comprehensive IT strategy aligned with business goals.

SAP's consultants provided the enterprise with the following:

▶ Technology strategy—in the form of a feasible IT plan

▶ IT portfolio management—recommendations for where to increase or decrease IT investments

▶ Security strategy—analysis and specification of an appropriate level of information security

▶ Rollout plan—helping to define and plan implementation projects, including timelines, milestones, and dependencies

▶ Software change management—helping to organize and control the implementation of changes to software and associated processes

6.2.4 Detailed Findings

SAP Consulting's experts identified and documented the following problems.

Forecasting and planning

The company's planning and forecasting processes were handled using heterogeneous systems and required spreadsheets and considerable manual effort. Consequently, it was unable to generate timely, reliable forecasts and lacked the high-quality information necessary to develop accurate business plans.

The sales-planning process used by the company could not balance supply and demand effectively over periods of several weeks or for individual products. Moreover, it took many weeks to create a demand plan. Considerable time and effort was also required to plan, gain consensus across business units, and link demand signals to revenue goals. As a result, planning and forecasting was confined entirely to the short term.

The enterprise had only limited insight into demand. It constantly had to resolve problems, and planners lacked time for strategic and contingency planning. Furthermore, manual processing made it impossible to forecast demand down to the levels of stock keeping units (SKUs) and locations.

Production planning and scheduling

The company has some 1,350 work centers with 900 injection molding machines at its five production facilities. Work-in-process materials had to be routed through two to six work centers. Any individual step for a particular product can be executed at one of several work centers. The enterprise faced the challenge of efficiently scheduling its work centers, effectively tackling the many possible product-routing permutations, planning manufacturing in line with capacity constraints, and prioritizing production.

Low productivity These difficulties were compounded by the organization's schedulers having to deal with non-core tasks, such as answering incoming phone calls. Consequently, there were issues with high work-in-process inventory, inconsistent utilization of work centers, and low employee productivity. Nevertheless, utilization was high at those work centers where work-in-process inventory was queued upstream and high levels of safety stock were maintained.

Tracking work-center performance and tracing the source of products

To meet certain customers' requirements, the company needed to certify the quality of specific products and record the work centers they passed through during the manufacturing process. Furthermore, the company had to find ways of identifying the root cause of product quality issues. It also needed to monitor and enhance the performance of work centers. But, the company's existing processes provided only limited visibility into operations at individual work centers, impacting its ability to identify and resolve problems. Due to rapid growth over a period of years, the company was still operating equipment with widely divergent capabilities— some of it dating back to the 1980s, and some acquired very recently.

Order fulfillment

The company has several hundred customers and generates some 7,500 bills of lading every month. Order values and the numbers of line items and customers vary considerably at the individual business units. The company lacked standard order-handling processes. Order fulfillment and associated processes had become particularly complex due to the high number of SKUs (around 38,000 in 2004).

Inventory of finished goods

The company's products have lifecycles of two or more years, and some can be held in inventory for several years. As a result, the company placed little emphasis on managing its inventory of finished goods, believing that what it manufactured would eventually be sold. But it had no real understanding of what this attitude was costing. Although products did eventually move, they sometimes remained in stock so long that storage costs had eaten up the entire profit.

High storage costs

Raw materials

The approximately 650 raw materials that the company uses account for around 50 percent of its product costs. The most important of these are thermoplastics. Fluctuations in the price of raw materials have a considerable impact on profitability, and competitive pressures in the company's markets make it difficult to pass cost increases on to customers. While it uses only a small number of different grades of thermoplastics, the company tended to maintain excessively high buffer stock to ensure it had sufficient material to meet demand.

Perfect order rates

The enterprise discovered it had limited ability to deliver finished goods in full and on schedule, including all necessary paperwork such as invoices. The company worked jointly with SAP's business consultants to define a perfect order rate as a composite of order fulfillment characteristics. This revealed significant opportunities for improvement across order-related dimensions. The consultants also discovered that the various production sites had adopted different approaches and processes, and therefore recommended developing standard processes across all units.

Develop standard processes

6.2.5 Preparation for Implementation

On the basis of these findings, SAP's consultants and the company went on to examine how best to standardize processes and procedures, increase transparency, and eliminate structural weaknesses to enhance the company's competitive edge.

Applying lean enterprise principles

The enterprise also worked closely with SAP's business consultants to evaluate its order-to-cash (O2C) and manufacturing processes. The main objectives included minimizing costs, enhancing customer service, and maximizing throughput across the complex network of work centers. In accordance with lean enterprise principles, they focused on increasing the efficiency of business processes and eliminating any steps that did not add value. The company realized the importance of improving IT in this endeavor. This would drive optimization by providing additional information and greater visibility into daily sales activities, sales trends, days' sales outstanding, manufacturing, compliance with production schedules, and general efficiency.

IT infrastructure

Further assessments conducted by SAP Consulting revealed that it would also be necessary to optimize the IT landscape. The individual production sites operated their own IT systems with local data storage, which were synchronized with headquarters on a daily basis. Therefore, it was impossible to adapt plans rapidly to accommodate changing orders, which significantly impacted the flexibility of the company's production.

6.2.6 Suggested Approach

On the basis of these findings, SAP's consultants proposed the following approach:

▶ Begin by adopting a step-by-step approach to optimize O2C and to model it within the ERP system. In a second phase, migrate production planning and control and logistics to a flexible, state-of-the-art system. The software recommended for this purpose was mySAP Supply Chain Management (mySAP SCM), which delivers comprehensive support for the new, integrated, and lean processes.

▶ Prior to implementing these changes, enhance the company's existing SAP R/3 software and upgrade to mySAP ERP—enabling the new production processes to be integrated seamlessly with the other business units. Implement data warehousing on the basis of SAP NetWeaver Business Intelligence.

- SAP's consultants strongly recommended consolidating the IT landscape and introducing central data management (SAP NetWeaver Master Data Management).

- In the second phase of the project, following completion of the preceding activities, focus on optimizing the entire supply chain and introducing mySAP SCM.

ROI potential analysis

The objective of this step was to identify and quantify a number of key figures that would be improved by the implemented software. Besides standard financial indicators, process-related values, in particular, were identified and determined. The analysis conducted by SAP Consulting found the following opportunities to improve the company's business processes:

Optimize business processes

- Forecast accuracy
  At the time of the analysis, the accuracy of demand forecasts was 21 percent. Following completion of the project, it was expected to rise to at least 45 percent.

- Financial closing cycle
  The organization initially required 10 days to close its books. The goal was to reduce this to five days short term and one day medium term (see also Section 6.2.8).

- Inventory
  The target was to cut the value of stock in inventory from 85 million Euro (approx. 101 million USD) to less than 40 million Euro (approx. 48 million USD).

- Perfect order rate
  The objective was to increase the perfect order rate by at least five percentage points (from an initial figure of some 78 percent).

- Utilization
  An increase in production utilization of at least 15 percent was forecast.

6.2.7 Approach and Implementation

On the basis of their project planning, the SAP consultants proposed a 10-month timeframe for the first phase of the implementation. The subsequent phase, optimizing the supply chain, was scheduled to take an additional 11 months. Between the two phases, an interim period of three months was slated for going live and subsequent checks. The milestones (largely based on SAP's tried-and-tested ASAP methodology) are shown in Figure 6.3.

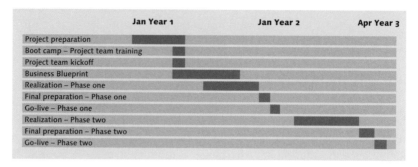

Figure 6.3 Overview Project Plan

Project preparation

The six-week stage of project preparation included all the analysis and planning tasks outlined above. It was driven primarily by SAP's Business Consulting experts and set the stage for the subsequent implementation. During this step, project standards were established and initial decisions were reached regarding organizational change management.

Boot camp—project team training

A vital element of preparation focused on assembling the project team and on training for all involved (provided by SAP Education). It was decided that a joint team would be established, with SAP Consulting in charge of project management. The team comprised SAP consultants (project managers and technical and applications specialists), as well as experts from the company's IT organization and user departments. The project as a whole had the sponsorship of the company's CEO—a decisive factor in ensuring the success of initiatives of this kind. The heads of IT and production chaired the steering committee.

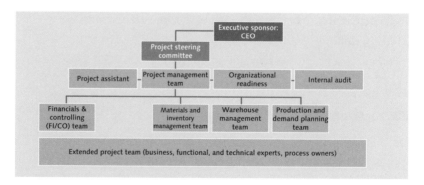

Figure 6.4 Structure of the Project Team

During the Business Blueprint stage, a document was created collating the results of the assessments outlined above, as well as the findings of an additional requirements workshop. Thanks to in-depth analyses conducted by SAP's consultants during the preceding stages, the project team was able to design the business processes and IT landscape in detail.

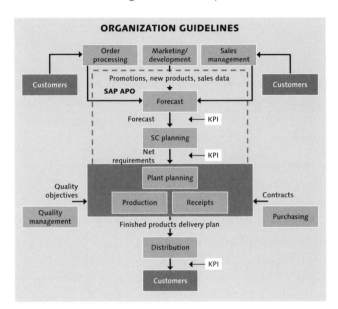

Figure 6.5 Project Structure

Services delivered by the SAP consultants included *SAP Technical Analysis and Design* to verify the feasibility of the company's solution. SAP Consulting aligned the technical design with the customer's business requirements, project-specific goals, timelines, and budgets, ensuring that the system architecture would deliver tangible business results. As part of *SAP Technical Installation*, the SAP experts built a foundation for implementing the SAP solution successfully and running it reliably over the long term. The service ensured that the customer's IT environment would be configured properly for maximized performance, availability, and flexibility.

Two-phase implementation

Phase one—Lay the foundations for the O2C process (10 months): The company completed its upgrade to mySAP ERP and introduced support for subprocesses, such as purchasing, order entry, warehouse management, shipping, accounting, and spare-parts management. mySAP ERP functions implemented included finance and accounting, sales and distribution, materials management, and purchasing. The enterprise also introduced the data-warehousing capabilities of SAP NetWeaver Business Intelligence (SAP NetWeaver BI).

Phase two—Enable supply-chain planning and execution processes (11 months): The company introduced mySAP SCM for a number of subprocesses, such as demand planning, supply network planning, production planning, and detailed scheduling. It also deployed SAP software for plant maintenance, as well as available-to-promise capabilities.

As part of the *SAP Test Management Consulting* service, the SAP experts provided the company with a detailed testing plan. Next, they guided the customer through solution testing to ensure a successful go-live. The consultants also delivered:

▶ **SAP Technical Migration, helping the customer to make an efficient and cost-effective transition to a new solution**
The service helped the enterprise move data from legacy systems to the new SAP solution and to migrate operating systems and databases.

▶ **Removing non-value-added activities**
As the company proceeded through phases one and two, it closely scrutinized individual process steps in accordance with lean enterprise principles. The goal was to determine opportunities for eliminating non-value-added activities. SAP's expert consultants worked together with the customer's team to develop the corresponding process maps. They analyzed all individual steps of the relevant transaction and determined the information necessary to support them. Where the company intended to eliminate steps, SAP's consultants helped to identify the implications for information systems. Although it made sense to remove steps that did not add value, the consultants still had to ensure that the resulting reduction in information would not impact decision-making. The team included experts from the company who knew the implications of eliminating these steps, and informed the management team about proposed changes.

Together with SAP's consultants, the customer's project team painstakingly mapped out the process flows to identify potential enhancements. These included opportunities for pooling inventory, areas where visual kanban signals could be used to manage production flow, and areas where sources of production orders could be consolidated.

Decision-making processes also offered scope for improvement. The project team was able to move routine decisions to a lower level of the company's hierarchy, thereby saving time and improving accuracy. Due to the complexity of the 1,350 work centers, it was particularly important to examine each individual step and the associated transactions. The company has now eliminated all unnecessary transactions. By considering the financial and operational significance of each transaction, looking closely at every step, and adopting a highly granular approach, the company has been able to capture vital information on each work center. This is now leveraged to streamline operations.

▶ **Rationalization of product lines**
During the implementation, SAP Consulting helped the customer to reduce its 38,000 SKUs to streamline processes, reduce costs, and minimize activities that did not add value. The company defined two categories of materials: core and non-core. The former are Make-to-Stock (MTS); the latter are Make-to-Order (MTO). To enable more accurate production scheduling, lead times were determined for the production of non-core materials. The rationalization has reduced the total number of SKUs to 5,800.

During the project, the team recognized that rationalization raised issues, because the company firmly believed it needed vast inventories to meet commitments to customers. The transition from large volumes of costly inventory to lean production with very low inventories was a cause for concern in the enterprise. To address this concern, the project team recommended initiating a subproject for change management to accompany the project rollout. This was built on the *SAP Project Organizational Change* service, allowing the customer to manage modifications and enhancements to its IT infrastructure effectively and thereby ensuring a smooth transition. Furthermore, employees acquired valuable knowledge and skills, enabling them to maximize the benefits of the SAP solution.

Organizational change management

Within the scope of the change management subproject, SAP's consultants looked into:

▶ **Change requirements**
To identify possible gaps between current and future processes, benefits of changes, and organizational impact

▶ **Potential media and channels**
To evaluate the effectiveness of communication channels, including cost-benefit analysis and planning

▶ **Communication requirements**
To set out key messages, planning, and communication channels between the main stakeholders and target groups

The project team then drew up plans for user training and knowledge transfer, focusing on users' real-world requirements.

Training   SAP's consultants and the customer's project staff realized that training would have to be developed at an early stage and continue beyond go-live. Moreover, they determined that some just-in-time training would be needed in the run-up. The project managers recognized that the majority of business-process design documents would have to be completed before training materials could be developed.

The company provided 80 key users with comprehensive training on the business processes enabled by SAP solutions. Another 20 employees at its production facilities were upgraded to provide colleagues with training in accordance with local requirements.

6.2.8 Results

Sales and operations planning   The implementation enabled the enterprise to enhance its process for planning sales and operations, improve the balance between supply and demand, integrate production constraints into planning, and align operational plans with revenue commitments in its business plan. Forecast accuracy—a key factor in planning—improved significantly, rising from 21 percent to 52 percent, and planners now have better information and tools for their day-to-day work. The company also has a far better insight into profitability per product and per customer, and into its overall financial situation. Financial closing has been cut from 10 days to five, and the customer expects to slash this number to just one day.

Manufacturing, planning, and scheduling   The company leverages the powerful functions of mySAP SCM to schedule the manufacturing of thousands of products at its 1,350 work centers. Because of the extremely large number of possible routings for each product, it needed an effective solution for scheduling and for presenting the information required by management. The majority of its 900 injection-molding machines can perform identical tasks. Together with the sheer number of products, bills of material, and routings, this made it impossible to manage master data without an integrated solution. But, the SAP software enabled the company to group products, reducing the number of routes through the work centers from hundreds of thousands to just 38. Moreover, by establishing 15 capacity centers, each comprising multiple work centers, the SAP consultants were able to improve the customer's rough-cut planning and manage capacity constraints better.

This approach, which included careful mapping of products and work centers to SAP data structures, enabled the company to master the complexity of its products and production processes using standard SAP functions. It can now leverage a vast quantity of data to create plans and identify planning options, without having to employ large numbers of staff to maintain master data. Moreover, it can now trace the source of finished goods, if certification is required, and identify the cause of quality issues.

Since the project kickoff, enhancements to the way the supply chain is planned and executed have reduced the company's finished goods inventory (see Figure 6.6), and the value of raw material in inventory has been cut by three million Euro (approx. 3.6 million USD). There was a slight increase in inventory toward the conclusion of the implementation due to a strategic decision adopted by the company. Nevertheless, inventory quality improved and most slow-moving or obsolete products were eliminated.

Inventory management

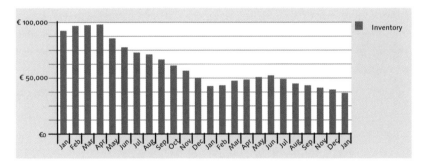

Figure 6.6 Reduction in Finished Goods Inventory

mySAP SCM's standard available-to-promise functions are used for individual customer orders. If the product ordered or a preferred location product is unavailable, the software uses rules to propose alternatives. This helps to reduce inventory and enhances customer service.

Available-to-promise

As shown in Figure 6.7, perfect order rates continuously improved throughout the implementation as the enterprise streamlined its planning and execution processes. Results varied according to business unit. Through improvements in order fulfillment and associated areas, there was an 83 percent reduction in backorders.

Improvements to perfect order rate

The average utilization of work centers immediately increased by 12 percent. During the second year, a 17 percent improvement was achieved.

Work-center utilization

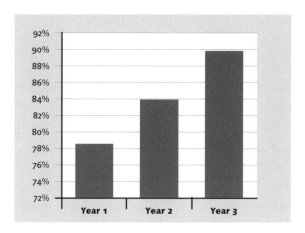

Figure 6.7 Improvement of Perfect Order Rate

Project governance and organizational change management The company established a governance committee to oversee implementation and guarantee compliance with company goals. While it invested considerable resources—including around 30 employees—it recognized that effective change management would be vital to the project's success. The initial challenge was to ensure that people understood the project was primarily about business processes, and not merely software.

SAP Consulting moderated and drove the change management effort. The customer focused on communicating the changes to all levels of the organization, generating widespread buy-in. To boost awareness, the company issued publications and held meetings to ensure that everyone was up to speed with progress, the current focus, the business processes to be reengineered, and the possible effects on individuals and organizations. Moreover, it guaranteed that all relevant decision-makers were closely involved and could provide input.

Conclusion The company's new mySAP solution and the expert services provided by SAP Consulting enabled the company to pursue its growth strategy, consolidate its IT, and streamline key activities more effectively. Integrated, standardized processes meant that it had the necessary flexibility to respond rapidly to changing customer needs and market conditions.

6.3 Standardized Process for Implementing an SAP Solution

A midsize company registered in Europe successfully develops products for the special pharmaceuticals and dietary supplement markets, with pharmaceuticals accounting for approximately 70 percent of sales revenues. The drugs developed in this business area must be licensed by the respective regulatory authorities of the country in which the product is marketed and, for the most part, are available only by prescription. Regulations regarding dietary supplements are significantly less stringent. The company develops vitamin and mineral preparations on a natural basis, which it sells primarily through direct marketing.

The company is by no means new to SAP: In an extensive project in 2001, the entire IT system landscape was revised and changed over to SAP, including the business processes. Sales revenues quadrupled in 1999 and 2000, the years of expansion and rapid growth, and the company found itself with a complex network of different applications and customer developments, unable to cope with future requirements. Effective planning and control became elusive goals. Consequently, the decision was made to move human resources, accounting and cost management, and production planning and control to SAP solutions as soon as possible in order to secure future success. Aided by SAP Consulting, the entire project—from planning to going live—was realized in just eight months and proved to be a real success.

Unmanageable network of applications

All this placed the company in an excellent position to tackle the challenges that arose from continuing growth over the next few years. In 2003, the company's sales revenues cleared the one billion hurdle for the first time and continued to rise in 2004. A particularly dynamic sector during that time was the market for natural dietary supplements; the significant increase in demand was attributed to intensive marketing activities at the start of 2005. The newly printed catalog, which included an editorial, coupled with a direct marketing campaign, seemed to have targeted the right customers at the right time. This progress was not without considerable preparation, however. Even the subsequent analysis of the direct marketing activities relied primarily on manual procedures—an area identified by the marketing and sales managers as in dire need of an efficiency boost.

This growth was accompanied by a real increase in the sales organization, particularly for special pharmaceuticals, because employees in this area conduct one-to-one sales meetings with doctors and pharmacists. They distribute product samples and promotional materials to increase awareness of the products and to demonstrate their effectiveness. This practice, however, is subject to legal requirements. In recent years, different countries have revised their requirements. The observation of these requirements, however, and documentation about compliance are essential for the pharmaceuticals industry. Figure 6.8 illustrates a section of the company's current structure.

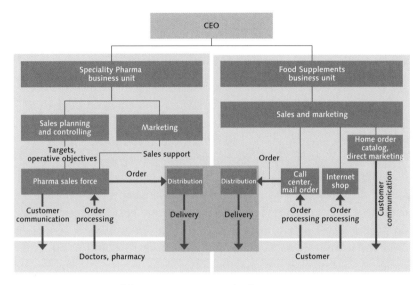

Figure 6.8 Overview of the Business Areas Involved

Deficits A critical analysis of sales performance conducted by the company's management body has uncovered serious deficits that cannot be resolved simply by restructuring the sales organization, due in part to the organization's growth and in part to increased demand. An initial analysis of the pharmaceuticals area revealed that employees spend far too long documenting their visits and that efficiency could be boosted if more flexible options for entering and processing orders were introduced. The time-consuming and reactive processes currently in place lead to delivery bottlenecks one minute and excess capacity the next, which can even result in whole batches being wasted due to product expiration dates.

In the dietary supplements area, which relies primarily on direct sales, it is revealed that the Internet shop cannot cope with rising customer demand. The call center will also need to expand in the near future, since callers already experience long waiting times at peak periods—an aspect identified in a customer survey as most in need of improvement, along with the Internet shop's poor user guide. The complicated user guide and performance problems have recently been the cause of increasingly more lost orders as customers have canceled transactions. With all these factors to consider, rapid action is vital.

6.3.1 Strategy and Planning

The management body sees an urgent need for an effective IT solution capable of boosting efficiency while also promising new and improved customer service options, especially as ideas have also been suggested to dovetail the two business areas more effectively. The sales managers regard direct contact between pharmaceuticals field staff and pharmacists as a potential sales channel for vitamin products. According to an internal analysis, this area harbors substantial cross-selling potential; however, it remains unexploited, because the data and processes from the two areas are not yet integrated. The plans for improved customer service also include a hotline for doctors and pharmacists, enabling them to contact the manufacturer directly with urgent queries. The idea here is to run the hotline in the call center. Since the hotline will not be implemented immediately, the new solution must be flexible enough to accommodate it quickly and without excessive external input.

Cross-selling potential

With an SAP solution already in place and the experience gained from working with SAP Consulting on tap, the company opts for mySAP CRM, leaving planning and realization to the SAP specialists. Industry experts from SAP Consulting conduct an initial analysis to determine the company's requirements and examine the current situation. They establish that the company plans to achieve the following objectives by implementing mySAP CRM:

mySAP CRM

▶ Improve sales processes through more reliable planning, simpler procedures for order entry, and more readily available information

▶ Retain customers better through enhanced customer service for end customers, doctors, and pharmacists

▶ Improve performance in the new Internet shop to cope with future requirements

▶ Ensure complete data and process integration with the back-office systems

▶ Plan, execute, and control marketing campaigns better

In view of these specifications, the experts propose implementing mySAP CRM with the data warehouse components from SAP NetWeaver Business Intelligence (SAP NetWeaver BI). They recommend SAP Mobile Sales for the mobile sales force and SAP E-Commerce for SAP R/3 as a basis for the Internet shop; the result is a solution that can be realized quickly and cost effectively. In order to be up and running for the fall and winter season—the company's most important time of year—IT manage-

BI and Mobile Sales

ment has drafted an aggressive schedule, leaving just seven months to implement the system. On the advice of SAP Consulting, it divides the overall project into two subprojects. The first subproject targets short-comings in the current Internet shop, with the new shop expected to yield real success in a short space of time. The bulk of the implementation project falls in the second subproject, with the implementation of mySAP CRM with SAP Mobile Sales and SAP NetWeaver BI. Campaign manage-ment and the Interaction Center are scheduled for a later stage.

SAP Solution Manager The company and SAP Consulting decide to use SAP Solution Manager to implement and later to run the solution, since the company has already obtained satisfying results with the implementation function available with this platform. SAP Solution Manager offers preconfigured content, tools, and methods to ensure high standards during the implementation and quality assurance phases. The objective is to use functions from SAP Solution Manager consistently to reduce costs and optimize the duration of the project.

The standardized implementation method ASAP is to be used throughout to bring the entire project to a prompt and cost-effective close. This approach is supported by the Implementation Roadmap, which is an inte-gral part of SAP Solution Manager. The company also intends to use Best Practices when implementing mySAP CRM, such as process templates and Business Configuration Sets.

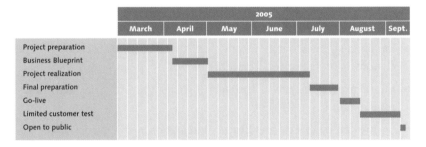

Figure 6.9 Project Plan for the Design and Realization of the Internet Shop

6.3.2 Project Realization

The first step is the project preparation phase, which involves document-ing the business environment, creating a project charter, and defining how the project is to be planned and organized. This is also the time for setting standards for documentation, reporting, and testing, as well as deciding which tools to deploy. Initial strategies for user training and documentation are also compiled in this phase. Once the technical requirements and design are complete, the phase is concluded with a kickoff meeting.

The company and SAP Consulting decide to take advantage of services from the support program *SAP Safeguarding*, which aim to minimize the risks involved with the performance, hardware sizing, and technical stability of interfaces and database systems. They appoint a Technical Quality Manager (TQM) from SAP to supervise the project throughout to the go-live date and to coordinate the Safeguarding services with the project team.

SAP Safeguarding

Once the company has assembled a project team—a total of five people from the IT department and the sales and marketing areas—an initial workshop is held in April 2005 to begin compiling a Business Blueprint for the Internet shop and CRM implementation.

The Business Blueprint is at the core of the second project phase. It contains detailed plans and drafts for realizing all the customer's requirements. By the end of this phase, the team should have a Business Blueprint that documents in full all the tasks that must be completed during the project realization phase and that the appropriate decision-makers have signed off. When compiling the blueprint, the team discusses a wide range of issues relating to the forthcoming realization phase:

Business Blueprint

▶ Necessary organizational changes and communication of such changes

▶ Ongoing training for the project team

▶ Development of user training materials and documentation

▶ Design of an appropriate business and process structure

▶ Definition and development of authorization concepts

▶ Development and design of user interfaces and portals

▶ Documentation, definition, and initiation of any other necessary developments

▶ Development and documentation of the technical and integration design

▶ Definition of procedures for system administration

▶ Structure of the development environment

▶ Elaboration of technical support procedures

This is a critical phase in the project, because it is the stage at which point all decisions concerning the functions and performance of the future solution are made. The extensive experience gained by the consultants in various other pharmaceuticals projects proves extremely useful to the company's team, making many decisions easier and reducing the time required to model processes and organizational structures. An efficient link between the web shop and the mySAP ERP system renders additional developments and additional costs redundant. This is reflected in the concept for the system architecture.

All information about the blueprint and a description of the processes and interfaces to be implemented are recorded in SAP Solution Manager. At the end of the Business Blueprint phase, the TQM organizes the first Safeguarding service. The *SAP Feasibility Check* assesses the technical viability and any existing risks. A team of three SAP experts checks the blueprint, focusing on the plans for implementing the business processes and interfaces. They draw their information from interviews with the project team, as well as from SAP Solution Manager. The service provides the project team with recommendations for technical optimization. A service plan identifies areas for which additional services would be beneficial. One particularly critical issue is the mobile sales application for use by the mobile sales force. Performance and technical stability are deemed to be problematic.

Details of the project scope can now be ratified by the steering committee. Based on the description and documentation of the processes to be implemented, the plans for configuration and testing, as well as the interface design for the web shop and the development system, the project realization phase is given the go-ahead to begin in just three weeks.

Realization phase All the plans, designs, and content contained in the blueprint are put into practice in the realization phase and prepared for use. The initial focus is on the Internet shop. While the company's team receives training for this phase, the experts initiate the first steps towards organizational change and subsequent user training. They compile a training plan for solution-specific aspects and gather information for the contents. This plan is also the basis for the ensuing user training, which the company will provide itself using the train-the-trainer concept.

The basic system is set up and configured. A user interface is designed for the web shop, which adheres to the requirements identified during the workshop, and external web designers are engaged to create a modern and appealing interface. Careful thought must be given to legal regulations governing the sale of dietary supplements; customer information and the associated documentation for this are the primary considerations.

SAP Consulting is able to draw on its pharmaceuticals experience to propose a proven and reliable solution that complies with all legal requirements.

The next step involves planning and preparing to integrate the new mySAP CRM solution and the existing mySAP ERP system. One of the solution's key advantages comes to the fore here, in that the customer's processes are connected to the back-office system. The current solution is extremely susceptible to losing information, because the data is transferred manually.

The project realization phase is also the time for planning and executing a range of integration tests, whereby the extensive system and solution tests are not planned, prepared, or conducted until the next phase. The e-learning functions in SAP Solution Manager are deployed for user training, including SAP Tutor. This tool allows you to record training material and make it available to users for private study or documentation.

Finally, the processes and transactions have to be completed and the functions developed especially for the company's web shop have to be tested. At the same time, planning gets underway for the hand-over strategy and final rollout. The system is scheduled to go live at the end of July for a limited number of test customers and be rolled out to all customers at the start of October if the test phase is successful. By the end of the project realization phase, the new production environment has been fully installed and configured, the processes and structures implemented, and the test plans completed.

The TQM now prepares the *SAP Technical Integration Check*. SAP experts work with the project team to identify any problems relating to the processes and interfaces that have been implemented. They complete an action plan detailing how the SAP specialists can help the project team during the forthcoming integration tests with regard to the performance and technical stability of the interfaces.

The final preparation phase covers user training (provided by SAP Education) and concluding tests. A complete functional and performance test is conducted with selected users, who took part in the first training course mid June. The final performance test and assistance from the SAP experts can optimize performance by 30 percent. During the *SAP GoingLive Check*, the final technical parameters are configured for the SAP application components and the database systems in use.

Final preparation phase

This is accompanied by final preparations for going live:

▶ All users attend the relevant courses. Basic training helps the company reach its goals much faster, by ensuring that the solution is used effectively and productively from the outset.

▶ The results from the SAP GoingLive Check and other functional and system tests are checked and documented.

▶ Support structures are put in place for the production system.

The documentation for the technical landscape and the business processes is used to set up monitoring functions for the solution in SAP Solution Manager. System monitoring focuses on the technical infrastructure, whereas business process monitoring targets technical aspects of the business process with regard to performance and error scenarios. The *SAP Business Process Management* support service is available during this phase and gives the company's project team and support team access to advice from SAP experts.

User support   The service desk is set up in SAP Solution Manager to provide technical support for users. The technical help desk therefore has access to the information in the documented processes and interfaces. The company's support organization can also forward issues that it cannot resolve to SAP.

The production solution is handed over to the users mid July, two weeks before the planned date. A few days later, the Internet shop is opened officially, initially for 50 selected test customers. It is opened to general customers as early as mid September.

6.3.3 Implementation Results

In the months immediately after going live with the new solution, the company reported that Internet sales were up by almost 20 percent, and had not impacted negatively on other channels. The number of customer complaints fell by 65 percent. Feedback from various customers shows that many older customers are now ordering over the Internet, because the Internet shop is easy and intuitive to use. Efficiency has been boosted in the back office, too. Three or four employees used to enter Internet orders in the mySAP ERP system, whereas now, only one employee is required to monitor and control the process. These extra resources will be valuable in the company's planned call center.

ROI in the   Direct access to the knowledge and industry expertise of the consultants
second year   from SAP Consulting enables the solution to be implemented in record

time at minimal expense. The company can put the advantages to use in the same year in its most important sales period, contributing greatly to the amortization of the solution in the second year. With its hard work affirmed by this success, the project team can turn its attention to new projects, such as implementing SAP Mobile Sales and the Interaction Center.

6.4 Creating a Custom Composite Application

Our fictitious enterprise is a large multinational organization. Like many companies, it was under pressure to strengthen its risk-management practices. Regulatory requirements like the Sarbanes-Oxley Act, KonTraG (German business supervision and transparency act), and Basel II called for a corporate-wide process for managing risk. In addition, risk-management practices were increasingly influencing the company's business decisions, external negotiations, and capital market ratings.

The enterprise did not have strong reporting capabilities for corporate risk management to help it achieve its business objectives. It therefore began by creating a corporate risk-management model that defined a process for managing risk and described the high-level organizational prerequisites for sustaining risk-management capabilities. The model contained the following process steps:

Risk-management model

▶ **Risk planning**
To determine the approach to risk management in each business area or project

▶ **Risk identification**
To detect the operational risks facing each business area or project before they become problematic

▶ **Risk analysis**
To evaluate risk attributes and prioritize the risks

▶ **Risk response**
To decide how to handle risks

▶ **Risk monitoring**
To keep track of risks and evaluate the effectiveness of response actions

Risk planning primarily involves defining processes and rules. All but this first topic needed to be included in the new risk-management application.

Figure 6.10 Model for Risk Management

Working together to develop a composite application

After considering its alternatives, the company decided to create a custom composite application. This allowed it to combine elements from existing applications that already covered particular risk-management practices and create a corporate business procedure for managing operational risk without having to start development from scratch.

The company chose *SAP Custom Development*, part of SAP Services, to build its new custom composite application, because it had never built one before. It worked closely with SAP Custom Development throughout all phases of development, including specification, design, realization, and testing to ensure that it was leveraging the latest SAP technologies in the most efficient and effective ways.

Evaluation criteria | When evaluating the development of this custom composite application, the company had to consider the following criteria:

▶ **Independence**
To introduce risk-management functions without interfering with existing business applications

▶ **User friendliness**
To ensure user acceptance

▶ **Security**
To ensure the highest level of data protection

▶ **Flexibility**
To be able to adapt to changing business/regulatory requirements

▶ **Visibility**
To ensure management visibility of risk exposure

▶ **Practicality**
To leverage the existing IT infrastructure

▶ Cost effectiveness

To maximize the value of existing investments

The first step in designing and implementing the composite application was to define a "to-be" data model for the application. Target processes and screen layouts were also created. These steps took place independently of the current landscape and did not differ from a "start-from-scratch" development. Next, the team analyzed the new data and process models for corporate risk management against existing applications. The analysis considered the following aspects:

Data and process model

▶ Sourcing

To identify which current applications already had some part of the data, functions, or processes required

▶ Structure

To determine how existing data was structured in comparison to the target data model

▶ Services

To ascertain how existing data and functions were accessible—specifically, whether synchronous service-oriented access was supported

▶ Security

To establish the security requirements related to existing data and functions

Taking the "Actual Project Activity" object as an example, the enterprise followed the process below to create its composite application: It sourced or derived the "Actual Project Activity" object from several existing SAP systems, including the company's mySAP CRM environment, Collaboration Projects, and Controlling, as well as from third-party sources and manual input. It analyzed the project data structures of the different sources. When matched against the "to-be" data model of the "Actual Project Activity," the parts of the data were identified that remained "remote" with the existing applications. For the remaining data that was new to the risk-management business practice, the company defined a composite, application-specific, detailed data model.

Next, existing services for remote object access were identified and defined in the Integration Broker. This technical definition was driven mainly by the availability of the services for either push- or pull-oriented data transfer. For example, data coming from mySAP CRM and Collaboration Projects was pushed asynchronously to the composite application, while the projects from Controlling were pulled synchronously.

Push and pull

Security rules In this context, the team also defined security rules for access to the services from the risk-management composite application. The rules considered role-based access to data (both at object level and instance level), as well as trust relations between existing applications and the new risk-management application.

While analyzing the data and process model, the company concurrently addressed the user interface layout for the different user roles in the risk-management application. Users were responsible for risk identification, analysis, and response. Their skills were highly varied and it could not be presumed that they had any application experience. For this group of people, a web-based people-centric user interface was implemented. This pattern provided them with a similar look and feel throughout the different steps of the risk-management process.

Unit managers were responsible for monitoring risks. They typically had managerial skills and, again, it could not be presumed that this group of employees had any application experience. For this group, web-based SAP NetWeaver Business Intelligence queries were used. This allowed for flexible searching, filtering, grouping, and graphing, without requiring any installation at client level.

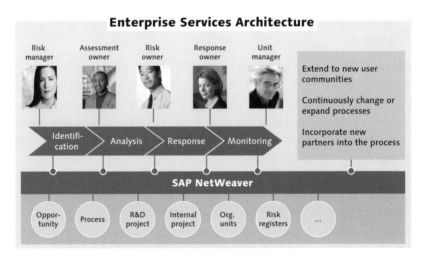

Figure 6.11 Structure of the Composite Application

Finally, the corporate and regional risk managers had to be considered. Their primary roles were to set up the risk-management processes and to monitor the risks. They were typically business experts with limited application experience. For this group, SAP GUI backend transaction screens were used. This allowed the company to maximize the use of existing backend transactions and user interfaces in order to minimize development time and reduce development cost.

By working with SAP Custom Development and creating a custom composite application to fulfill its need for a solution for operational risk management, the company was able to connect its new application to existing applications without changing them. The application now enables tighter cross-team collaboration on cross-functional risks, and risks are now introduced directly from their original business applications. Automated cross-source data consolidation has improved the quality of work delivered, and the flexible environment now allows for new risk data sources to be added dynamically. All of this has resulted in greater efficiency and cost savings with regard to the processing time for gathering and analyzing risk information.

Improvements

In short, the enterprise has faster and greater visibility into the organization's aggregate risk exposure, thereby enabling it to make better decisions that affect the long-term success of the company.

✓	Cross-functional optimization	Connects the composite application to existing applications without changing them
✓	Tight interaction with co-workers	Enables cross-team collaboration on cross-functional risks
✓	Compliance with corporate policies	Automatically considers risk-relevant business objects from their original business applications
✓	High quality of work	Enables automated cross-source data consolidation
✓	Flexibility in dynamic environment	New risk data sources can be added dynamically
✓	Efficiency and cost savings	Reduces process time for gathering risk information
✓	Visibility to management	Aggregates risk exposure information across business applications
✓	Extension of current infrastructure without disruption of existing applications	Solution exists in SAP NetWeaver AS and is independent of individual business applications and release schedules

Figure 6.12 Advantages of the Composite Application

6.5 Global SAP System Rollout with Provision for Smooth Operations

A chemicals group with 11 production sites across different countries in Europe, the United States, and Asia, as well as subsidiaries around the globe, has decided to implement a uniform SAP solution at almost all of its sites in order to create more organizational flexibility and standardize its processes. The plans exclude the two production locations in Germany and Belgium, which already run up-to-date solutions. One of the group's goals is to make it easier to relocate the manufacturing of single products by making recipes and work instructions available at all the sites.

The group's decision affects a total of 15 offices and production sites in different time zones, all of which have different needs: Employees in certain offices are already familiar with recent SAP components, while others have very little experience. The number of users varies at the different sites and the users come from a variety of cultural backgrounds.

6.5.1 Standardizing the SAP Systems

SAP Managed Services

The group wants a fast rollout, but lacks sufficient internal resources for the project; the answer is *SAP Managed Services*. Its consultants will set up the solutions in SAP Implementation Hosting, support and optimize the systems after implementation, and provide second and third-level support for users and applications. A building block concept allows the group to choose how much support it receives—to decide which regions, times, solutions, and subcomponents are to be covered and to what extent. The chemicals group will pay only for the services it actually uses. After the rollout, the internal IT department will gradually resume responsibility for supporting the European systems. To enable the team to perform the task as effectively as possible, internal support structures will first be modernized and the processes will be optimized.

Service levels

Before planning begins, SAP Managed Services examines the current IT solution's performance, structure, and support, and defines service levels with the customer, including service and response times as well as report contents.

System architecture

During this stage, the team also meets with the IT department to draft the new system architecture, design the infrastructure, and ascertain network and data transfer requirements. SAP Managed Services uses the rollout plan to make preparations for implementing the different solutions in the SAP data center. At the same time, the group's employees approve the template with the different international subsidiaries. Their principle is to keep to the standard system as far as possible and allow changes only where dictated by conditions on site. In this way, the systems should be implemented quickly and be easier to maintain later on.

The rollout begins in Europe, because the systems in Asia cannot go live until they have been migrated to Unicode. With the chemical company's IT department largely occupied with rollout activities and approving the template, SAP Managed Services assumes the task of supporting the users in Germany and Belgium (where new SAP applications are not being implemented) for the next 18 months. The SAP specialists optimize the systems while they're in use and make any necessary adjustments and updates.

At the branch in India, proceedings are delayed due to discussions about the new processes. The company swiftly changes its implementation schedule to advance the rollout in the United States. This means that SAP Managed Services will need to provide support for the United States earlier than originally planned.

Schedule changes

Once the systems have been implemented in the different countries, the team from SAP Managed Services oversees second and third-level support, as well as ongoing monitoring for the systems and applications. The consultants also respond to calls for first-level support, and help key users fix minor problems, while also equipping them to do so independently in the future. Past experience shows that the number of such requests falls as users learn how to resolve problems themselves.

6.5.2 Lighter IT Workload with Application Management

The global planning and sales processes mapped in the SAP R/3 system and SAP Advanced Planning & Optimization (SAP APO) must be available at all times. SAP APO consolidates stock information in real time for over 200,000 location products from different ERP systems and calculates the best delivery date/time. The company relies on this procedure to process over 1,500 sales orders daily.

SAP APO

Automatic business process monitoring based on SAP Solution Manager 3.1 ensures that processes and process chains run smoothly and on time. If a logical error occurs in back-order processing or requirements planning, for example, the system terminates the respective job, without starting any dependent processes. Therefore, any system error affects numerous processes and various business areas within the company. Business process monitoring not only enables SAP experts to detect problems in a business process early on and proactively, it also allows them to address the causes of these problems quickly. The system immediately indicates critical jobs if they're not completed within a certain time frame, which prevents major problems from the outset.

Automatic business process monitoring

SAP Managed Services also provides support for the SAP Enterprise Buyer (SAP EB) component. Since the EB processes are not as mission-critical for the chemicals group as is sales order processing in SAP APO, the company decides not to provide a weekend hotline for SAP EB and restricts global support to 16 hours, five days a week.

In the early stages of the project, the group receives a weekly report on all the support services. As the project progresses, employees from the chemicals company become more adept at filtering out the key figures needed to control the services and refine the reports. SAP Support Portal lets the company see the status of all support requests and shows when difficulties were reported and processed, as well as the type of problems encountered most frequently by its employees. This enables the company to take organizational countermeasures if the number of first-level support requests does not decline.

Implementation in India completes the project and the global rollout goes ahead, as planned, within 20 months. SAP Managed Services prepares a knowledge transfer program for the in-house IT department, which gradually resumes responsibility for supporting the European systems. Satisfied with its recent experiences, the company decides to leave key applications in the care of SAP Managed Services.

New support structures and processes To boost efficiency in the IT department, SAP Managed Services helps the company to review its support structures and processes. The team brings employees up to speed with the latest developments and helps them to devise the best possible structure for the SAP Customer Competence Center (SAP CCC, see Section 4.2.1). SAP Managed Services uses the reports to determine the number and type of support requests received daily and the number of suitably qualified employees needed to complete the work promptly. The modifications also target the processes, workflow, and reporting, as well as organizational and authorization structures.

Aided by SAP Managed Services, the IT department has selected service and support tools for monitoring the business processes. SAP Solution Manager allows diverse processes—for example, from requirements planning, back-order processing, or product allocation—to be automated, reducing the time and effort required by approximately 50 percent. This is accompanied by lower operating costs, while continuous business processing monitoring keeps system performance at a consistently high level. Weak spots and bottlenecks are identified quickly, leaving the supply chain obstruction free.

6.6 SAP MaxAttention: Risk Reduction and Continuous Optimization

A global corporate group with more than 30,000 employees has been an SAP customer for many years and currently deploys the following solutions: SAP R/3 with all modules fully configured, as well as SAP Strategic Enterprise Management (SAP SEM) and mySAP Supply Chain Management (mySAP SCM). The company already uses SAP Solution Manager in some areas, which greatly facilitates technical support in distributed systems. The company has its own in-house IT department.

Implementing mySAP Customer Relationship Management (mySAP CRM) is the company's next major step. It has entrusted the implementation project to an SAP partner, who is responsible for the actual project and for system management. This project is already underway and others are in the pipeline.

SAP's role is limited to that of software provider. In addition, the company draws on SAP Standard Support, as agreed upon in its maintenance contract. In all, SAP's involvement in this project is essentially reactive in nature, as illustrated in Figure 6.13. The partner implements mySAP CRM; there is no direct communication with SAP. SAP support does not come into play unless a problem arises. Nor does the project organization provide for all parties coming together for discussion; the customer deals with the different parties separately: its implementation partner, SAP Sales, SAP Consulting, and SAP Active Global Support.

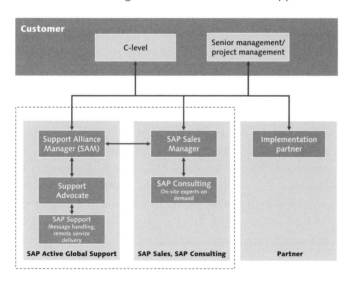

Figure 6.13 Organization at the Start of the Project

SAP Active Global Support has received messages from the customer, as well as from SAP Sales indicating that since upgrading its solutions, the customer has been experiencing serious performance problems, inconsistencies, and functional deficiencies. Further discussion confirms this to be the case.

6.6.1 Strategy

SAP Solution Management Assessment
SAP starts by conducting an *SAP Solution Management Assessment* (SMA) to identify problems and action areas and to propose suitable solutions. The assessment reveals a need for specific services as well as continuous optimization, which is only possible through close collaboration between the company and SAP. The current problems need to be resolved as soon as possible, which, in turn, can reduce potential risks. Over the long term, the company needs to transfer knowledge from SAP to the IT organization in order to complement these measures. Close collaboration would also allow the company to align its own release plans with SAP's release strategy, and to better plan its other outstanding projects.

SAP MaxAttention
Given these stipulations, the company opts for *SAP MaxAttention* (see also Section 4.9.1), a particularly intensive form of SAP engagement that eliminates problems in the short term, while strengthening collaboration and optimizing the SAP solution in the long term. SAP MaxAttention is fixed for a period of three years and comprises management and expert services components, a tailored, joint release strategy, and a service level agreement. As part of the engagement, plans are also drawn up to revise the organizational structure so that the parties involved work as one unit. SAP's role has now changed from that of software provider to active partner and trusted advisor. A Technical Quality Manager (TQM) is appointed to act as the company's permanent on-site SAP representative.

SAP Solution Manager
From now on, SAP Solution Manager will be put to greater use so it can improve organization and communication within the company and its projects. Its functions, tools, and content cover the core aspects involved in providing, running, and optimizing an SAP solution and reduce the total cost of ownership (TCO). SAP Solution Manager is also integral to successful communication and collaboration between the customer and SAP, which is why the system landscape, the solution, and the business processes were documented in SAP Solution Manager during the SAP SMA. This documentation provides valuable technical information for the customer, partner, and SAP, and might also be useful for the expert services mentioned below or for troubleshooting. Problems are collected in

a central issue list in SAP Solution Manager before being processed and resolved in cooperation with SAP.

The scope of SAP MaxAttention makes it impossible for us to detail every aspect in this example; as such, only short-term measures are described here.

Execution of the SAP SMA

The SAP SMA comprises three phases: preparation, on-site analysis, and recommended follow-up activities. In the preparatory phase, an SAP expert evaluates the relevant SAP systems via remote connection. If they have not done so already, production systems undergo an *SAP Early-Watch Check* at this point. In the second phase, an SAP team analyzes the solution landscape and core business processes on site. In the final phase, the team compiles a report and discusses it with the customer. The report describes:

▶ The status of the system landscape

▶ Issues that could impair core business processes

▶ SAP's recommendations for resolving these issues

Together with the customer, the SAP team formulates an action plan aimed at optimizing the solution landscape and critical business processes.

Three phases

SAP SMA Results

The assessment revealed the following problems at the example company:

▶ General performance problems in SAP R/3

▶ General performance problems in SAP APO

▶ Process problems in SAP R/3 between the FI and CO modules

▶ Inconsistencies in SAP Business Information Warehouse (SAP BW)

▶ Process problems in SAP APO

▶ Problems managing and operating the systems

In this example, the action and service plan drawn up after the SAP SMA to help tackle the identified weak points is used to tailor SAP MaxAttention to meet the company's requirements.

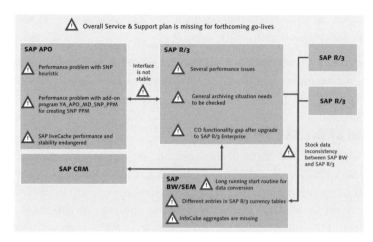

Figure 6.14 Problem Areas in the Company's IT Solution

6.6.2 Organizational Changes with SAP MaxAttention (Management Component)

In the first step, the parties involved agree on restructuring project organization. With the new structure, the company receives proactive support with all those involved working closely together. A front office is set up on the company's premises and communicates permanently with a back office at SAP. This setup enables different specialists from the SAP network to process problems quickly and also lets experts be called in at short notice to help out on site.

SAP experts

The Technical Quality Manager (TQM) controls the joint project on site. The company is also allocated a Support Alliance Manager (SAM), who together with the TQM, regularly presents future plans and the latest findings to the management body for approval. In the background (SAP back office), a Support Advocate forms the interface to SAP, which it uses to arrange for additional SAP experts to be called in from the support, development, and consulting teams.

Changes in meeting structure

SAP integrates itself in the existing meeting structure and sets up new channels for coordinating proceedings:

▶ Daily consultation with the partner to assess how recommendations are being implemented

▶ Meetings as required with the company's IT manager and the partner to approve completed project steps

▶ Weekly management meeting (customer's CIO, heads of department, partner's managers, Support Alliance Manager, TQM, SAP Sales—SAP back office where appropriate) to discuss all measures and open actions

▶ Regular conference calls with the SAP back office

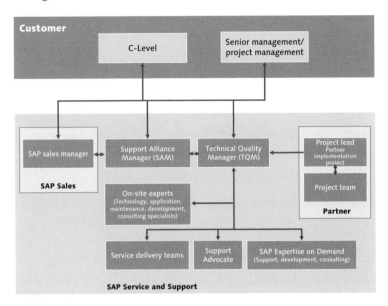

Figure 6.15 Reorganization with SAP MaxAttention

The reorganization transforms SAP's essentially reactive relationship with the company into a proactive one. SAP also works with the company and the partner to redefine escalation channels (see Figure 6.16).

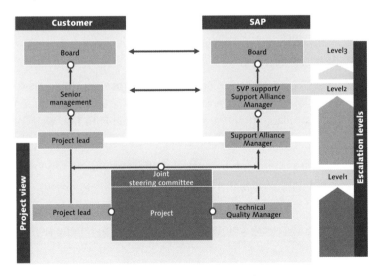

Figure 6.16 Clearly Defined Escalation Channels with SAP MaxAttention

6.6.3 Expert Services Component

The SMA revealed problem areas and weak points in the company's IT solution. SAP has therefore recommended services from its portfolio, which the company exploits in the form of expert services from SAP Max-Attention.

The following services are ordered for the production SAP solutions:

▶ *SAP Business Process Performance Optimization* (BPPO) for SAP R/3
▶ SAP BPPO for month-end closing
▶ *SAP Expertise on Demand*
▶ *SAP System Administration* for SAP APO
▶ *SAP Data Volume Management* for SAP R/3

And for the new mySAP CRM solution:

▶ *SAP Feasibility Check*
▶ *SAP Technical Integration Check*

These services are outlined below, along with their impact on the example company.

SAP BPPO

This optimization service is to target the following aspects of the customer's enterprise:

▶ General performance of SAP R/3
▶ General performance of SAP APO
▶ Weak points with SAP R/3 period-end closing

Focus on core business processes

SAP BPPO focuses on a company's core business processes. It strives to get them running optimally and ensures that they attain the required throughput in the available time frame. The goal here is to find ways of improving the technology without having to redesign business processes.

The individual process steps can be analyzed effectively using the information in SAP Solution Manager about the key business processes and their problems.

SAP BPPO assesses the weak points that are inclined to impede performance:

- Expensive SQL statements
- Customer developments and modifications
- Inefficient use of standard SAP transactions

Long running SQL statements are one of the most prevalent causes of performance problems. Not only do they cause long runtimes in the programs that they are called in, but also they indirectly lead to performance problems in other transactions. It is by no means unusual to find that a few expensive SQL statements account for 50 percent of a database server's total load. Expensive SQL statements are indicated by a high number of buffer or disk accesses; the buffer accesses place load on the database server's CPU, and the disk accesses place load on the I/O system.

SQL statements

The SAP BPPO service identifies, analyzes, and optimizes expensive SQL statements that cause performance problems throughout the entire system. Various monitors, such as SQL trace and the shared SQL area, can be used for identification and analysis purposes.

There is considerable scope for optimization in the following three cases:

- Some SQL statements cause many data records to be transferred from the database to the application server. Only by changing the ABAP program can this be optimized.

- Another kind of expensive SQL statement forces the database to read countless data blocks to determine whether data records meet the selection conditions, even when only a few data records are selected. This behavior indicates an inefficient search strategy. Adding a new secondary index simplifies the search and optimizes the runtime.

- A suitable index already exists; however, the database does not use it for the search.

SAP BPPO analyzes all three cases and proposes an appropriate solution.

Even with optimal database accesses, performance may still be unsatisfactory. Common causes include customer developments and modifications for the standard SAP system and user exits. SAP BPPO can also identify, analyze, and optimize such causes. With increased throughput and improved response times for long running transactions, core business processes can run smoothly and reliably. Experience shows that over 50 percent of all performance problems in ABAP programs can be traced back to a combination of inefficient database accesses and inefficient program algorithms.

Customer developments and modifications

Ineffective use of standard transactions

In addition to expensive SQL statements and customer developments, using standard SAP transactions ineffectively can also hamper performance and impede the throughput of core business processes. With SAP BPPO, SAP experts go to the customer to analyze the performance of individual steps in the core business processes and identify ways to optimize them. They focus on the following areas:

▶ Optimization of application functions

▶ Parallel processing, use of programs with mass data capabilities

▶ Database locks

▶ SAP enqueues

▶ Sizing

▶ Temporal distribution of load

▶ Distribution of load over database and application server

▶ Shared resources

All the findings from the analysis are documented directly in SAP Solution Manager during a service session, creating a central results bank that the customer and SAP employees can access at any time. The problems identified are recorded in the central issue list in SAP Solution Manager, along with the steps needed to resolve them. The analysis results are compiled into a service report containing a technical process description, a systematic action plan to optimize the system's response times for critical steps in the business process, and service recommendations.

The service is delivered on site, which gives SAP an opportunity to impart extensive expertise to the customer's staff and empower them to analyze and optimize other business processes in the SAP solution independently.

SAP Expertise on Demand

The customer's in-house support organization cannot resolve every issue reported. For one reason, many members of the support team have already been reserved for large and midsize projects, and simply don't have the resources to deal with the large number of less critical issues. Another reason is that many problems require very specialized expertise. This level of know-how is not available in-house and the company cannot justify the costs of acquiring such expertise.

Issue solving process

This is where the *SAP Expertise on Demand* service comes into play. A simple procedure is in place to report dedicated issues to SAP, which ensures that the right expert is found for the job. The information in SAP Solution

Manager regarding the problem and its environment, such as the business process, interfaces, and landscape, allows for effective troubleshooting. In certain cases, issues can be analyzed directly and straightforwardly in SAP Solution Manager. This could be the case if problems arise in the Java environment.

The customer is involved in the troubleshooting process. Collaboration tools such as Windows NetMeeting and WebEx, or videoconferences, enable the customer's employees to take an active role in the process and independently resolve similar issues in the future.

Depending on the type of issue and where it occurs, issues can be addressed remotely or on site. On-site problem-solving becomes an attractive option if an expert discovers that several documented issues are related and it is not a case of eliminating just one isolated weak spot. The specialist first assesses whether an expert service would fix the problem. If not, the specialist goes to the customer site to resolve the problem as soon as possible. In cases where the experts agree that resolving a particular request would not be the best course of action, for example, because the cost would be unjustifiable, they explain their decision clearly to the customer and propose alternative approaches if appropriate. In this way, SAP Expertise on Demand perfectly complements the expert services that target major, related problem areas.

SAP System Administration

Our example company has decided to order the *SAP System Administration* service from the *SAP Solution Management Optimization* program. It wants to assess and improve the way it manages and operates its SAP APO and SAP BW systems.

SAP System Administration analyzes and enhances the main aspects of SAP solutions at system level. While delivering this service, SAP passes on well-founded knowledge to the customer's staff, enabling them to react quickly and reliably to all queries relating to system operation in order to prevent problems, and therefore become proactive team members. The main focus of the service is on analyzing and optimizing the monitoring concept. SAP experts work out which technical indicators should be monitored for the business processes to be executed. They also explore the possibility of using suitable auto-reaction methods to automate monitoring. All in all, total availability and data security are enhanced as a result of using the SAP System Administration service. Over the long term, the company is able to reduce its operating costs substantially.

Optimization at system level

The service is divided into five phases:

1. **Kickoff meeting**

   Participants get to know one another and record the potential for improvement that has already been identified.

2. **Review of present situation**

   This phase determines weak points in system operation, paying attention to core business processes, responsibilities, and the need for coordination and training. It is possible to focus on specific areas, such as performance, system, and database management, change management, high availability, printing, or security.

3. **Workshops**

   Although the workshops are based thematically on standard training courses, their focus is on resolving specific problems. On-the-job training arms staff with the skills they need to operate the system efficiently. A System Maintenance Action Plan (SMAP) is created during the workshop. It describes the measures and activities required to get the solution running optimally, and allocates responsibilities.

4. **Closing presentation**

   Those who participated in the kickoff meeting meet to discuss the results.

5. **Review**

   The documents for the service are compiled—such as an Immediate Action Plan recommending high-priority actions—and made available to the company's employees.

SAP Data Volume Management

The company has also decided on *SAP Data Volume Management* (SAP DVM), another optimization service, to improve the way it manages and operates its SAP APO and SAP BW systems. The volume of data in systems and system landscapes usually accumulates steadily over the years. Searching for data becomes more time-consuming—and more costly—as the data volume increases. Large amounts of data also require more hardware resources (main memories, hard disks, and backup measures) and more personnel to cope with increased administration. The underlying database system also has to be monitored and adjusted on an ongoing basis, which adds to the costs for data maintenance. It follows that the data volume should be kept to a minimum. This is also in the interests of enhanced system performance and shorter downtimes when systems are being backed up or upgraded. Optimizing the data volume contributes to lower operating costs and increases the availability of the system solution.

SAP DVM comprises a comprehensive service package for optimizing the data volume in individual systems and entire system landscapes (advisable if the database volume is greater than 200 GB or the database grows by more than 10 GB each month). SAP DVM uses the following principles to create a data management and archiving strategy:

Data management and archiving strategy

▶ **Data avoidance**
Identifies and avoids unnecessary data wherever possible. The functions responsible for collecting this unnecessary data are identified for switching off.

▶ **Data summarization**
All applicable data is written in reduced form. This is usually most applicable with accounting and cost management data.

▶ **Data deletion**
Deletes out-of-date, redundant data.

▶ **Data archiving**
Archives obsolete data that is no longer required for business operations.

Existing strategies can also be assessed as part of the SAP DVM service. Its stated goal is to empower users to create and maintain a data management and archiving strategy; therefore, SAP DVM offers customized workshops. It also incorporates a target/actual comparison for analyzing and monitoring data-archiving activities.

The largest tables in a system are analyzed and the results are used to outline a data management and archiving strategy. The initial proposal is purely technical in nature and is discussed with the customer, taking account of specific business requirements. This phase is also a period of intense knowledge transfer for the customer.

Data analysis

In addition to the optimization services described above for the existing IT solution, the customer receives several assessments in order for the implementation project to minimize technical risk.

SAP Feasibility Check

SAP Feasibility Check, a service from the SAP Safeguarding program, has been selected to support the mySAP CRM implementation. It is provided at the start of the implementation project, as soon as the Business Blueprint and technical planning are complete. SAP Feasibility Check focuses on transferring knowledge from SAP to the customer and on identifying the project's critical success factors and associated risks as early as possible. Sizing, performance, and system infrastructure are the key factors in assessing the technical feasibility of the implementation project. Administration, the support strategy, and the conceptual design of the critical interfaces are also analyzed. If requested, core business processes can also be checked for functional deficiencies and potential risks.

Final report   The results of the SAP Feasibility Check are summarized in a final report, which contains a description of the planned business processes, as well as specific recommendations for minimizing identified risks. Another important part of the final report is the detailed risk management plan. It describes the tasks that are to be allocated to SAP, the implementation partner, and the customer in order to reduce risk in the new solution. A detailed service plan is also compiled. It specifically targets the risks associated with the implementation project that were identified by SAP Feasibility Check. All the information is documented in SAP Solution Manager and used for other services, such as the SAP Technical Integration Check.

SAP Technical Integration Check

To safeguard its mySAP CRM implementation, the company has also ordered another Safeguarding service: the *SAP Technical Integration Check*. Working closely with SAP experts, the company assesses the progress to date and clarifies who needs to do what. The core business processes and key interfaces must already be in place at this stage.

Examination of business processes   SAP employees first examine the core business processes to ensure that they are in accordance with the technical components. Then, they analyze the key interfaces within these business processes. The three stages of the service are preparation, on-site checks, and follow-up actions. In the preliminary phase, SAP experts analyze—via remote connection—the scope and current status of the implementation project. On-site analyses in the following areas of the SAP solution pave the way for smooth technical integration:

▶ Core business processes

▶ System landscape

▶ Key internal and external interfaces

- ▶ Administration of business processes and interfaces to ensure data consistency, performance, availability, and operation of the business processes and interfaces
- ▶ Strategy for running the solution before and after the start of production
- ▶ Status of data migration
- ▶ Project milestones
- ▶ Future support organization

Throughout the analyses, SAP specialists work with key members of the implementation team, such as the project manager, technical project manager, application and development team manager, implementation partner, and members of the support organization. The SAP team compiles a final report listing the results and actual follow-up actions for the customer. The SAP experts and the project team then assign each action to the appropriate person.

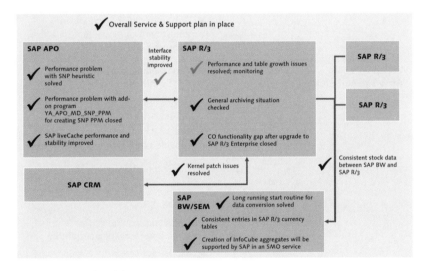

Figure 6.17 Results of the Support Services

Impact of the Services

The following table gives examples of the service results. Service plans compiled for SAP MaxAttention are considerably more extensive. The services listed here are only intended as examples.

Category	Service	Impact
General performance of SAP R/3	SAP BPPO	▶ Overall system performance improved by 10% ▶ Most important transaction improved by over 35% ▶ MRP run 30% faster ▶ Speed of certain customer transactions increased 250-fold
General performance of SAP APO	SAP BPPO SAP Expertise on Demand	▶ End users satisfied with overall performance of SAP APO, which improved 20% ▶ Overall performance of Core Interface (CIF) reached satisfactory level ▶ Performance of Supply Network Planning (SNP) improved by 15% ▶ Drill-down times reduced by 25% ▶ Creation of SNP Production Process Model (PPM) accelerated by 30 to 40% ▶ Runtime for CIF comparison/ adjustment of movement data improved by 55%
Weak points with SAP R/3 period-end closing	SAP BPPO	▶ Period-end closing activities up to 65% more efficient ▶ Revised system settings to prevent data loss ▶ Automatic valuation and planning provided by SAP development team
Inconsistencies in SAP BW	SAP Expertise on Demand	▶ Consistent data
Process problems in SAP APO	SAP Expertise on Demand	▶ Stable CIF ▶ Demand planning version monitored and reorganized monthly ▶ Scope reduced from 3.7 GB to 2.6 GB (30% reduction) ▶ Current scope of demand planning version satisfactory
General system administration and operations	SAP System Administration (SAP APO, SAP BW); SAP DVM	▶ Optimized system settings ▶ Higher quality system operations ▶ Knowledge transfer made possible

Table 6.1 Overview of Services and Results

Category	Service	Impact
mySAP CRM implementation project	SAP Feasibility Check SAP Technical Integration Check	▸ Potential project risks identified ▸ Recommendations for minimizing risks ▸ Proposals from both services incorporated in service plan

Table 6.1 Overview of Services and Results (cont.)

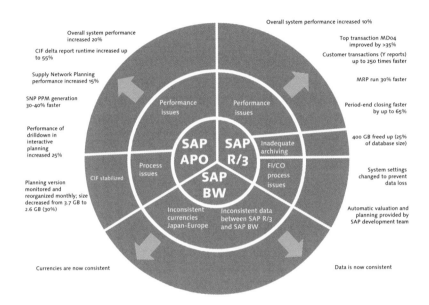

Figure 6.18 Overview of Improvements Resulting from SAP MaxAttention

6.7 Upgrading with SAP Ramp-Up

The mounting pressures of internationalized markets prompted a leading provider of high-tech products to upgrade quickly from SAP R/3 to mySAP ERP in order to handle processes across different countries and companies securely and effectively on the Internet. Research and development is a top priority at the company. Its key clients are aerospace and defense companies and public customers. As both a one-stop provider and a technology and program partner, the company is constantly expanding its international activities. It already operates in over 30 countries with more than 400 employees marketing its products primarily in Europe, the Middle East, South Africa, and North America.

Transition to mySAP ERP

6.7.1 Participation in the SAP Ramp-Up Program

The company's global business called for powerful systems and processes capable of linking partner companies online and communicating data and information about products and services quickly. Such partners include service providers who maintain equipment on the customer's site. Faced with increasingly shorter innovation cycles, constantly changing customer requirements, and the demand for all-around efficiency, the company needed to take urgent action. It already had medium-term plans for the transition from SAP R/3 to mySAP ERP, which it moved forward to create leading-edge and more effective IT structures. The upgrade project's key objective was to use web-based processes to improve collaboration with partners.

Present situation Until now, service partners around the world had accessed the company's SAP R/3 systems via SAP Internet Transaction Server (SAP ITS), a relatively difficult procedure. After the upgrade, SAP NetWeaver Application Server (AS), shipped with mySAP ERP, would fulfill this role. Web-based processes would then support all the procedures for servicing and maintaining the high-tech products for customers worldwide, resulting in much smoother processes thanks to the interplay between mySAP ERP, SAP NetWeaver Business Intelligence, and SAP NetWeaver AS.

Other processes would follow. The upgrade and the standardized system platform also presented an opportunity to reduce operating costs and the TCO of the IT landscape.

In all, the company was an ideal candidate for the SAP Ramp-Up program, because it wanted to use newly available or improved functions or technology quickly. The company's strategy called for more efficient web-based processes, attainable with the new ERP version.

Once the company had decided on the SAP Ramp-Up program, it informed its sales coordinator at SAP, who immediately contacted the Ramp-Up team and set the process in motion.

Analysis of project risks The SAP Ramp-Up team began by analyzing all the relevant aspects of the implementation, using information from the customer and SAP employees. This included planned scenarios, interfaces to third parties, and the technological basis.

Potential project risks were thus identified at the start and suitable measures were taken to prevent problems. The team had in-depth knowledge of the current situation and functional scope of each scenario in the solution. This was useful to the customer during planning and greatly accelerated the project.

After the analysis, the company received a document confirming its participation in the SAP Ramp-Up program. Once signed, the path was clear for the requested software to be delivered.

SAP Ramp-Up as an Accelerator

The Ramp-Up phase at SAP is usually limited to six months. It begins with the market launch of a mature product that has been validated by a neutral team of consultants and ends when the software becomes available without restriction to all customers. In this case, the company determined that the schedule for implementing the upgrade project to mySAP ERP 2004 would be only five months, due to special internal requirements.

For the IT manager, the time restriction for going live in the SAP Ramp-Up program represented an additional opportunity to create pressure internally. This proved useful in focusing and accelerating the activities within the enterprise. Once the external service provider responsible for hosting the systems had joined the team, the project was ready to get underway. With ongoing support from the SAP Ramp-Up team, the customer's team of four set about making careful preparations for the project. It examined potential alternative scenarios, defined milestones, and compiled reports and procedures for test scenarios.

Project preparation

The customer's project team quickly came to appreciate other benefits of the SAP Ramp-Up program, one being the chance to pass on feedback and ideas to SAP to enhance the solution. The feedback was sent directly to SAP's development department via the Ramp-Up back office. Various key figures were used to summarize the feedback and made it transparent for management. The result was not only that problems were resolved quickly, but also that the feedback was recorded and systematically fed into SAP's ongoing plans for further development. This feedback to SAP became a means by which companies could exert their influence when modifications were implemented into the standard software solution.

Feedback to SAP

6.7.2 Fast Track to Going Live

It took just four months for the customer's project team to complete the upgrade project and configure the new release in line with the company's specific requirements. The team was quick to summon all key users from the user departments to develop, map, and test all the relevant processes intensively. The *SAP GoingLive Check*, part of the SAP Ramp-Up service package for mySAP ERP, safeguarded the implementation even further. Besides analyzing the key business processes, the check ensured that the solution went live with the correct performance parameters and continued to run reliably.

Outlay and results The internal outlay for the upgrade project was approximately 225 person days. Feedback on the new mySAP ERP solution from the approximately 220 users and 17 key users has been very positive and the new SAP GUI 6.40 has been readily accepted. The CIO is also satisfied with performance, since the system is running reliably and has proved very powerful. The logs from *SAP EarlyWatch Alert*, which are evaluated daily, support this feedback. This fully automated diagnostics service monitors the key administrative areas of the SAP landscape and provides up-to-date information about system performance and stability.

Finally, the trouble-free upgrade project is attributable in no small part to the high quality of the solutions in the SAP Ramp-Up program. A number of aspects indicate that SAP solutions are of an extremely high quality, even at the start of the Ramp-Up phase. For instance, SAP has improved and standardized its development and production processes and added additional quality constraints and checks. In the validation phase, a neutral team of consultants implements the SAP solution before the Ramp-Up phase, and does so under the same conditions as a real customer project. SAP does not release a solution for the market—or the Ramp-Up phase—until the feedback from the validation team has been incorporated in the solution and it meets strict quality standards. As such, the solutions are fit for go-live from the moment they are launched on the market. The product versions used in the SAP Ramp-Up phase are the same as those that later become available with the general release.

Easy communication The rapid success of the project can be attributed both to the in-house team's in-depth knowledge of SAP products and to intensive collaboration with SAP developers. The SAP Ramp-Up coach ensured those involved could communicate easily without complications. As the central contact person from SAP Consulting, the coach accompanied the customer on site and ensured that urgent queries and customer messages always reached the right person at SAP. The coach was largely responsible for the excellent cooperation between internal and external staff, which saw the project duration slashed from five months to four. Project costs were also more than ten percent lower than the projected value.

The customer's project team utilized the training program—designed especially for Ramp-Up project staff (SAP Ramp-Up Knowledge Transfer)—to become trained for the new SAP product in record time. SAP repeatedly authorized access to its comprehensive e-learning program so that the company's employees could deepen their knowledge when it best suited them. The SAP Ramp-Up Knowledge Transfer program is also open to the customer's partners.

SAP Ramp-Up Knowledge Transfer

During the upgrade project, a special code in the header indicated the company's messages as coming from a Ramp-Up customer. Ramp-Up projects are now also indicated by a flag set in the Message Wizard on SAP Service Marketplace. SAP developers gave these messages preferential treatment during the project, thereby considerably accelerating their processing time. The company submitted a total of only 19 messages, with an average processing time of one and half days.

Quick response to customer messages

A key reason for the error messages being processed so rapidly during SAP Ramp-Up is that the Ramp-Up back office monitors and accelerates the handling of complex problems. Experts, who were usually directly involved in developing the solution, staff the Ramp-Up back office. SAP also documents all SAP Ramp-Up projects from around the globe in one central system. The data from this system is used to provide weekly updates to the SAP Executive Board about the progress of all market entries, as well as the status of all ongoing SAP Ramp-Up projects.

6.8 Planning and Executing Upgrades

A company from the oil industry uses SAP software to support key business processes—particularly in production planning and control, sales and distribution, financial accounting and cost management—and to handle human resources tasks. It is a global company with a centralized IT infrastructure and a total of 10 SAP systems, used by more than 25,000 users and supported primarily by the group's own IT service provider, which runs an SAP CCC. The SAP systems are based on a predominantly uniform and homogeneous platform.

Several years ago, the company decided to realign its IT strategy to reflect new market requirements and the geographical distribution of its SAP users. After upgrading to Release 4.6B, the company spent the next three years tailoring the central SAP R/3 systems to regional needs and rolled out several independent, regional SAP systems. The results of these rollout projects are documented in SAP Solution Manager.

System landscape

For key processes, the oil group uses special functions from SAP's industry solution SAP for Oil & Gas. The SAP R/3 systems deployed in America are linked to other SAP products in one solution landscape. In Europe, in particular, the company tailored standard SAP functions to meet its own needs through modifications and customer developments. It also mapped country-specific requirements in separate, independent HR systems.

Multi-display
multi-processing The international nature of the group's activities calls for multi-display multi-processing (MDMP) technology both at global level and in Asia. This technology allows different character sets, or code pages, to be used in one SAP system.

Recent group-wide analyses revealed that using SAP software more extensively could boost efficiency:

▶ Advanced reporting functions and better ad-hoc reports could make business activities more transparent.

▶ Scope for economic improvement by reducing the process costs for ordering C items, such as seldom required office supplies.

▶ Employee leave requests could be handled more efficiently.

The IT service provider has notified the group's top management that the ongoing acquisition of various small companies and the expansion of the current network of service stations will make it extremely costly and time-consuming to integrate or replace other enterprise software solutions with the existing SAP systems. This, in turn, will impede, or, at best, slow down, efforts to implement the acquisition strategy flexibly.

6.8.1 Feasibility Study

Software
evaluation Under these circumstances, the company decided to consider another release upgrade and assess the feasibility of the mySAP ERP solution. It enlisted three employees from the SAP CCC to conduct an initial in-depth analysis of any relevant application-specific and technical aspects from the perspective of program and project management. The preliminary study took 10 weeks and was supported by SAP Consulting. Its findings were as follows:

▶ Both the release upgrade and the subsequent addition of new functions from mySAP ERP call for a holistic organizational concept and a standard methodology (similar to the rollout phase) to ensure that the project is completed cost-effectively with minimal risk.

- Over a period of two years, a total of seven projects will be implemented, including central program management, to upgrade all the global and regional SAP systems to mySAP ERP.

- The initial technical and application-specific feasibility study confirmed mySAP ERP 2005 and its core component SAP ERP Central Component (SAP ECC) 6.0 as the ideal target release for the company.

- To standardize procedures as far as possible, SAP Solution Manager should be used across the group as a central infrastructure for handling the upgrade projects, and the SAP Upgrade Road Map should be used concurrently with the group's own project methodology.

- The savings and specific risks associated with each project need to be investigated and appropriate measures must be defined to minimize costs and risks (with SAP services, for instance).

- The project scope and upgrade path are critical to performing an accurate cost and effort estimate and a risk analysis.

- The program management team based in the SAP CCC will bear responsibility for each project, including initial preparation as well as quality assurance over the course of the projects.

Project efficiency (low cost, low risk) depends on the experience of the project team, as well as the complexity of the system landscape affected by the release upgrade. The potential cost drivers and risk factors depend primarily on the project scope; the challenges posed by a purely technical upgrade for a small, independent SAP system differ entirely from those for a large SAP system serving different regions. This is particularly true when, as in this case, the customer wants the upgrade to achieve the following goals:

Different project scopes

- Return modifications to standard SAP functions

- Replace the MDMP technology currently in use with Unicode

- Redesign the technical landscape so that new business scenarios such as Employee Self-Services can be released for a multitude of users when the upgrade goes live

Each target release has different requirements, which means that certain aspects may need to be analyzed and assessed separately for each project. Such aspects include adjustments to the IT infrastructure (e.g., hardware sizing), specific technical restrictions (e.g., availability of SAP add-ons and country versions), and affordable downtimes. As the central project management team responsible for quality assurance and project standards, the SAP CCC plays a pivotal role in identifying and exploiting savings.

The program management team has decided, in consultation with the respective project managers, to use SAP upgrade services to tackle specific problems, cost drivers, and risk factors. The company has signed a contract for SAP MaxAttention (see also Sections 4.9.1 and 6.6), which entitles it to a certain number of services for each project.

6.8.2 Preparing and Executing the Upgrade Projects

Most of the upgrade projects depend on the two centrally managed, global development systems being upgraded (projects 1 and 2). The plan is to first complete the technical upgrade for these solutions and then to develop a "solution design," which will be adopted in the SAP systems in the regional factories and refineries, as well as in the local HR/FI/SD systems.

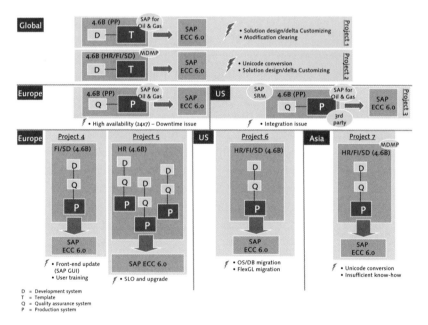

Figure 6.19 The Company's System Landscape

Project 1: Upgrade of the global development system for production planning and control

The project team has used the results from the initial feasibility study to make detailed preparations for the central development system (production planning and control). Its basic approach will be to complete the technical upgrade as quickly as possible and then implement a new solution design—including delta Customizing—which will be adopted in the regional SAP systems. In this and all subsequent phases, the group's policy is for all members of the project team to follow the SAP Upgrade Road Map.

The SAP Upgrade Road Map contains all of SAP's methodical expertise relating to upgrades. It lists project management tasks and provides the entire project team with application-specific information and technical details about upgrading to the target releases available. There are also other advantages of using the SAP Upgrade Road Map in SAP Solution Manager. One such advantage is that it enables individual responsibilities to be defined for relevant tasks, making it easier to track the progress of planned, ongoing, and completed project activities. Another advantage is that important information and project documentation can be assigned and managed for the tasks, making the overall project status transparent to all involved.

SAP Upgrade Road Map

In an initial step toward designing the new solution, representatives from the business departments have analyzed scenario descriptions for mySAP ERP in SAP Solution Manager, along with more detailed information from the Upgrade Information Center on SAP Service Marketplace (*http://service.sap.com/upgrade-erp*). The precise business requirements also need to be identified and specified, and therefore the project team that is specialized in applications has decided to draw on SAP expertise in the form of the following two SAP upgrade services:

▶ *SAP Accelerated Value Assessment*

▶ *SAP Modification Clearing*

SAP experts work through detailed checklists with employees from the business departments to ascertain how selected mySAP ERP business scenarios could benefit the entire group. This is a quick check, which also entails the SAP experts conducting on-site interviews, and provides the company with a clearly structured, customer-specific overview of the enhanced mySAP ERP functions. In accordance with group policy, the findings and all other documentation of the solution design are stored in SAP Solution Manager so that they can be used in subsequent project steps, such as system configuration (delta Customizing) and testing.

SAP Accelerated Value Assessment

The solution design for the SAP system for production planning involves returning costly, high-maintenance customer developments and modifications to the SAP standard, at least for application areas that are not part of the group's core business processes.

Unfortunately, the company kept very little documentation when it made changes to SAP software or developed its own programs and reports, and its procedure for managing change requests was less than satisfactory. Furthermore, since many of the programmers have left the company, the group does not have a clear picture of the modifications in the global production planning system. Therefore, the project team has decided to use the *SAP Modification Clearing* service to purge the system of modifications and custom developments.

SAP Modification Clearing   In this service, SAP experts follow a tool-based procedure and begin by analyzing the extent to which the SAP system has been modified. The results are documented across the business processes available in SAP Solution Manager. They essentially show which of the current custom developments and modifications are actually used. The length of this identification phase depends on how much the system has been modified, although the experts usually define a course of action within one week.

The appropriate application-specific project team discusses the findings with SAP's technical experts to decide which of the modifications can and should be returned to the SAP standard. The result of the modification analysis phase is a categorized list of the SAP objects affected, including proposed solutions and estimated workload.

In the ensuing clearing phase, selected custom developments and modifications are returned to the SAP standard. Again, application-specific adjustments of this kind are documented in SAP Solution Manager with reference to the appropriate business processes.

SAP GoingLive Functional Upgrade Check   This project, like all other upgrade projects, will be accompanied by the SAP Safeguarding service, *SAP GoingLive Functional Upgrade Check,* consisting of three remote sessions. Once the preliminary phase is complete, the first session—"planning"—identifies potential critical success factors and evaluates the technical risk involved in the project. In addition to analyzing general problem areas, the session ensures that there are no technical restrictions regarding the target release, such as platform availability or country versions.

Depending on the outcome of the planning session, SAP may recommend closer collaboration in the form of additional on-site services, particularly if a project is deemed critical. For non-critical projects, ongoing remote support ensures that performance bottlenecks do not occur after the upgrade. One such form of support is the analysis session of the SAP

GoingLive Functional Upgrade Check, which is performed six to eight weeks before the upgrade is due to go live. A load analysis is conducted on the basis of real system data and extrapolated for the target release. The result is that bottlenecks in the system configuration, memory, processor, and hard disk capacity of the application and database servers are identified and eliminated early on.

Approximately four weeks after the production system has been upgraded, these technical performance indicators are checked again in the verification session of the SAP GoingLive Functional Upgrade Check.

Project 2: Upgrade of the global development system for HR, FI, and SD

Upgrading the second global development system poses two specific challenges for the project team: the first challenge lies in the migration from MDMP to Unicode; the second challenge is in the changes that the solution design will entail for the technical landscape.

As of SAP ECC 6.0 in mySAP ERP 2005, SAP has adopted Unicode technology—the industry standard—to enable the use of multilingual "cross-code page" applications. Unicode technology is required by Java applications in particular, such as SAP NetWeaver Portal. The company's decision to upgrade all of the group's SAP systems to mySAP ERP means that the systems in Asia, which use MDMP, have to migrate to Unicode. From a technical perspective, Unicode migrations are comparable to OS/DB migrations; although they entail a multitude of preparatory and review tasks and usually require hardware resizing for the systems concerned. The project team has decided to book the *SAP Unicode* workshop, with a focus on consolidating its understanding of Unicode and familiarizing itself with SAP Best Practices.

This is a one-day workshop in which SAP experts explain the following topics:

SAP Unicode workshop

▶ Basics of Unicode and its use in SAP solutions

▶ Methodology and tools to facilitate efficient Unicode migration

▶ Discussion of the customer's specific procedure, with an emphasis on the strategy for rolling out Unicode in multiple SAP systems

After the Unicode workshop, the project team can estimate how much additional project outlay to anticipate for Unicode-related issues. It will need to cooperate with representatives from the business departments, particularly when it comes to adapting SAP programs, which, in Unicode systems, are subject to stricter rules in syntax checks, and when creating the vocabulary to convert the data to Unicode format. The workshop also brought other critical aspects to light; namely, that the team would have to schedule two periods of downtime for the regional, live MDMP systems—one for the Unicode conversion and another for the technical upgrade. Furthermore, it became clear that the team would have to take great care when adjusting the IT infrastructure in order to prevent performance-critical bottlenecks from occurring. The new findings were sent to the project team responsible for upgrading the MDMP systems in Asia.

SAP Evaluation Workshop for mySAP ERP Transition and Upgrade The department responsible for this phase, Human Resources, suspects that extending the current HR systems to include Employee Self-Services (to enhance the way leave requests are processed, for instance) will have a considerable impact on the present technical design of the SAP systems in question. This issue is clarified in a special three-day evaluation workshop that SAP offers for selected strategic business scenarios: SAP Evaluation Workshop for mySAP ERP Transition and Upgrade. The workshop comprises a thorough business analysis and studies the impact of the different technical deployment options in an existing SAP landscape.

Following the global projects, the project to upgrade the regional production systems (production planning and control in the factories and refineries) gets underway, as specified in the overall program management plans.

Project 3: Upgrade of the regional test and production systems (production planning and control)

An initial detailed analysis of the project situation showed that, owing to the high availability required of the production planning and control systems, any delays would be critical to the success of the project. It also indicated that the technical upgrade of the SAP industry solution currently in use could be problematic. The project team has therefore acted on a proposal from program management to consult an SAP Upgrade Coach.

SAP Upgrade Coach *SAP Upgrade Coaches* are experts in SAP-related upgrades. They have a wealth of knowledge about methodologies and technology and can provide invaluable on-site support during critical release upgrade projects. The areas and tasks on which an upgrade coach focuses are dictated entirely by the individual requirements of the project. The coach is essentially the project manager's main contact person for any technical and planning issues relating to the upgrade. At the start of the project, the coach holds a three-day initial assessment with the project and sub-project managers to plan milestones and to identify which tasks are critical for the project. The information attained from this assessment is used to design strategies, for example, for upgrading all the test and productions systems as quickly as possible with minimal expense.

The upgrade coach attends the reviews for key project milestones; for example, to analyze the results of a test upgrade that was based on a copy of the production system, or to review plans for testing and the model for user training. Of course, the project and subproject managers can contact the coach by telephone throughout the entire project. The services of an upgrade coach, as described here, can be booked for a minimum of 10 days; however, they can be provided for longer periods if required.

Given that downtime must be kept to a minimum in the production systems, and based on initial results from the test upgrade, the SAP upgrade coach and the technical project managers have decided to invest further in optimizing technical downtime, which current estimates indicate is approximately 19 hours. They have chosen to order *SAP Downtime Assessment* from their service "allowance."

SAP Downtime Assessment

Although the introduction of the System Switch Upgrade procedure (available for target releases based on SAP Web Application Server 6.10 and above) saw technical downtime almost halved—there is sufficient evidence to put the average time at approximately six hours for upgrades to SAP R/3 Enterprise and mySAP ERP 2004 (SAP ECC 5.0)—even shorter downtimes can be achieved with certain system constellations.

An analysis of the test upgrade, which usually takes up to three days, has detected two key factors causing longer than average downtimes. One is the time required to convert data from a specific SAP for Oil & Gas table, using execution of programs after import (XPRA). The other is transporting information about the new solution design after the technical upgrade. The SAP upgrade coach has therefore recommended the *Customer-Based Upgrade (CBU)* technique as being preferable to the standard upgrade procedure.

SAP Customer-Based Upgrade

This technique builds on the methodology and procedure used in the System Switch Upgrade. The CBU method is particularly effective at reducing downtime in projects that entail a large number of post-upgrade transports with cross-client objects, which can require time-consuming activation phases at database level.

Once a copy of the production system has been upgraded "normally," a system-specific data extract is exported from the system. Special tools are used to repackage any earlier changes into a customer-specific transport, along with any changes to the Dictionary and Repository caused by subsequent transports. In subsequent test runs and when the production system is upgraded, this transport is included in the relevant technical upgrade process of the System Switch Upgrade procedure. This method has almost halved the original estimate for downtime.

With regard to the production system in the U.S., which is connected to other SAP systems such as SAP Supplier Relationship Management (SAP SRM) and SAP Business Information Warehouse (SAP BW), the SAP upgrade coach advises the team to keep a close eye on integration aspects of the future landscape during testing. Unfortunately, the company has paid very little attention to integration testing in the past. On the advice of the SAP upgrade coach, the project team has therefore decided to order the *SAP Test Management Optimization* service and to search for specific ways of improving the company's current test procedures.

SAP Test Management Optimization

The service aims to apply SAP Best Practices and special tools to plan and carry out testing in a way that uses resources efficiently and guarantees top quality. Different versions of the service are available. For example, customers can request a simple assessment of their current test procedures, or, in addition, they can have the service determine ways in which technologies for automating tests might offer scope for improvement.

SAP Test Management Optimization has revealed that the test case descriptions don't follow standard guidelines. Moreover, the expected result of the test cases was not specified adequately, which meant that the quality of the integration tests for the related SAP systems was not satisfactory. Furthermore, the scope of the test cases was too limited to ensure functional integration for the core business processes across all SAP systems.

To boost efficiency and minimize the amount of testing required, and also for later test phases, the project team has been advised to use SAP Solution Manager. It increases transparency when preparing for and monitoring tests, which leads to significant time and cost savings.

Project 4: Upgrade of the test and production system (sales and distribution and financial accounting) in EMEA

The project team's very restrictive budget has forced it to reduce the project scope to a minimum and take appropriate action to contain all critical cost drivers early on. For this reason, this upgrade project has been limited to being a purely technical release. Prior to the beginning of the project, the manager of the technology subproject indicated a potential bottleneck involving up to 2,000 desktop PCs whose dated hardware configurations were not suitable for a new SAP frontend. Another key cost driver that was identified during the planning phase is the training required for SAP users, since the employees affected (approximately 3,500) are spread across 12 different locations.

One of the first lines of action is to prepare a detailed estimate of the cost for the overall project. For that reason, the company has booked a standardized service called *SAP Quick Upgrade Evaluation*.

In addition to a two-day on-site workshop in which interviews are held to document the exact project status, the service entails a tool-based analysis of the SAP systems involved. The assessment of the modifications and general complexity (enhancements and customer developments) is used to forecast the project milestones and estimate the costs and effort, in particular, for testing and user training. The results are presented to the customer in a second on-site workshop. The *SAP Knowledge Transfer Optimization* service establishes precisely how much the company stands to save by changing its training concept and using e-learning methods and tools.

SAP Quick Upgrade Evaluation

The study conducted for the SAP Knowledge Transfer Optimization service has shown that, owing to the vast number of users affected and their different locations, classroom-training sessions would exceed the allotted project budget considerably. Since the changes caused by the technical upgrade are minimal, the subproject manager has been advised to consider e-learning training methods for all non-critical application areas and for transactions in which the user interface will change only slightly. The power users responsible for producing the training materials and the members of the project team who are responsible for user training are trained in using *SAP Tutor*—SAP's simulation tool for creating e-learning materials. The e-learning management functions integrated in SAP Solution Manager are also presented and activated.

SAP Knowledge Transfer Optimization

The two services described above have confirmed the project team's original resource planning and simultaneously reduced the cost for user training by around 25 percent.

An *SAP GoingLive Functional Upgrade Check* is also carried out in this project. The analysis session confirms the technical project manager's concerns; around 2,000 desktop PCs fall short of the system requirements for the new SAP frontend (SAP GUI 6.40). To avoid having to replace the machines and incur additional hardware costs, the project team has been advised to implement a Citrix concept, which would permit the desktop PCs to access an up-to-date SAP GUI with the existing hardware.

Allowing plenty of time before the going live weekend, the project manager has decided to book *SAP Upgrade Weekend Support* to safeguard against unforeseen risk.

SAP Upgrade Weekend Support   With SAP Upgrade Weekend Support, customers can call on a designated contact person from SAP Support for a period of at least 60 hours over the weekend when the production system is being upgraded. The contact promptly handles any issues that affect the upgrade and ensures that the right support experts from SAP are always available to analyze and resolve any problems that may occur. Thanks to all established measures, the project is completed on time and within the tight budget.

Project 5: Consolidation of the test and production systems (human resources) with technical release upgrade in EMEA

The project group working on the HR systems needs assistance from *System Landscape Optimization* (SLO). When the SAP systems were localized, six separate systems were set up in Europe for human resources processes in various countries. The program management's feasibility study showed that consolidating the systems to build one central HR system would not only be technically viable, but also much cheaper to operate. A more detailed investigation of the technical and economical feasibility of the project has shown that consolidating the systems to mySAP ERP (SAP ECC 6.0) would result in substantial advantages.

Migration Workbench   Over the course of the project, the team benefits from the SLO consultants' expertise and from the integrated procedure supported by the *Migration Workbench* (MWB) for migrating clients across different releases. The MWB's migration technique uses a Dictionary mapping process to transport data from a sending system to a receiving system on the basis of RFC technology. It supersedes all client-specific activities required for a release upgrade. The target system must be built using the SAP upgrade procedure, to enable cross-client objects such as the Repository to be converted to the new release.

SLO consultants accompany the project throughout all the planning and execution stages involved in optimizing the system landscape and simultaneously upgrading to mySAP ERP 2005 (SAP ECC 6.0). Thanks to their expertise, the project runs smoothly and the consolidated system goes live without any hitches.

Project 6: Technical upgrade of the local production system (HR/FI/SD) in the U.S.

Owing to the degree of modification in the current solution and the multitude of interfaces to other SAP systems and third-party products, the project managers have rated this project as critical. In accordance with corporate guidelines, an upgrade coach is called in to provide support in this case as well. The technical assessment conducted in the preparation phase indicated that the current combination of operating system and database is not approved for the target release mySAP ERP 2005 (SAP ECC 6.0).

Faced with the necessity of migrating the OS/DB before the actual upgrade, the technical project team and business departments seize this opportunity to use additional measures to optimize the size of the current database and curtail future growth. The SAP upgrade coach arranges for other SAP experts to provide *SAP Data Volume Management*, a five-day service that identifies specific areas for cost-cutting and proposes future action.

This service reduced the size of the database by approximately 20 percent by deleting redundant document data such as IDocs, once the database had been reorganized. Changes in Customizing will prevent such data from being stored in the database in the future. This has an extremely positive impact in a subsequent project phase. Reorganizing the database has reduced a large database table that would otherwise have been time-critical during the upgrade (due to modified table structures); the downtime that would have been required to convert the data has been reduced accordingly.

SAP Data Volume Management

Beyond the purely technical release upgrade, advanced functions that affect certain central sales and financial accounting processes have also been included in this release. The subproject managers therefore feel that the employees concerned should receive intensive training at a nearby SAP training center. The course is a one-stop source of first-hand information about key enhancements and new developments in the SAP software, such as the new general ledger for financial accounting.

Project 7: Technical release upgrade and Unicode conversion in the regional production system (HR/FI/SD) in Asia

For target releases as of mySAP ERP 2005 (SAP ECC 6.0), Unicode technology must be deployed to use multiple languages in one SAP system. Therefore, the company needs to consider how the regional SAP solution will be operated in the future. The number of local IT staff has fallen considerably in recent years and knowledge of new technologies and application areas has not been built up in-house. Nor can timely IT support be provided for all the locations. The group has therefore decided to stop managing the production system in-house and switch to an application-hosting provider when it upgrades to the new release.

SAP Hosting   The company has elected SAP as its hosting provider, on the basis of its regional presence and coherent upgrade-hosting concept. During the technical upgrade, SAP Hosting uses additional upgrade services to enhance the way the project is planned and carried out and to ensure cost efficiency. Migrating to Unicode, in particular, is demanding in terms of sizing and of keeping downtime to a minimum. Standardized upgrade services such as SAP Data Volume Management and SAP Downtime Assessment also come into play.

6.8.3 Outcome

By upgrading its SAP R/3 systems to mySAP ERP, the group has laid the foundation for a future-proof IT infrastructure that will enable it to leverage new technologies and innovative business changes to rise to the challenges of a global economy and adapt flexibly to changing market conditions. The seven projects that were guided by central program management highlighted a wide range of possible upgrade variants and confronted the respective project teams with different challenges. In addition to their own know-how, the expertise provided in SAP's upgrade services and tools such as SAP Solution Manager were instrumental to the success of the SAP landscape upgrade.

6.9 System Landscape Consolidation

This example studies a company from the metal and plastics processing industry with production locations in Belgium, France, Great Britain, Switzerland, the Czech Republic, India, the United States, Canada, and Singapore. The company is planning to consolidate its processes to achieve consistency along the entire value chain—from production and procurement at supplier level (supply chain management) to logistics processing through delivery to the end customer (customer relationship management). It also wants to integrate industry-specific processes, such as end-to-end batch tracing, quality management, EDI communication with partners, and period-end rebate processing. These processes are accompanied by a harmonized accounting system and an enterprise management system typical of the industry.

The international company is focusing on the requirements of an ever-changing global market, concentrating particularly on Europe and North America. This, in turn, places new demands on the group's system landscape. The company has successfully combined competence, commitment, creativity, and a world-class design concept with high quality and excellent service to become a world leader in its field. To secure its market leadership and to expand in certain areas, its managers have also decided to explore new IT possibilities.

At the start of the project, the situation is as follows: Three regions (Europe, North America, and Asia) with different production locations and sales structures, four sales centers in Germany, eight marketing companies in Europe and 10 abroad, as well as numerous sales partners worldwide, are distributed over 11 SAP ERP systems, one SAP CRM system, and one SAP APO system. One system with two separate clients is assigned to Asia, four systems to North America, and six to Europe. The advantage of the European systems is that they are already supplied with data from one development system. In view of this complex system landscape, the management body has decided to reduce and consolidate the number of SAP ERP systems.

System landscape

Other objectives include:

▶ Redesigning business processes to improve efficiency
▶ Restructuring the organizational structure
▶ Integrating a new manufacturing company
▶ Reducing the TCO

Harmonizing
strategy

The company has also declared its intention to complete the groupwide consolidation project in a series of parallel subprojects over 24 months. All the legacy systems were upgraded to SAP R/3 Enterprise in an earlier project. The task of consolidating this extremely heterogeneous system landscape will be shared by the enterprise's IT company and business departments and specialists from System Landscape Optimization (SLO). Project 1 will not cover the central SAP CRM system or SAP APO. The global harmonization strategy is based on a multistage concept. Three regional systems will be set up first. The next step will involve standardizing the business processes and cleansing the data. This will be followed by technical changes made to the processes in SAP APO and SAP CRM.

6.9.1 The SLO Procedure Model

SAP has put together an extensive portfolio of SLO services (see also Section 4.8) ranging from procedure selection and project planning through design and realization. Having decided to utilize these services, the company begins by filling out and submitting the SLO questionnaire on SAP Service Marketplace. The information from the questionnaire is used in a preliminary meeting to ascertain the general conditions and to clarify the project details and course of action.

Pre-analysis

When systems are merged, for instance, various factors determine how much time and effort is required. They include differences in the systems' Customizing and Repository settings, the size and functions of the systems and clients, and the exact changes that have to be made. A reliable estimate of the outlay for the entire project cannot be made until these factors have been analyzed and evaluated. Consequently, SLO initially presents a quotation for a preliminary analysis. During this analysis, experienced SLO consultants use proven technical tools to check all the relevant areas, such as Customizing, in the clients and systems concerned. The appropriate business departments and the company's IT organization also participate in this stage. The consultants clarify whether all the conditions are met for the intended client/system merge. Specific aspects such as archiving and workflows are also tackled in the analysis.

At the end of the analysis, the SLO experts propose the best way of consolidating the clients and systems. They also compile an annotated list of areas requiring particular attention. They hold a workshop to explain the results to the company's representatives and present the solution proposed by SLO. This information is used by SLO to prepare a quotation for the overall project as well as a project plan.

Named contact persons from SLO's team of consultants are available during the preliminary stages and all other project phases to support the company's project team with technical and application-specific issues. In highly complex projects of this scale, the importance of testing and accepting the test results must not be underestimated. It is vital that the right test strategy is used and the results be verified. The usual approach is to carry out numerous test runs and check the results each time, although the exact schedule depends on the complexity of the requirements and the volume of data to be transferred. Only when the final test run has been completed successfully can the team ensure maximum security for the system data during the switch to the live system. Additional test phases have to be scheduled until this occurs. As soon as all the tests have been completed, the data in the production system is usually scheduled to be converted on a weekend or public holiday.

6.9.2 Project Phases for System Consolidation

The following table provides an overview of the planned projects and their objectives:

Measure	Focus	Criteria for success
Project 1: System consolidation to merge 11 ERP systems into three ERP systems 1. Subproject Asia: Consolidation of one system with two separate clients 2. Subproject North America: Consolidation of four systems 3. Subproject Europe: Consolidation of six systems	► Mapping of the three regions in which the company operates ► Higher degree of integration ► The systems have become very different over the years; the new systems should be based on a uniform business process	► Much lower operating costs as a result of fewer systems ► More effective international cooperation
Subsequent project 1: Standardization of business processes Identification and elimination of duplicates	► Uniform use of material numbers, accounts, and similar data ► Cleansing of master data	► Synergies created by standardized business processes ► Better reports for cost accounting ► More efficient processing of system data

Table 6.2 SLO Project Overview

Measure	Focus	Criteria for success
Subsequent project 2: Modification of processes in SAP APO and SAP CRM	► Cross-system design and standardized processes	► Standardized processes ► Centralized maintenance procedures ► Reduced TCO

Table 6.2 SLO Project Overview (cont.)

Project 1: System consolidation to merge 11 SAP ERP systems into three regional ERP systems

The company is keen to reduce the high costs it incurs for operating the 11 SAP ERP systems across Europe, North America, and Asia. By setting up three regional systems, it hopes to provide centralized system support from its headquarters. Centralization would facilitate data management and make the company's financial and sales data more readily available across the group. Long-term objectives to be realized as part of Project 1 include standardized business processes and uniform, global reporting procedures.

A concept has already been elaborated for the company's future SAP system landscape with development, quality assurance, and production systems. Once the group's favored overall concept for Project 1 has been presented, the different teams kick off the subprojects with a technical analysis and consult the company's nominated contact persons to clarify which changes need to be made when the systems are merged. The analysis examines interfaces, in particular, Application Link Enabling (ALE) interfaces, and communication control issues. The relevant systems must also be examined in detail to ascertain differences between Customizing and Repository objects—such as user exits, append structures, and customer developments.

The teams begin by identifying the right target system for each region and use the input from the pre-analysis to determine which changes need to be made. Next, master and transaction data and Customizing settings from the previously autonomous source systems can be transferred to the new target systems, using standard tools or SAP's expert tools such as the Conversion Workbench (CWB) and the Migration Workbench (MWB).

Subproject 1: Asia This subproject aims at merging the two separate clients in the Asian system via the *Client Merge* service.

Owing to the low volume of data being consolidated, the group regards the task of merging the two clients in the Asian system as a pilot project.

Furthermore, as the two clients have not been in production use for very long and have similar Customizing settings and business processes, they lend themselves to consolidation. Since the clients are already in the same system, the management body and SAP's SLO experts have decided to use the CWB during the Client Merge service. Another advantage is that ERP objects such as material numbers can be renamed in the same step. This is clearly reflected in SLO's estimated project time of nine months.

The goal of subproject 2 is to migrate the four North American systems to one target system with four clients, using the *Client Transfer* service.

Subproject 2: North America

Since the four SAP ERP systems in North America are extremely large and differ immensely in terms of structures and processes, the group's project managers and the SLO specialists have decided to transfer the American ERP systems and the Canadian ERP system to four separate clients in the target system. They have also opted for consolidation on a purely technical level using the MWB. Using the MWB enables data to be transferred automatically and very efficiently.

Another advantage of the Client Transfer service is that the business processes and client-dependent Customizing settings do not have to be harmonized initially. Once the business processes have been harmonized, they can be merged into one client at a later stage. Simply reducing the four independent systems to one system has enabled the company to cut operating costs by approximately 25 percent.

The management body has already planned a re-engineering project to harmonize the clients. Before transferring the data, the team compares the cross-client Customizing and Repository settings.

Subproject 3 focuses on combining six European SAP ERP systems, using the *System Merge* service.

Subproject 3: Europe

The SAP ERP systems in Europe were implemented at different times at locations in Belgium, Germany, France, Great Britain, Switzerland, and the Czech Republic. They have been supplied with data from one development system for some years now. Three of the systems also have one, uniform Customizing client, from which they receive data via the development system. Certain Customizing settings for the business processes in the remaining systems differ considerably. The project team wants to take this opportunity to identify the best business processes, and thereby the primary system, before the systems are merged. It has therefore decided to set up a single-client system and simultaneously transfer the complete history from the source systems.

The system in Germany will absorb the data from the other five systems. A panel of experts from different business departments has been nominated to ascertain the most efficient business processes and solutions; the different countries confirm the final selection and it is implemented in the target system. After determining the issues and required target structures for the future European system, the team has decided to use the MWB and the CWB during the System Merge service.

The System Merge service has the following advantages:

▶ Use of preconfigured change scenarios; for example, for renaming material, customer, and vendor numbers or for converting charts of accounts

▶ Use of the technical migration features of the SLO tools; this enables cross-release migration projects—if the source and target systems are on different releases—as well as transfer to a Unicode-enabled system

▶ Reduced system downtime because application-specific changes take place in parallel with the technical migration

All SLO contact persons will remain on hand throughout the project review phases.

The two subsequent projects to standardize the business processes, to identify and eliminate duplicates, and to modify the processes in SAP APO and SAP CRM are still in the decision-making phase.

6.9.3 Advantages of the SLO Services

SAP Legacy System Migration Workbench

In the past, the usual way to merge clients was to transfer data from the source client(s) to the target client, using the *SAP Legacy System Migration Workbench* (LSMW), for example. Master data, as well as open items and transactions, was transferred from the source clients for a particular key date. This is a sound approach if the processes in the clients involved are very different and new common structures are being created from scratch; however, it can have serious consequences. Conventional data transfer processes don't permit detailed historical data to be migrated; only key date values, summarized values, and open transactions can be transferred. Because transactions cannot be transferred with their complete predecessor processes, additional technical or organizational solutions are often required for day-to-day activities during the transition period. In many cases, the legacy systems continue to be operated in parallel during the transition period.

SLO has developed solutions that are not subject to such restrictions and represent clear value added for customers. They include the services described in this case study—Client Merge, Client Transfer, and System Merge. Customers benefit because any data and its history can be transferred at any time. These solutions also permit individual objects to be selected for transfer.

The special technical tools developed by SLO—the MWB and CWB—contain program logic that builds on application-related expertise already defined in existing conversion packages. The rules can be preconfigured ready for use—additional objects and customer developments are identified and integrated over the course of the project. The objects affected in any mySAP Business Suite applications are converted consistently, quickly, and irrespectively of a key date. Once the data has been transferred, users can access all data and functions as usual. This means, for instance, that the entire document flow remains consistent and complete.

MWB and CWB

6.10 Improving Operations and Support for SAP Solutions

A global enterprise with around 10,000 employees has been an SAP customer for many years. It currently deploys an SAP R/3 system with all the modules fully configured, as well as mySAP Supply Chain Management (mySAP SCM). Two separate internal organizations, set up during the implementation projects, are responsible for running and developing the two SAP solutions.

The enterprise is eager to do all it can to improve its internal processes, aiming ultimately to increase efficiency and reduce costs. Also high on the agenda is active participation in the SAP CCC program (see also Section 4.2.1), which the company hopes will result in close collaboration with SAP and the international SAP CCC Community. Considering its situation, the company decides to order services from the SAP Empowering portfolio (see also Section 4.2.3).

6.10.1 Strategy

Together with SAP, the company defines the following roadmap:

1. SAP is to conduct an *SAP Operations Competence Assessment*, incorporating SAP CCC certification.

2. As part of empowering, they will work together to create a plan for transferring support-specific expertise.

The SAP Operations Competence Assessment is designed to identify problems and action areas associated with running and supporting SAP solutions, thereby ensuring that the certification criteria for the SAP CCC program is also checked carefully. The resulting action plan is the basis for "empowering engagement"—support-specific knowledge transfer from SAP to the customer.

6.10.2 SAP Operations Competence Assessment

The service centers on the customer's current SAP operations and support structures. SAP identifies the potential for optimization and suggests how the recommendations might be implemented. Rather than focusing on the SAP solutions already in use, the analysts concentrate on the processes, functions, and expertise needed to run and support the solutions, and on the tools deployed. The assessment comprises three phases: preparation, on-site analysis, and follow-up.

Preparation The preparatory phase is critical to the success of the service and involves clarifying expectations with a sponsor from the company. A decision is made to examine the two environments that run the solutions and to interview representatives from the IT team, as well as from the key business areas affected. The considerable amount of time and detailed planning necessary to interview so many people pays off later. The customer has clear expectations: The enterprise wants to know where there is scope to improve the way it runs and supports the solutions, and the extent to which its support organization meets the criteria for SAP CCC certification.

The SAP experts contact colleagues who act as the company's personal contacts. They also assess whether the criteria for SAP CCC certification is met and evaluate previous service reports. In addition, they gather detailed information on specific topics from the customer.

On-site analysis Over a period of three days, the people responsible for the different aspects of operations and support are interviewed on site, based on information gathered during the preparatory phase. The SAP experts cover the topics defined in SAP IT Service & Application Management—support strategy and service management, application management, and SAP operations. If they discover capacity for improvement in this early phase, they discuss viable alternatives and propose optimization measures. In the example we are using here, the following action areas are discussed, verified with all the participants, and signed off:

▶ Two operating organizations are responsible for the two SAP solutions, impacting significantly on costs.

▶ SLAs have not been defined for all business areas and those that have are based only on technical measurements.

▶ The support process for incident and problem management is not consistently defined from end to end, and various tools are used for these processes (this is also relevant in terms of SAP CCC certification).

▶ Responsibilities and processes have not been defined for contract administration—also relevant for SAP CCC certification.

▶ A business process management concept, covering monitoring for key business processes, is not in place.

▶ There is more than one procedure for implementing changes to the SAP solution, which can lead to changes being implemented that are not compatible.

The SAP Operations Competence Assessment team compiles a final report covering the following elements:

Follow-up

▶ The overall condition of the operations and support environment for each area

▶ Identification, documentation, and recommendations for eliminating any weak areas that compromise or jeopardize the way the SAP solutions are run, supported, and developed; SAP's recommendations for eliminating these weak areas

▶ An action plan for implementing the measures, including, where relevant, other recommended SAP services; any tasks relevant for SAP CCC certification are also indicated

The final step is to sign off the contents of the report, in particular, the next steps based on the action plan.

6.10.3 Empowering Engagement

SAP and the customer use the prioritized action plan to initiate a tailored process of engagement. The recommendations provided enable the customer to complete certain items from the action plan independently. Other tasks call for more detailed analyses and additional input from SAP experts, which are delivered via SAP Empowering workshops or certain other services.

In this example, the customer uses documentation provided by SAP to optimize the way contracts are managed. With regard to the two separate operating organizations, the customer decides to work on improving its processes in one organization first, with the intention of using the enhanced processes for both SAP solutions later. The company benefits because it was SAP who highlighted this potential and it can use the information to evaluate the extent to which organizational change improves efficiency.

Workshops and services

SAP offers the company a range of workshops and services to undertake the remaining action areas:

▶ The SAP Empowering workshop *Advanced Problem Solving for Customer SAP Support* to help create an end-to-end support process; the SAP Empowering workshop *SAP Service Desk Skills* to deal with the requirements of a service (help) desk

▶ The SAP Empowering workshop *Change Request Management with SAP Solution Manager* to establish a standard, consistent, and tool-based software change process

▶ The *SAP Business Process Management* (BPM) service to create a tool-based concept to ensure that mission-critical business processes run smoothly

The action plan is worked through and the recommended workshops and services delivered, leaving the company well equipped to run both SAP solutions effectively. With all the criteria relevant to SAP CCC certification implemented, SAP also awards the enterprise an SAP CCC certificate. As a recognized and certified SAP center of excellence, it shows its own company as well as SAP that the support organization is continuing in its efforts to provide first-class solution support. Consequently, the company enjoys close partnerships with SAP and the international SAP CCC Community, with the common objective of continuously optimizing the IT services and processes that support key business processes.

6.11 Planning to Source Selected Support Tasks for Operations and Applications

A European automotive supplier with subsidiaries in eight countries has taken over three production locations in the United States and Brazil, whose IT systems need to be migrated as soon as possible to the SAP system deployed throughout the group. The solution currently in use is SAP for Automotive, with the modules Finance and Controlling (FI/CO), Sales and Distribution (SD), Materials Management (MM), Warehouse Management, Production Planning (PP), Plant Maintenance, and Project System. The specific product liability requirements faced by the U.S. automotive supplier indicate that the Quality Management (QM) module also needs to be implemented. Furthermore, the company wants all of its financial accounting units worldwide to comply with U.S. GAAP.

The IT department now faces completely new challenges. It has to build up new resources quickly to support the additional users. The service times are also different. So far, support has been available 12 hours a day, which is no longer sufficient because the support team now has to cater to additional time zones. Moreover, the team has to prepare for migrating the systems, consolidating the data, and implementing the QM module. In addition, the IT department has discovered that it needs to increase the current level of system availability from 93 percent to 99.5 percent to meet future requirements. Yet the budget for maintenance and support must not exceed current expenditure, despite the fact that the IT department has new tasks to fulfill.

New challenges

In the face of these challenges, the IT department is debating whether to outsource certain system operation and application management tasks in order to make its costs more transparent and free up resources for its new responsibilities. There has also been talk of using this opportunity to upgrade the system to mySAP ERP 2005, though the viability of conducting such a project at this stage has still to be confirmed. Together with SAP Managed Services, the company discusses various options for tackling the requirements.

6.11.1 Cost Analysis for Operations and Support

First, SAP Managed Services works with the company to determine the cost structures of the current support organization, pinpointing cost drivers as well as potential for profitability. Next, the consultants analyze the additional tasks that will arise from supporting the production locations in the United States and Brazil. The results show that the costs incurred for in-house support are set to rise by around 26 percent, due in part to increased service times.

The IT department uses these findings to negotiate with the management body as regards the additional tasks and planned funding. It succeeds in securing extra funding to the tune of around 15 percent, initially for 12 months. This means that the IT department must cut its costs substantially in a short space of time. The analysis indicates that SAP Managed

Cost reduction

Services can help reduce costs for the long term. The following services would be beneficial:

▶ Outsource support for the applications at the production locations in the United States and Brazil; with extended service times, these applications cause most of the extra costs and will create the most work directly after the changeover.

▶ Ongoing application management for the modules FI/CO, SD, MM, PP, and Supply Chain Management for the eight European subsidiaries, including support in implementing new functions, since these applications will be affected by the most modifications when the new locations are integrated.

▶ Hosting from SAP Managed Services for the prototype and the implementation environment for the production locations in the United States and Brazil. This would allow hardware sizing to be defined once the requirements for production operation are clear. With such an approach, the template would be developed faster and the rollout would be accelerated, since the prototype can be set up within three weeks and the implementation environment within 10 days.

▶ Hand over application management for the QM module to SAP Managed Services, since internal resources and expertise are insufficient.

Monthly flat rates are agreed on for all items and the service levels are defined. This entails defining report contents and service and response times, for example.

6.11.2 Upgrade to mySAP ERP 2005

It would be in the company's best interests to migrate to mySAP ERP 2005, not least because the standard system already offers functions that would make it easier to meet corporate governance and compliance guidelines. However, the solution is currently in the Ramp-Up phase.

SAP Ramp-Up To participate in SAP's Ramp-Up program, a company must have—among other things—a suitable infrastructure and a competent team to set up and run the (test) solution. However, the example company does not have sufficient internal resources to meet these requirements. In a matter of weeks, SAP Managed Services can provide a suitable system environment and take care of the sizing and design of the IT landscape. The company would then be well prepared for the production phase and the transition to its own systems. The prices for the infrastructure, as well as for running the system securely and reliably, are all fixed. The team from SAP

Managed Services supervises the upgrade project from the planning phase to the system going live. As a result, the automotive supplier doesn't need to define hardware and sizing until the test systems are running satisfactorily with original data. Therefore, the company could free up internal resources and concentrate exclusively on mapping specific business processes. Knowledge transfer from SAP Managed Services ensures that the internal IT department is up to date. The company would also be able to actively participate in product development at SAP.

6.11.3 Increased Availability

Faced with the task of increasing system availability at short notice, the company opts for a two-day *SAP System Fitness Check*. A team from SAP Managed Services analyzes the SAP systems for performance, stability, utilization, and operability before presenting its findings and proposing solutions. It finds, for instance, that the new availability requirements could be met quickly if existing IT resources were utilized more uniformly and the solutions in use were parameterized more effectively. Finally, the team shows the IT staff how to check the key system parameters so it can do this by itself in the future.

6.12 Steps Toward a Best-Run IT Organization

A multinational enterprise has already implemented SAP solutions in various countries. It now wants to deploy the solution in other international subsidiaries and set up a new data warehouse. The extra users will increase the anticipated system load.

6.12.1 Review and Evaluation of Present Situation

A review of the present situation has caused the following issues to surface:

▶ IT organization, processes, and tools
Users find it difficult to locate the right contact person when errors occur. The enterprise is currently investigating ways of handling support requests and problem messages more effectively.

▶ SAP Application Management
A general evaluation of the system landscape's capacity has shown that a single landscape will still suffice, even if the data volume and business activities increase in the coming three years. In fact, the landscape has extra capacity in the application server layer, but a bottleneck has

been found in the database layer. Upgrading from a 32-bit to a 64-bit CPU on the database server could ease the bottleneck, as could a faster CPU, more memory, or a distributed database solution. In view of the current conditions, the enterprise has decided that the benefits to be gained from separating the landscape would not justify the technical effort required. It has requested advice for improving the way it manages its applications.

Since working with a single solution landscape is generally riskier, SAP advises the company to include performance monitoring and data archiving in its standard administration tasks.

The company's plans for expansion and its new, more exacting requirements make it necessary to review the availability concept and consider additional time zones.

Depending on the desired result and the components in question, there are various ways of increasing the availability of the solution; for instance, by using a switchover solution or standby database and a failover data center, whereby the effectiveness of the respective high-availability solution must be checked regularly.

▶ SAP NetWeaver Management
The group has asked SAP for assistance in investigating why response times are too long. They hold a joint workshop and establish that the hard disk system cannot cope with the input/output (I/O) load, which results in long wait times when data is accessed. In addition to close monitoring, SAP recommends a faster disk system that can handle more I/Os. Spreading the database files (such as online redo logs) of the instance over different media could achieve similar effects.

The experts also uncovered the following problem: Many Controlling reports are created using an SAP system, which places disproportionately high demands on the database and results in too many I/Os. The load could be reduced if the reports were created more efficiently using consolidated data from the data warehouse. They also propose checking the effectiveness of the algorithm used in the reports to extract data.

The customer wants to know whether the system could be recovered within eight hours in the event of an error (unplanned downtime). SAP finds that recovering the database following a serious error would actually take several days. This is because it takes too long to recover data from the tape and to reconstruct the archive redo logs. Also, too many redo logs have to be used. The customer could achieve the target recovery time of a maximum of eight hours by using faster tape storage systems, suitable database parameters to reconstruct redo logs faster, and two or three full database backups as opposed to just one. Increasing the number of backups indirectly reduces the number of archive redo log files required between two backups. If a recovery does become necessary, fewer archive logs have to be reconstructed.

In addition, maintenance tasks are causing excessively long downtimes. Though planned, they are hampering day-to-day activities. Upgrading to a more recent database version would allow more administrative tasks to be completed online and bring the availability of the entire landscape closer to 24/7.

6.12.2 Enablement and Realization

To address these problems, SAP proposes the following training measures.

▶ **IT organization, processes, and tools**
SAP offers a wide range of Empowering workshops, one of which, *Effective Management of SAP Support Organizations*, is described below as an example. The workshop shows IT managers the optimal way to set up a center of excellence to support and enhance SAP solutions. It discusses principles, functions, and case studies for managing and running a support organization or SAP CCC. It focuses particularly on key topics such as the management of technical processes and business processes, suitable key performance indicators, service level management, change management, and service desks. SAP advises the customer to adjust its organization and underlying processes. Doing so substantially boosts transparency and efficiency throughout the service organization.

▶ **SAP Application Management**
The customer's support staff participates in the course *SAP Application Management*. It covers SAP application change management, business process monitoring, and business process performance monitoring, and results in certification of the participants.

▶ **SAP NetWeaver Management**
The customer's support team attends a training course on profiles in SAP NetWeaver management. The course covers the basics of system management, system administration and batch processing, firewall management and security administration, application services, as well

as user and authorization profiles. It also results in certification of the participants.

By the end of the enabling phase, the customer is well equipped to implement the recommendations.

6.12.3 Optimization

SAP delivers the following services to optimize the SAP solution landscape:

▶ **SAP Business Process Management**
The *SAP Business Process Management* service analyzes core processes with regard to the systems and interfaces involved. A strategy for business process management is drawn up, encompassing object monitoring, procedures for error handling, and escalation channels. During the service, SAP passes on expertise for expanding the strategy so that the methods can be applied to other areas. By implementing the recommendations, the company has been able to meet growing needs more effectively with its existing service organization and to create synergies for business process management.

▶ **SAP Data Volume Management**
This service reduces the size and growth rate of the database used by the SAP solution. It is described in detail in Section 6.6.3. In this example, by changing its disk systems and access strategy, the company is able to slash response times as well as costs by utilizing hardware more effectively.

▶ **SAP System Administration**
The *SAP System Administration* service is also described in Section 6.6.3. The company has decided to implement a standard and, where possible, automated concept for application monitoring, to use a professional change management tool, and to design a high-availability strategy.

Two months later, SAP checks whether the original problems have been resolved and whether the company has seen a tangible improvement.

7 SAP Service and Support Infrastructure

SAP Ecosystem holds information and service offerings tailor-made to participants' needs. Two high-performance communication and cooperation platforms constitute the lifeblood of this ecosystem.

SAP has forged ahead with extending its service and support infrastructure to provide participants in the SAP Ecosystem with the information and services that they need. This infrastructure consists of SAP Solution Manager, which is integrated into the customer's system landscape, and SAP Service Marketplace, operated by SAP. SAP Service Marketplace, including its portals, enables a tight interlocking of your company-specific service and support processes with those of SAP; for example, in the area of ordering services and problem solving (see Section 7.2). It also grants you access to all base functions that you need in order to use SAP's support offering.

The interface with SAP Solution Manager, the second main pillar within SAP's service and support infrastructure, reaches into the interlocking of electronic workflows across platforms, into detailed implementation tasks, and the operation of your company solution (see Section 7.3). In addition, SAP Solution Manager offers important additional functions, such as support during an implementation, monitoring functions, and a service desk with functions for creating messages professionally.

7.1 SAP Solution Manager

Because most companies are now integrating a variety of systems, IT infrastructures are becoming increasingly complex. The number of interfaces to Web services and software products—from a broad range of vendors—has also increased dramatically. Bearing this in mind, SAP aims to help companies run their SAP solutions as cost-effectively as possible and with minimal technical risk. Curbing total cost of ownership (TCO) and accelerating return on investment (ROI) are important ways in which to achieve this goal.

Until recently, if a company had a reliable telephone or email-based workflow up and running—with the software or hardware vendor for dealing with error messages—you knew its support strategy was well

New requirements

organized. Today, however, the goalposts have moved, and if customers, providers, and their partners are to collaborate effectively and smoothly, a host of different requirements must be met.

Some time ago, SAP began connecting all its live customer systems to the SAP support infrastructure. Today, SAP can make the unique claim of having connected almost 95% of its customers. This link means that SAP's customers can always rely on quick responsive support in critical situations that potentially could affect their core business.

New challenges   In the age of globalization and the Internet, and at a time when entire business scenarios are being completely restructured, companies must reassess their existing infrastructures and look for new ways to implement systems for specific objectives and provide efficient support. Implementing and running individual systems is important, but not as vital as ensuring that all the core business processes flow smoothly across the group by using a reliable, effective software solution. This new challenge calls for a holistic view of all the components in the IT landscape and the cross-company connections; the entire lifecycle of the solution must be considered. The interplay of technical and functional aspects is also essential for effective communication between the IT organization and the business areas within the company.

New collabo-
ration scenario   With SAP Solution Manager, SAP has created a completely new way of collaborating effectively with customers and partners. SAP Solution Manager's primary goal is to provide SAP customers with optimum support during the implementation, go-live, and operational phases, as well as when tailoring their solutions to meet new requirements, and to proactively deliver high-quality, timely services that fulfill customers' needs. Because requirements have changed, it is vital—from SAP's point of view—that a tool is provided that can absorb all the necessary data from the customer's entire IT landscape and core business processes, and make this data available when it is needed. This is precisely what SAP Solution Manager does within a customer solution. IT-related decisions are made on the basis of this central collection of data, which minimizes risks. Furthermore, SAP Solution Manager builds an important foundation for IT governance by allowing the IT dimension to approximate the business process view, by enabling IT processes to be standardized and monitored, and by creating transparency.

As a collaboration platform between customers and SAP, SAP Solution Manager offers entirely new possibilities to optimize this cooperative work. Results collected by SAP are stored in SAP Solution Manager and are available to the customer. The identified problems and fields of action (top issue management) are tracked with the help of experts from the customer and SAP, who can be called in if necessary and written off from a pre-booked contingent. The application area ranges from continuous business process development to technical system optimization. SAP Solution Manager thus offers support during the entire process—from documenting open questions to communicating via the latest collaboration scenarios such as "application sharing" to documenting results and managing the implementation.

The comprehensive amount of information found in SAP Solution Manager is also the basis for many additional functions, which ensures that customers can implement and run SAP solutions optimally and continually identify the scope for technical enhancements. The key functions are listed below and explained in greater detail later on:

▶ Provision of implementation methodologies and tools
▶ Monitoring and graphical representation of the IT infrastructure and core business processes
▶ Portfolio of services and Best Practices for Solution Management
▶ Service Desk
▶ Change management and upgrades

Figure 7.1 Scope of SAP Solution Manager

7.1.1 Implementation

SAP Solution Manager provides the necessary methodology and tools to help companies set up their implementation projects, implement the functional and technical aspects of the software solution, and ensure that the implemented solution goes live successfully. SAP Solution Manager can help you:

▶ **Provide procedure models for implementation projects**
  SAP Solution Manager uses roadmaps to show who is assigned to particular tasks and how the tasks should be carried out optimally within an implementation project. Roadmaps are structured collections of documents, which cover everything from general procedures to application-specific details. They show you when specific services would be useful for your company. In addition, they describe how the teams, which are responsible for implementing the functions for your business processes and for setting up the necessary infrastructure to run the solution, collaborate to ensure that your projects go live with minimal risk. Roadmaps are available for implementing mySAP Business Suite or for setting up administration procedures for SAP solutions.

▶ **Define the project, including the required system landscape**
  SAP Solution Manager uses a business process repository and a landscape directory for this purpose. These contain considerable information about SAP components and examples of business processes from different SAP solutions that you can use as a template for your projects. You can also manage selected project information, such as project time frames and personnel resources.

▶ **Create a business blueprint for the corporate solution you want to implement**
  In addition to the predefined business processes in the above-mentioned business process repository (see Figure 7.2), SAP Solution Manager offers a broad range of documentation and documentation templates.

▶ **Configure your system using an implementation guide, distribute the configuration settings across systems, and verify that they are consistent**
  SAP Solution Manager includes Business Configuration Sets (BC Sets), which you can reuse as copy templates for configuration settings in other systems.

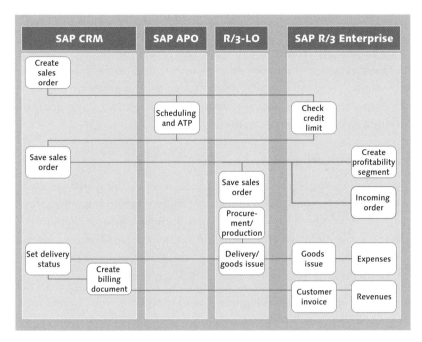

Figure 7.2 Example of a Predefined Business Process

▶ **Define, automate, and manage test cases using the Test Workbench**
The business processes defined when the business blueprint is created are used as templates here. It is important to test the system not only the first time you implement it, but also when you upgrade it and when you install Support Packages or Legal Change Packages.

▶ **Automate test cases using the seamlessly integrated test tool, Extended Computer-Aided Test Tool (eCATT)**
Using this tool, an enhanced version of CATT, you can record and run a wide range of applications. eCATT also has an interface for integrating tools from other providers.

▶ **Define and handle problems specific to implementation**
This function helps the project team to identify and eliminate potential risks.

▶ **Create and manage e-learning units for user training**
This boosts effective knowledge transfer. Role-specific learning maps enable users to gain the knowledge they require to achieve their particular objectives.

► Store information about the implemented business processes and the related solution landscape in the repository, which is also used by current operations

This means that the information does not have to be entered again. Therefore, you can use SAP Solution Manager's monitoring functions; for example, to oversee live business processes that were originally defined during the implementation phase.

7.1.2 Monitoring

Modular infra-structure

SAP Solution Manager features a modular monitoring infrastructure, which reflects the three main aspects of solution monitoring: service level management, system monitoring, and business process monitoring. Users, system administrators, and the customer's application management team can all benefit from this infrastructure. Four central functions of the monitoring infrastructure are particularly important:

1. It provides up-to-date, graphical documentation of your system landscape and business processes.

2. It bundles tools for monitoring and maintaining the system landscape.

3. It safeguards against system failures and inadequate performance.

4. It logs system and system landscape performance.

Graphical interface

SAP Solution Manager has a graphical interface with which you can view parts of, or the entire IT infrastructure, in varying degrees of detail. Most of the stored data is read automatically from the system landscape and processed in SAP Solution Manager. This saves you a lot of time, especially if a system landscape is highly complex. In addition to being able to view software and hardware, including all key technical data relating to systems and interfaces, you can now view actual business processes, which opens up a whole new dimension to documentation and monitoring. This allows you to map your core business as integrated processes across the company so that information can be exchanged optimally. You can also handle problems, upgrades, migrations, and major implementation projects more efficiently.

By providing tools and technologies, SAP Solution Manager enables you to monitor and maintain your system landscape centrally. You can organize your system administration tasks more effectively and verify improvements using an integrated reporting function. In this way, maintenance planning and implementation are supported and made more transparent. This includes SAP Notes, SAP TopNotes, SAP HotNews, and

Support Package Stacks. For example, you can compare your SAP application's current Support Package level with the recommended level. Then, you can initiate an approval procedure to import the Support Package. Next, you can download the Support Packages from SAP Service Marketplace and import them into the system. Further process steps such as testing and importing to the production system are also integrated in the maintenance process.

Monitoring is a cost-effective way of safeguarding against system failures and inadequate performance. Long-term monitoring alerts customers to looming problems, such as when capacity limits are in danger of being reached or hardware resources are being consumed too quickly. You can also keep track of the current status of your system landscape with real-time monitors. If the system issues a warning, you can navigate directly to the source of the problem and take preventive or corrective measures.

Safeguarding against system failures

Long-term monitoring uses key performance indicators (KPIs), which you can enter automatically in service level reports at regular intervals. The reports provide a basis for the Service Level Agreements (SLAs) that are drawn up between your IT department and the employees in your company who are responsible for business processes. They enable you to monitor the outsourcing partner maintaining your systems. The KPI data in the service level reports is obtained from the reports compiled with the SAP EarlyWatch Alert service. This data is sent automatically from your SAP systems to SAP Solution Manager via the Service Data Control Center (SDCC). If weak points have been identified in your system, SAP Solution Manager makes several suggestions for addressing them. Figure 7.3 shows the flow of data from the customer's system landscape to the technical monitoring infrastructure to the point at which it is processed in SAP Solution Manager.

KPIs

In SAP Solution Manager, you can combine business processes and system landscapes graphically with the system monitoring functions. Technically speaking, real-time system monitoring is based on the Computing Center Management System (CCMS, see Figure 7.3). When required, the CCMS activates alerts in the graphical display of the IT infrastructure and the system landscape. This helps you to safeguard your business processes, because even when a system's performance is satisfactory, the core business process for which the systems have been deployed may not necessarily be running smoothly. The correct monitoring functions must be selected and combined so that the system administrators can see from the business process display whether a system warning pertains to a crit-

CCMS

ical business area. Should problems arise, such information can be vital to your company.

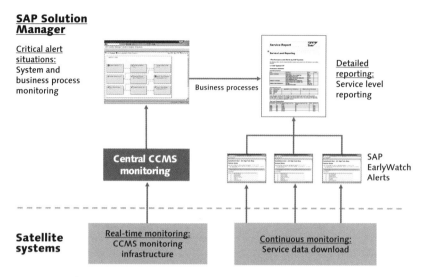

SAP Solution Manager

Critical alert situations: System and business process monitoring

Business processes

Detailed reporting: Service level reporting

Central CCMS monitoring

SAP EarlyWatch Alerts

Satellite systems

Real-time monitoring: CCMS monitoring infrastructure

Continuous monitoring: Service data download

Figure 7.3 Infrastructure for Monitoring SAP Solutions

It is not just the technical environment of a software solution that is critical. The mutual reliance of IT and business areas and how individual processes are mapped to the existing infrastructure are also extremely important. Therefore, SAP Solution Manager focuses on the customer's core business. SAP's new service and support infrastructure represents the next generation of optimum service and support functions, which can localize a problem to exactly where it occurs.

In practice: items GmbH

items GmbH, a full-service IT company operating in the German cities of Münster, Bocholt, and Lübeck, offers services for all SAP solutions used in the German utilities industry, and several specialized systems for various other tasks. Operating company and customer systems in the company's computer center once required a great deal of administration. To reduce this admin work, items GmbH decided to implement SAP Solution Manager and SAP CCMS, which offers tailored functions for monitoring SAP and non-SAP systems.

The project team that was led by Alfred Vorst, director of basis technologies at items GmbH, and which comprised the company's employees and consultants from SAP Consulting, successfully implemented SAP Solution Manager in just a few months. "Our collaboration with SAP Consulting was very good, and their dedication and competence were integral to the project's success. We implemented the system monitoring and reporting concept together in a very short time," says Vorst. Involving items' own employees in the project was also very beneficial, says Vorst. "The knowledge transfer worked perfectly."

To items GmbH, the benefits of the new solution are clear: Implementing basic initial system monitoring, which monitors system availability, backup status, and update task and job terminations, quickly led to a significant reduction in administration—and as a result, in costs—particularly for operations. "Our system administrators now save more than an hour a day and use the extra time for service-oriented tasks," says Vorst.

7.1.3　Service Delivery

In the operations area of SAP Solution Manager, customers can access a wide range of SAP services centrally. A standard set of service procedures is provided for evaluating, implementing, running, and continually optimizing your SAP solution. In this case, SAP Solution Manager functions as a central platform for delivering these services. The benefits of this are:

▶ Self-services and cross-solution services are provided.

▶ The focus is on your core business processes.

▶ The proactive and documentary nature of the services is enhanced.

The services can be divided into three different categories: self, remote, and on-site services.

The customers perform self-services themselves. The tools for self-services are integrated in SAP Solution Manager. This type of service contains mainly documented instructions on how to carry out the service, as well as recommendations for strengthening any weak points. Customers usually acquire the knowledge required to carry out a self-service by participating in an SAP training course. Consequently, instead of having SAP perform the service, they can save money by using their own personnel, while still benefiting from SAP's expert knowledge.

Self-services

On-site services   When SAP experts perform an on-site service, they work on the customer's premises with direct access to the SAP Solution Manager system and to the current business processes and system landscapes stored in it. Consequently, the service delivered reflects customer requirements much more accurately, the recommendations made are better, and the proactive nature of the service is enhanced.

Remote services   If a service is delivered from a remote location, SAP experts log on to the customer's SAP Solution Manager system through a remote connection. SAP Solution Manager provides SAP experts with the necessary information regarding the customer's solution and secure access to the individual components of the solution.

You can order remote and on-site services using SAP Solution Manager on SAP Service Marketplace (see Section 7.2). SAP employees deliver the appropriate service and then, in SAP Solution Manager, document the results, the procedures they employed, and any changes to the customer's system landscape or business processes. Customers can call up the results as reports at any time in SAP Solution Manager.

Cross-solution services   Cross-solution services are another key benefit of SAP Solution Manager. Until recently, for example, the SAP EarlyWatch Check could be delivered for individual systems only. With SAP Solution Manager, it can now be used for entire solutions encompassing several systems. Cross-solution services like these can be delivered only with SAP Solution Manager because this platform is the first of its kind to provide customers with a standardized service and support infrastructure that is integrated centrally in their solutions. This shows that SAP has also given ample consideration to complex, distributed solution landscapes. The more sophisticated a solution, the harder it is to identify problems without using a central infrastructure that recognizes the solution's processes and systems. In the future, SAP Solution Manager will be inextricably linked to the services and support provided for these solutions.

Best Practices   In addition to the services, the operations area of SAP Solution Manager offers document-based *Best Practices for Solution Management*. These are descriptions of complex procedures that you carry out when you implement and run your SAP solution. Best practices are available on topics such as system copies, backup and recovery, and data consistency between various SAP components. The purpose of best practices is to transfer expert knowledge that SAP and its partners have built up and continually optimized through their years of experience in handling customer projects.

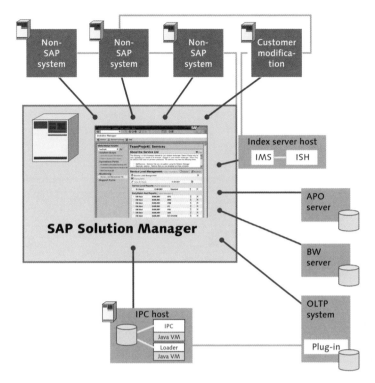

Figure 7.4 Integrating SAP Solution Manager in the Customer's Software Solution

To ensure that the information on offer is always up to date, SAP Solution Manager contains just a series of links; the documents themselves are stored on SAP Service Marketplace. Whereas SAP Service Marketplace lists the full range of Best Practices for Solution Management, SAP Solution Manager displays only those that are relevant to the customer's solution. The services function in a similar way. The SAP Service Catalog (see Section 7.2) lists all the services on offer. With SAP Solution Manager, customers do not have to conduct tiresome searches for the entries specific to their solution, because the system offers only a selection of entries that is relevant to their purpose.

7.1.4 Service Desk

The Service Desk in SAP Solution Manager assists the customer support process and offers effective user support for an SAP solution. SAP Solution Manager provides you with the complete infrastructure you need to set up and run a help desk with the associated internal support organization.

In addition to conventional help desk functions, the Service Desk offers access to:

▶ A customer solution database (if used in SAP Solution Manager)

▶ SAP Service Marketplace

▶ SAP Notes Search

▶ Tools for detecting the cause of disruptions (root cause analysis)

▶ Other support tools, such as SAP Note Assistant

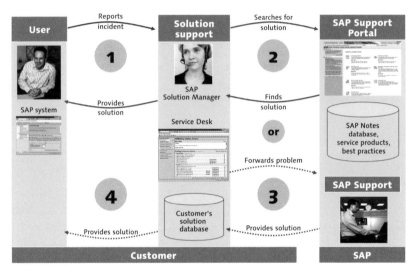

Figure 7.5 Message Processing Between the Customer's Users, the Support Organization, and the SAP Back Office

The greatest benefit of the Service Desk is that it accelerates and optimizes message processing, saving both time and money. Anybody using an SAP solution can send a message directly from his or her own working environment to the Service Desk in SAP Solution Manager. SAP Solution Manager provides employees in the customer's support organization with a fully integrated help desk system encompassing a wide range of features for solving problems. This includes the SAP Notes Search, access to the customer's solution database, and an automatic data collector that collects all the key data from the user's system, such as transaction, release, status of the Support Packages, and database version. This ensures that the messages contain all the necessary data so that the support employee does not have to contact the user again, thus saving time at both ends and enabling disruptions to be remedied swiftly.

A significant aspect of message processing is the root cause analysis. An integral part of SAP Solution Manager designed specifically for this purpose—Solution Manager Diagnostics—offers suitable analytic tools for Java-based applications. The result is that sources of disruptions can be ascertained faster and remedied sooner. Finally, Solution Manager Diagnostics improves the availability of applications.

If required, the customer's support employees can forward the message to SAP's support organization via a direct link. SAP Solution Manager, which is installed at the customer site, provides the support organization with an exact picture of the customer's situation. SAP's support employees can carry out online evaluations of the data gathered by the data collectors. If an SAP employee changes the message in any way, for example, by proposing a solution, the changes are updated automatically in the original message at the customer's Service Desk.

If you do decide to set up an internal solution database, SAP Solution Manager is the perfect platform for communicating SAP specialist knowledge for the various user roles in your company. Thanks to its open architecture, you can also connect external tools for message processing to SAP Solution Manager at any time.

The Service Desk in SAP Solution Manager also allows SLAs to be monitored automatically. This function is particularly important for service providers, such as SAP Customer Competence Centers (SAP CCCs), and support organizations who have completed SLAs with their customers. The monitoring function optimizes the availability of critical customer installations and systems.

SLA monitoring

SLAs are defined in the Service Desk within service agreements for support or consulting services. These agreements contain binding conditions for the service to be delivered. If the customer reports a problem to its service provider, and an SLA exists for the relevant area, the Service Desk will already be aware of this as soon as the customer registers the problem. The time limits for handling the service procedure are set automatically in accordance with the SLA. Service providers can see at a glance which messages have top priority and can organize their workload accordingly.

Contractual agreements

From the customer's point of view, the direct link between the contractually agreed SLAs and the actual services provided makes it more likely that agreed-on response times will be adhered to.

As far as the service provider is concerned, prioritizing inquiries in this way makes it easier to handle critical service procedures, and ultimately helps to boost customer satisfaction.

Another major advantage of this solution is that the support costs incurred can be allocated directly to the party responsible, such as a cost center, with the appropriate tools. This makes costs transparent, and gives customers, who want to cut back on services or support, enough time to take suitable countermeasures (such as user training).

In practice: itelligence AG

itelligence AG, a leading IT service provider, uses SAP Solution Manager to simplify and enhance the support it offers to both its external customers and internal users.

SAP Solution Manager helped itelligence AG to centralize its heterogeneous infrastructure, which included multiple solutions for help desk and support activities. Previously, the solutions were integrated in SAP R/3, or based on either websites or email, depending on the particular location, and required various interfaces and integration tools. Thanks to the SAP Solution Manager support portal—which unifies help desk and proactive support—that has all changed.

"It was crucial to us to have a central, integrated, international platform for all hotline, support, and remote services," said Oliver Schreiber, Director of Outsourcing and Services. "By using SAP Solution Manager, we can offer our customers a web-based support portal that is very easy to access. It provides them with all the necessary support-related information, such as SAP EarlyWatch Alert reports and service level reports. So far, customer acceptance of the solution has been very good. This web-based support portal for our customers is also a very important differentiator on the market for itelligence. It is a unique selling proposition."

7.1.5 Management of Change Requests and Release Upgrades

SAP Solution Manager also helps customers with projects regarding software change management and upgrades. To stay ahead in the ever-changing world of business, it is imperative to be able to manage changes in business processes and software effectively. You can achieve this by continually adjusting your IT solution to new business and technical requirements. Whether they involve importing Support Packages, upgrading to new software releases, or modifying business processes, all changes have a common thread. They must be implemented quickly and cost-effectively with minimum disruption to operations.

With the range of functions offered by SAP Solution Manager, you can manage change requests and release upgrades, from project management activities to technical implementation. The roadmaps (see Section 7.1.1) describe procedures for carrying out change management projects. Upgrade projects are dealt with in a separate roadmap, comprising step-by-step instructions for the work packages and activities required for the release upgrade (see Section 6.8).

Change processes are triggered by change requests from the business area (for example, to optimize business processes) and the IT organization (for example, to import Support Packages). The requests are analyzed before a decision is made. A workflow in SAP Solution Manager outlines and documents all the considerations and decisions to be made by those responsible within your company as part of the approval procedure.

Once approval has been obtained, you can set up a project to implement the change requests. This is necessary only when extensive changes are being made, for instance, in the case of a release upgrade. First, the scope of the changeover from the current status to the new solution is examined in detail. You will find the function for creating a business blueprint, which is available in SAP Solution Manager and also used in implementation projects, useful for this analysis. If you deployed SAP Solution Manager when you implemented the solution, you can now base this phase of your change project on the project documentation that was created previously.

When implementing the changes, you must consider the following two aspects: First, the functional changes must be tailored to the configuration of the applications; the procedure here is the same as it was for implementation (see Section 7.1.1). Second, the changes have to be realized technically. This includes, for example, activating customizing changes in the actual production systems after they have been tested successfully in the test systems. Some projects require you to import SAP Notes and Support Packages. If you're managing an upgrade project, a technical release upgrade is required. SAP Solution Manager provides an array of functions that simplifies the procedure for implementing business-related changes and incorporating them in the release. These functions also minimize the risk of impeding current operations.

If a release upgrade affects several components, special attention must be paid to their interdependencies. When implementing the changes, you must perform the individual substeps in the correct order. To do so, you need detailed information of the current environment and the planned solution. SAP Solution Manager contains information about the current solution and the future business blueprint, which you can use as a basis for analyzing and coordinating activities.

Testing Testing is a key task in projects for implementing change requests or release upgrades. You can use the Test Workbench in SAP Solution Manager to check whether the changed business processes are running correctly. You will find it helpful when organizing tests and actually testing. If you have used SAP Solution Manager before to test your business processes, for instance, in the course of an implementation project, you can reduce the time and work required by reusing previous tests.

E-learning When migrating from the previous solution to the new solution, you can considerably lessen the loss in productivity by informing users beforehand about the changes, and the impact these changes will have on the procedures. However, user training is a major cost driver in many change management and upgrade projects. Fortunately, the e-learning management function provided by SAP Solution Manager helps you cut costs in this area. You can record training courses using SAP Tutor and make them available to employees as Internet or intranet-based e-learning courses. You can also combine the courses with other documents or presentations to create role-specific learning maps, which provide users with an overview of all the changes relevant to their role.

Overall, SAP Solution Manager enables you to implement changes effectively in your SAP solution. Standardized procedures and consistent controls accelerate the project, reduce costs, and lower the risk of disruptions to current operations. In addition, enhanced quality and stability mean that your production system is not adversely affected by the changes. Experts in the technical and functional departments of your company can improve collaboration thanks to the integrated working environment. The impact of the planned changes on the particular solutions and business processes can also be recognized much more proactively.

In practice: hameln pharmaceuticals

hameln pharmaceuticals, a global pharmaceutical specialist, upgraded its ERP system from SAP R/3 4.6B to SAP R/3 Enterprise.

The legal requirements for companies active in the pharmaceutical industry stipulate extensive testing and detailed project documentation for release upgrades.

A major factor in hameln pharmaceuticals' decision to implement SAP Solution Manager was access to standard SAP methodology. This is not surprising when you consider that the support platform can be used as the working environment in all project phases and is seamlessly integrated into the testing environment, which reduces the complexity of test management and testing.

Rainer Meine, manager of the SAP upgrade project at hameln pharmaceuticals, summed it up as follows: "SAP Solution Manager enabled us to base our project on clear methods and model our business processes centrally. The integrated test environment also greatly simplified testing. All in all, it didn't take us long to upgrade our release."

7.2   SAP Service Marketplace and Portals

The current SAP Service Marketplace houses all the information about the world of SAP, bundled into individual portals. As a joint Internet platform for customers, partners, and SAP, it gives SAP Ecosystem members easy and central access to information, services for SAP solutions, and support applications that SAP provides online.

Central entry point

SAP Service Marketplace contains information about diverse SAP solutions, consulting and training offerings, and communities of various user groups. It also provides access to the following portals, whose offerings are tailored to meet the needs of specific interest groups:

▶ SAP Support Portal

▶ SAP Developer Network

▶ SAP Channel Partner Portal

▶ SAP Business One Customer Portal

▶ SAP Partner Portal

▶ SAP Help Portal

▶ Customer-specific portals, where appropriate

The SAP Service Marketplace offers users the following advantages:

Advantages

▶ Central access via the Internet, any time, any place

▶ Single Sign-On (SSO), allowing users easy and secure access to the different portals without having to log on again

- User-friendly, intuitive navigation in all portals, thanks, in part, to harmonized layouts
- Numerous personalization options and proactive notification services so that you receive precisely the information you need
- A personal inbox that stores all the replies to your messages centrally

To access the SAP Service Marketplace, you need a user ID and a password. You can apply for both on the initial page of the SAP Service Marketplace at *www.service.sap.com*. A more convenient option is using Single Sign-on in connection with SAP Passports, a digital certificate enabling you to log on securely without a user ID or password.

Functions A few general functions of the SAP Service Marketplace will now be explained, before its content is described in detail:

- You can tailor this Internet platform to meet your individual needs by using the personalization options. In your personal profile settings, you define which information is relevant to you, in which language, and for which country.
- You can subscribe to a newsletter and be actively informed about the latest SAP news. Or, you can subscribe to certain subject areas and documents, in which case you're automatically sent a message notifying you of new information in the sections for which you have subscribed.
- If you need information, but don't know where to look on SAP Service Marketplace, the search function can help you find it.
- If you want to access a central source of information quickly, you can call it up directly by typing in a quick link instead of having to navigate there yourself. A quick link is a type of keyword that you enter in the address field of the browser. The most important quick links for SAP Service Marketplace and the portals are listed in Appendix A.

Information Offering for All Users

In addition to the aforementioned portals, SAP Service Marketplace provides areas with content relating to all users, to special offers for user groups, and to customers with SAP CCCs.

Solution Details The *Solution Details* category (in the "Education, Consulting, Solutions Area, and More" section) provides you with valuable information about industry and cross-industry solutions, including details on infrastructure, technical components, and releases. The industry solutions include SAP for Automotive, SAP for Banking, or SAP for Telecommunications. Examples of cross-industry solutions, on the other hand, are mySAP Customer Relationship Management (mySAP CRM) and mySAP Supply Chain Management (mySAP SCM),

The *Consulting* section contains information about the consulting services available for the entire lifecycle of an SAP solution—from its design, implementation, and ongoing operation, to its optimization.

Consulting

The *Education* section gives you access to SAP's entire education offering via the Online Training Catalog. You can register for courses or workshops, order documentation, or request recordings of training sessions, which you work through by yourself. Furthermore, you can book courses online. Then, an electronic order confirmation is sent to you, without your having to contact SAP directly.

Education

Information from and for members of SAP's user groups worldwide is posted under *Communities* for specific target groups. These communities include Deutschsprachige SAP-Anwendergruppe (DSAG) e.V. (German-speaking SAP User Group) and Americas' SAP Users' Group (ASUG), whose members exchange experiences, knowledge, and ideas, and make their common interests known to SAP. SAP is provided with valuable feedback on the technical and functional areas that interest users and, consequently, can take into account users' requests and suggestions in future developments. Functions for entering development requests are available to SAP user group members, as well as key account customers with SAP CCCs. The *SAP Customer Competence Center Net* (SAP CCCNet) is also a source of useful information for them.

Communities

SAP Support Portal

No modern support portfolio is complete without online services. In the *SAP Support Portal*, you'll find all the information and applications required to install, run, and continually enhance your SAP solution. For example, you can download best practices, learn about SAP's maintenance strategy and SAP Solution Manager, and place orders. The main support functions provided are:[1]

Support functions and services

---

1 You can access all the functions marked with an asterisk (*) without having to enter system data manually; data that has already been maintained appears automatically. This facilitates fast and convenient operation of the relevant support functions.

- System data maintenance
- SAP Notes Search*
- SAP HotNews*
- SAP TopNotes*
- Customer messages*
- SAP Software Distribution Center, from which you can download Support Packages directly

The following services are independent of the support services:

- User data maintenance for SAP Service Marketplace
- Catalogs enabling you to order software and services online

System data maintenance

To ensure that the system data is consistent and correct, SAP has integrated all its official product master data into the system data application; in other words, all the product versions, their software components, releases, and Support Package levels. If you use the SAP EarlyWatch Alert service, your system data is compared automatically to the product master data and updated; however, your system administrator can also enter the data manually. The advantages of properly maintaining system data are obvious:

- Better quality results when searching for SAP Notes with reference to a system
- Problem messages can be created faster and more cost-effectively and, depending on the accuracy of the information, SAP Active Global Support can resolve problems faster

SAP Notes Search

SAP provides solutions to problems that have already been identified in a central solution database—*SAP Notes*. The convenient search function enables you to select the relevant SAP Note for your system and to restrict your selection further using additional information. Any stored system data is loaded automatically into the search form. This saves you time when entering information and, due to the conciseness and improved quality of the search results, you can navigate through the list of SAP Notes faster.

SAP HotNews

SAP HotNews contains high-priority SAP Notes. The instructions help you solve or preempt problems that could cause systems to shut down or data to be lost; therefore, it is extremely important that all customers read them.

Using the workflow in SAP Support Portal, you can subscribe to certain SAP HotNews for your specific area of interest. The system then displays only those SAP HotNews items that are relevant to you. You can also receive SAP HotNews by e-mail so that you're always in tune with the latest developments. Once you have carried out the described measures, set the relevant SAP HotNews to "completed" in the SAP Support Portal so that these items will not be displayed again.

SAP TopNotes are the ten most important SAP Notes for each component. A new list is compiled every month. As with SAP HotNews, you can subscribe to specific components and view relevant SAP TopNotes in the SAP Support Portal. You can also arrange to have them sent by e-mail. Familiarizing yourself with the latest SAP TopNotes helps you to identify problems more easily, resolve them independently, and prevent them from occurring in the first place.

SAP TopNotes

If you cannot find a suitable SAP Note for your problem, you can send a customer message to SAP from the SAP Support Portal. You can now complete these two steps without having to enter your data twice, because the new SAP Message Wizard includes a facility for searching for notes before you create any messages. You should also note that including the context of the problem enhances the notes search and enables the problem to be classified clearly. When you enter your message, additional specific questions are displayed that correspond to the application area you selected, which saves time later because the SAP support specialists don't have to contact you for more information.

Customer messages

In the SAP Message Wizard, you can rate SAP Notes and thereby contribute to improving their quality. Any notes that you have read are added to the message so that the support staff can record the problem quickly and isolate it more effectively. You can save your search results and messages temporarily at any time and retrieve them from your central inbox when you're ready to continue editing them. Your inbox also contains the status of your message and replies from SAP. If you have included your email address in your user data, you can be informed as soon as your message has been answered. This saves you time because you don't have to keep checking the status of your message.

These enhancements are the first step toward establishing a comprehensive facility for searching for solutions. SAP is currently working to integrate other sources of information in the SAP Message Wizard, such as SAP Online Help and discussion forums.

SAP values your feedback on the quality of message processing. You can evaluate this in a short questionnaire sent when you confirm your message. To continually improve support services, SAP analyzes all customer feedback thoroughly.

SAP Software Distribution Center SAP Support Packages, which contain software corrections, boost the performance and stability of your SAP solution. In the SAP Support Portal, you can download these SAP Support Packages and other patches (such as binary or database patches) to your local PC or by using the download basket in the SAP Software Distribution Center, and import them to your system using standard SAP tools. Since the structure of the navigation tree varies depending on the SAP software license your company has purchased, the display is customer-specific. It is also very easy to download Support Package Stacks recommended by SAP, which are bundles of Support Packages for particular products.

You can also subscribe to information about SAP Support Packages for products and releases that are of interest to you. As soon as a new Support Package matching your requirements becomes available, a message is sent to your inbox.

Other functions In addition to the support functions described above, the SAP Support Portal contains other functions, which will be mentioned only briefly. These functions allow you to open service connections and request license keys or developer and object keys, which are necessary for modifying SAP source code. You can also maintain user data in this portal.

User data administration *Central user data administration* in the SAP Support Portal enables both SAP customers and partners to manage their user data themselves. The employee chosen as administrator is granted the appropriate authorization and can then request users free of charge for his or her colleagues and assign authorizations to them for the support functions. Users that are no longer required can be deleted.

Online catalogs Various providers offer services for SAP solutions through a wide range of channels; however, only the SAP Service Marketplace and its portals provide central access to the entire service offering of SAP and its partners. This saves you time when you're looking for the right service, an appropriate training course, or a suitable partner for a particular service. Because the services are available online, you can access them at any time and from any location, and place your order; you don't need to worry about contacting the providers during their official business hours. You can order support services and software in the SAP Support Portal.

SAP Service Catalog contains SAP's comprehensive range of support services. You can access fee-based services and services included in the maintenance package. Each service is displayed with details of its scope, price, and delivery conditions.

SAP Service Catalog

Once you have ordered an on-site service, an SAP specialist will contact you to adapt the content and scope of the service to meet the specific requirements of your SAP solution. If you ordered a service that is delivered over a remote connection, you'll receive an order confirmation as soon as you place the order. You can retrieve any other information relating to service delivery, such as confirmation of the delivery date or a questionnaire for indicating how the services should be prepared, from your inbox. Not only does this save you time, but also you don't have to make any unnecessary inquiries at your local Customer Interaction Center.

You can also purchase the SAP software you require from an online shop in the SAP Support Portal. The SAP Software Shop stocks software DVDs for almost all SAP products, which are available for a variety of platforms supported by SAP. To place orders, a user needs authorization, which you can assign yourself. This allows you to decide who is authorized to order software in your company.

SAP Software Catalog

SAP Developer Network

The *SAP Developer Network* (SDN) is the technology-focused portal for SAP customers and partners. SAP has been promoting knowledge transfer between consultants, developers, and administrators for over 30 years. The SDN was launched for TechEd 2003 to provide online access to technical expertise regarding SAP products and to facilitate sharing of this knowledge with customers and other consultants.

For the first two years, the SDN was designed for developers and consultants, focusing, in particular, on the new SAP NetWeaver technology platform and SAP xApps. Since the second half of 2005, additional discussion forums and weblogs for all SAP products have been added, making the network attractive to application consultants, software architects, and business process analysts as well. The SDN has also been networked with the other SAP portals to create a truly integrated offering.

Users can access the following information and services:

▶ Product information, how-to guides, tutorials, documentation, roadmaps, articles relating to future technology (such as ESA), tips, and SAP Notes (for customers only)

- ▶ Test and evaluation software for downloading, such as SAP NetWeaver components for a limited period of time, coding examples, and business packages for the SAP NetWeaver Portal

- ▶ E-learning units, such as recordings of technical presentations for events like TechEd, and access to SAP Online Knowledge Products

- ▶ Information exchange with the SAP Ecosystem through:

    - ▶ Discussion forums for particular topics and products

    - ▶ Collaboration rooms (protected areas accessible only to certain users and offering project or product-related applications and information) for individual customers and projects

    - ▶ Weblogs (frequently updated websites with informal diary-like entries) from experts, to which users can submit queries or comments

- ▶ A search function that accesses the SDN and the Help and Support Portal to provide an integrated overview of all key information

- ▶ A personal business card for every member, facilitating contact with other members of the community

- ▶ A points system to recognize the authors who contribute most to specific topics

Examples of collaboration

One of the objectives of these offerings is to further reduce installation times and thereby improve TCO, while facilitating collaboration with and between SAP customers. The following examples are testament to the success of these offerings:

- ▶ Close collaboration between SAP product managers and software architects and customers' developers resulted in new features for Business Server Pages (BSPs)—a part of SAP NetWeaver—being incorporated in the platform almost 1:1. Without the open communication afforded by the SDN, this would not have been possible.

- ▶ The average response time in ABAP and BSP forums is currently 10 minutes. More than 1,000 new topics and queries are opened or replied to daily in all the forums. The vast majority of top contributors to forums and weblogs are developers and consultants of customers or partners.

With 350,000 registered users and over 12 million page views per month, the SDN has grown over the last two years to become the main platform on which the SAP Ecosystem shares technology-related information and other expertise.

From the outset, the SDN is built on SAP technology. This was a strategic decision, not only to demonstrate the power and flexibility of SAP NetWeaver, but also to give SAP customers living proof of all the capabilities of this new technology:

Built on SAP technology

▶ The SDN pages are based on SAP NetWeaver Portal.

▶ Knowledge Management, a subcomponent of SAP NetWeaver Portal, is the foundation for content management and the collaboration rooms.

▶ The cross-portal search facility builds on the comprehensive TREX (search and classification) functions.

▶ The discussion forums and weblogs are non-SAP products that have been fully integrated in SDN.

▶ The portals are accessed using SAP Passport or SSO.

Future SDN services will be aimed at the special needs of the new target groups—business process analysts and software architects. The further development of ESA will result in the SDN handling a large portion of communication for the enterprise services processes. The necessary functions will be implemented during 2006.

SAP Channel Partner Portal

The *SAP Channel Partner Portal* (*http://channel.sap.com*) is the central e-collaboration platform for all SAP Channel Partners. In addition to providing the latest information and promoting knowledge transfer, it comprises sales, consulting, and support applications. It is instrumental in promoting direct and close collaboration between SAP and its Channel Partners, who can access the relevant information in the portal to ensure that customers receive an optimal service.

Users can choose from the following key areas:

Key areas

▶ **Manage my Partnership**
SAP Channel Partners can check the status of the partnership, edit their company profile and contact data, and handle their annual business planning.

▶ **mySAP All-in-One & SAP Business One Solutions**
This area supports the Partner Solution Network and promotes communication between partners. Users can access all the development tools and information they require to develop their solutions.

- ▶ **Partner Networking**
  This area of the portal allows all SAP Channel Partners to network with other partners. Specific partner areas present all the details of a partner's solution and services. This promotes and supports business relationships between partners.

- ▶ **Education**
  Focuses on e-learning components, because it is critical for small and midsize enterprises (SMEs) to have a training offering that is cost-efficient as well as being independent from time and location.

- ▶ **Support Service**
  Helps partners to set up their own support processes and offers central services for handling problems consistently and quickly.

Due to the significance of local markets, the SAP Channel Partner Portal has a very regional structure. The global SAP Channel Partner Portal is supplemented by various national portals featuring information and services, which are tailored to the local market and available in the respective native language.

At present, the portal has around 30,000 registered users. With more than 70,000 hits a week, the SAP Channel Partner Portal is an integral part of business processes between SAP Channel Partners and SAP.

SAP Business One Customer Portal

The SAP Business One Customer Portal is the main source of information and the platform for web-based support for customers who use SAP Business One. It provides all the information they need to resolve standard problems independently for SAP Business One. This information is available in the:

- ▶ SAP Notes database (includes SAP HotNews, SAP TopNotes, and FAQ Notes)

- ▶ SAP Business One Knowledge Base (release-dependent collection of documents on various topics)

- ▶ E-learning units (SAP Tutor recordings, flash books, and similar)

FAQ Notes provide solutions to standard problems in a particular module or submodule from the SAP Business One application. Users can locate useful information quickly for the exact area of the application they are currently using.

The portal provides access to the core support and administration applications that users need for their day-to-day activities. The only prerequisites are Internet access, a user ID, and authorization for the relevant application. The following applications are available:

▶ Message tool

▶ System data maintenance

▶ Installations and updates

▶ User administration

▶ License key request

If customers still require more information, an integrated message application allows them to request help easily from SAP or from the SAP partner assigned to them. Key system information is recorded automatically when the message is created, which simplifies and accelerates the support process. Customers can choose to be informed by email when SAP or the SAP partner replies, so that they don't have to continuously monitor the application.

SAP Partner Portal

With more than 100,000 accesses each month, the *SAP Partner Portal* is the main platform and best single source of tools, information, and Web services for SAP partners—excluding SAP Channel Partners, for whom a separate portal is available. In addition to current news, distributed via the SAP Global Partner Newsletter and Newsflash, the SAP Partner Portal comprises the following areas:

▶ **Events**
Content
The SAP Partner Portal announces events that are dedicated to inspiring, enabling, and offering several key opportunities for partners. It informs partners about events that are specifically for them, and provides information about SAP solutions and showcases for the latest business strategies focusing on their needs. In addition, partner-tailored information about key corporate international and national events is available.

▶ **Marketing & Sales**
The *Marketing & Sales* area provides tools and information for SAP and partners to undertake joint marketing and sales activities. The marketing section offers valuable assets such as the partner branding guide, partner recognition programs, SAP PR policies for partners, and guidelines for joint marketing activities.

In addition, the sales section contains offline demos for partners, partner playbooks, partner sales kits, and information about the Joint Sales Engagement—a process that facilitates communication and information exchange between the SAP sales force and its partners so that they can cooperate in the field.

▶ **Ramp-Up**
SAP Ramp-Up processes play an important role in incorporating partners' feedback to enhance products and services for the launch of SAP's most recent software editions. The Ramp-Up section of the SAP Partner Portal is the platform that informs SAP partners about Ramp-Up news, processes, and how they can get involved in SAP Ramp-Up. It provides information about Ramp-Up contacts, active and upcoming Ramp-Ups as well as Ramp-Up partner guidelines and knowledge transfer. Furthermore, it offers partners online services such as nomination forms, learning map order forms, and online Ramp-Up project feedback.

▶ **Test & Demo Licenses**
The Partner Portal *Test & Demo Licenses* section offers SAP partners a globally valid licensing agreement that grants access to the full spectrum of SAP solution packages and components for testing, demonstration, and partner-internal training purposes. Partners can select the licensing model that best fits their requirements, based on their SAP partner status. The SAP Partner Portal offers a streamlined process for ordering test and demo licenses with a unified and simplified order form and gives partners access to a complete list of available packages and components.

▶ **Education**
The *Education* section provides a full array of educational options for partners to ensure they have the latest information they need for implementing, supporting, and working with SAP solutions. It also contains guides to educational programs and services, providing information, curriculum, and delivery options to fit any educational need for the latest SAP solutions.

▶ **Support**
The *Support* section informs partners about SAP's unparalleled support service portfolio, which offers customers the necessary assistance to optimize their software solution, to enhance their business processes, to achieve lower TCO, and to accelerate the ROI. Furthermore, the Support section provides access to software downloads, as well as information about maintenance tools, SAP Solution Manager, and the

SAP Implementation Quality Program. In addition, partners will find information about SAP's worldwide support centers, the SAP Support Academy, and remote connections to SAP.

▶ **Partnering with SAP**
Because partnering is important for mutual success, SAP has worked with partners to develop a strong partner ecosystem and provide customers with solutions and services that add value. This section describes the different partner categories and the partner program in the *Partnering Guide*. Moreover, partners have access to information about SAP partners and their offerings in the SAP Partner Information Center. Partners will also find information about the application and certification process, as well as an online application form.

SAP Help Portal

Knowledge in terms of a structural, corporate resource is useful only if, when required, it is easily accessible, comprehensive, and well structured. At *http://help.sap.com*, the SAP Help Portal offers you the entire documentation for all SAP solutions and products.

Web-based access to documentation

Members of the SAP Ecosystem can retrieve these documents at any time or place without having to install the entire content locally, using a documentation DVD, for instance. Such easy access is practical when you require only a small amount of information from various areas. Another advantage of the portal vis-à-vis conventional media such as DVDs is that the downloads offered for documentation patches and updates are always the latest versions.

Besides documentation for implementing, customizing, installing, and upgrading, the SAP Help Portal also features a glossary of over 22,000 SAP-related terms. Thanks to the latest search technology developed by SAP, huge volumes of data—currently over nine million documents—instead of being overwhelming and therefore trying on your patience, can be searched, prepared, and displayed clearly in a matter of seconds. Essentially, members of the SAP Ecosystem can access the entire SAP Library and therefore obtain any documentation they need at any time, which means that it's often not even necessary to request support from SAP.

Due to the smooth interaction between the SAP Help Portal and other platforms, such as SAP Solution Manager or the SAP Developer Network, users are offered content that meets their current needs. In the future, additional functions will be in place to accommodate customer-specific requirements even better:

▶ Option of connecting directly to the system and comparing the content automatically

▶ Documentation accompanying each phase throughout the entire product lifecycle

Customer-Specific Access to SAP Service Marketplace

Large companies that carry out SAP projects on a global scale have a greater need to exchange information with SAP. By providing customer-specific access to the SAP Service Marketplace, SAP gives them new impetus for intensifying collaboration. The SAP Service Marketplace includes areas designed as customer portals. In the interest of improving communication between employees, customers can also provide information here that is relevant to the target group.

In practice: DaimlerChrysler AG

At the beginning of 2004, the DaimlerChrysler SAP Service Marketplace was created as part of a pilot project and was made available to DaimlerChrysler AG as an SAP portal. Members of DaimlerChrysler's SAP Community can use the portal as a central, company-specific source of all SAP-related information.

"The idea behind developing a company-specific SAP portal was to simplify and, simultaneously intensify global collaboration at company level," explained Stefan Helbing, head of the Training & Know-How workgroup at DaimlerChrysler SAP C4 (Corporate Customer Competence Center). "It is advantageous for our employees to access the marketplace, because they can use quick links or the SAP C4 homepage to obtain information fast." On the DaimlerChrysler SAP Service Marketplace, employees can also view and book the training courses held at the training center in Walldorf.

Furthermore, all DaimlerChrysler employees working in tandem with SAP on global projects can directly upload large, project-related documents—such as definition collections and presentation documents—to special sections to make them available to other project participants.

DaimlerChrysler can also draw attention to topics that are relevant to the company in the news section. The global availability of Daimler-Chrysler SAP Service Marketplace is another advantage for users.

Helbing summed it up as follows: "For our staff, DaimlerChrysler SAP Service Marketplace is an ideal platform in the SAP environment. It renders cross-company collaboration less complex, permits us to exchange information with SAP, and enables us to access SAP support applications quickly."

Although only the key aspects have been highlighted, you should have an insight into the diversity of information, collaborative services, and functions that the SAP Service Marketplace and portals currently offer. Despite this impressive offering, SAP is continuing its efforts to enhance information management and to develop new customer-oriented functions. To provide you with optimum support for your SAP solution, SAP also intends to strengthen the link between the support platform SAP Solution Manager (see Section 7.1) and the SAP Service Marketplace even further.

7.3 How SAP Solution Manager and SAP Service Marketplace Interact

The customer's SAP Solution Manager is connected to SAP Service Marketplace via the Internet and an RFC data connection, which enables electronic workflows spanning both platforms. Interaction between SAP Solution Manager at the frontend, which has direct access to the customer's landscape, and SAP Service Marketplace at the backend of SAP's global support organization, establishes a platform for professional, collaborative service and support processes. These processes, in turn, enable the provision of proactive services, which are tailored to meet the customer's individual needs and requirements. This maximizes the reliability and performance of the customer's software solution and ultimately helps to reduce operating costs and accelerate ROI.

Support infrastructure

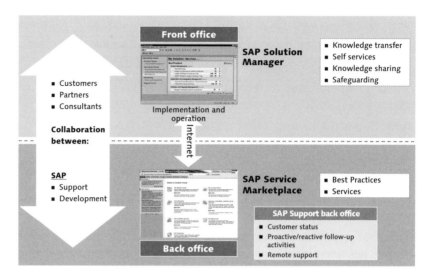

Figure 7.6 Interaction Between SAP Solution Manager and SAP Service Marketplace

7.3.1 Cross-Platform Service and Support Processes

The following section describes some examples of cross-platform service and support processes, some of which are already being used by most SAP customers.

SAP EarlyWatch Alert

SAP EarlyWatch Alert (EWA), a service for monitoring SAP systems, was originally delivered via SAP's support systems. SAP Solution Manager, however, now enables this service to be carried out at the customer site, allowing you to make your processes more efficient.

Automated flow   Once you have set up the EWA in SAP Solution Manager, it is fully automatic and monitors the status of your SAP systems at regular intervals. Using this proactive analysis, SAP Solution Manager generates regular status reports for your IT management team. Details of serious problems are documented in the report and forwarded to SAP Active Global Support so that they can help you further. The information is transferred automatically via a link between SAP Solution Manager and the SAP Service Marketplace.

SAP EarlyWatch Check   If a red warning signal is displayed, SAP provides you with the SAP EarlyWatch Check remote service to analyze the situation in more detail. As part of the SAP Standard Support offering, you can use this service up to twice a year for each of your live installations.

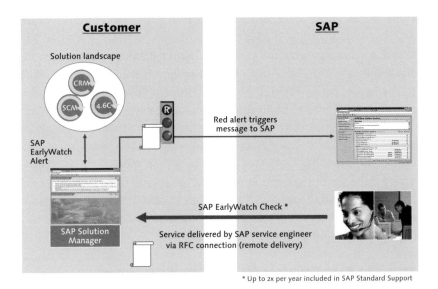

Customer   **SAP**

Solution landscape

CRM

SCM   4.6C

SAP
EarlyWatch
Alert

Red alert triggers
message to SAP

SAP Solution
Manager

SAP EarlyWatch Check *

Service delivered by SAP service engineer
via RFC connection (remote delivery)

* Up to 2x per year included in SAP Standard Support

Figure 7.7 Connection Between SAP EarlyWatch Alert and SAP EarlyWatch Check

Where appropriate, the EWA report recommends services for analyzing and eliminating problems and provides links to the SAP Service Catalog, which contains detailed descriptions of the recommended services and enables you to order them online. Orders are sent directly to SAP's service delivery team. Further communication regarding orders takes place via the SAP Service Channel—a two-way communication medium between you and SAP. SAP Service Channel messages are sent both to employees' personal inboxes on SAP Service Marketplace and directly to SAP Solution Manager.

Even if the monitored systems are running smoothly, SAP Solution Manager sends a monthly status report to the SAP support team via the SAP Service Marketplace. Based on the findings in this monthly status report, a generic status report is created every quarter in the SAP back office. This report is, in turn, supplied to the customer's IT management team via the SAP Service Channel.

Message Processing

Message processing was described in Section 7.1.4, which focused primarily on the Service Desk in SAP Solution Manager. We'll now take a brief look at how the process is distributed over SAP's two support platforms, enabling customers and SAP to collaborate more effectively.

When a user enters a problem message, it's sent to the customer's own SAP Solution Manager system. The customer's support employee can look for a suitable solution in the SAP Notes database on SAP Service Marketplace and use the Note Assistant to import the relevant SAP Note to the appropriate system. If necessary, the employee can also forward the message directly to SAP's support organization via SAP Solution Manager. If the SAP specialist has to analyze the problem in greater detail, he or she can log on to the customer's SAP Solution Manager system via a data connection. This provides access to all the monitors and analysis tools for the various systems in the customer solution. To reconstruct the problem, the SAP specialist can access the desktop of the customer's support employee or even the desktop of the user who originally reported the problem, using an application-sharing tool.

Access to Best Practices for Solution Management

SAP Solution Manager offers you Best Practices for Solution Management tailored to your SAP solution. These are documents that can help you implement and run your SAP solution. You choose the relevant document and then proceed to SAP Service Marketplace, where you can download it. This is where SAP always posts the most recent document versions.

7.3.2 Enhanced Support Infrastructure to Enable New Processes

iView The SAP NetWeaver Portal has a role concept that lets you provide specific groups within your company with specialized information to support their day-to-day activities. SAP plans to provide an iView (portlet) that you can install in your SAP NetWeaver Portal to facilitate even greater integration of the support infrastructure in your working environment. The iView, which is part of the portal solution, extracts data from applications, documents, and the Internet, and displays it in the portal. It is installed in your portal and assigned to certain user roles. Users then have system-based access to the relevant support applications and information.

Each user personalizes the iView just once, by selecting the relevant installations from the list of all those available. This configuration data is stored locally in your portal. When an employee logs on to the portal, the iView automatically connects to the SAP Service Marketplace and updates the information. Single Sign-On (SSO) means the employee is logged on to SAP Service Marketplace automatically without having to enter a user ID or password.

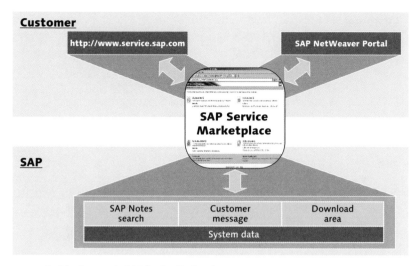

Customer

http://www.service.sap.com SAP NetWeaver Portal

SAP Service Marketplace

SAP

SAP Notes search	Customer message	Download area
System data		

- Direct access to SAP Service Marketplace
    - All required support functions are available
    - Support application based on customer's system data
- Support applications integrated in customer's portal (optional)

Figure 7.8 Support Applications with SAP Service Marketplace

iView features include:

Features

▶ Display of all the service reports about the customer's system

▶ SAP Notes Search for a particular system

▶ System data maintenance for a selected system

▶ Message entry for a selected system

▶ Status overview for customer messages for a selected system

▶ New downloads for a selected system

▶ Display of SAP HotNews and SAP TopNotes for a selected system

The information is updated at defined intervals and, if necessary, can also be updated by users at the click of a button.

Customers who use SAP Solution Manager can easily incorporate information from SAP Solution Manager in the iView; for example, they can display performance data for the key transactions or warning messages about critical system statuses. Consequently, system administrators can check the current status of their systems at a glance, without leaving their familiar working environment.

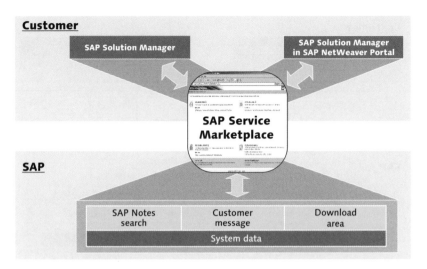

Customer

SAP Solution Manager

SAP Solution Manager
in SAP NetWeaver Portal

SAP Service Marketplace

SAP

SAP Notes search	Customer message	Download area
System data		

- Implementation, solution monitoring, Service Desk with SAP Solution Manager
- Support applications based on business processes in customer's solution
- SAP Solution Manager integrated in customer's portal (optional)

Figure 7.9 Support Applications with SAP Solution Manager and SAP Service Marketplace

	SMP	SMP, NP	SMP, Sol. Man	SMP, NP, Sol. Man
Basic functions				
All necessary support functions available	✓	✓	✓	✓
System data automatically updated by EWA	✓	✓	✓	✓
Access to all information on SAP Service Marketplace	✓	✓	✓	✓
Support applications based on customer's system data	✓	✓	✓	✓
Role-based access to information		✓		✓

* SMP   – SAP Service Marketplace
* NP   – SAP NetWeaver Portal
* Sol. Man – SAP Solution Manager
* EWA   – SAP EarlyWatch Alert

Figure 7.10 Comparison of Functions for Different Scenarios—Additional Functions Are Available Only if SAP Solution Manager Is Implemented (1)

	SMP	SMP, NP	SMP, Sol. Man	SMP, NP, Sol. Man
Additional functions				
Implementation			✓	✓
Solution monitoring with integration in Service Desk			✓	✓
Powerful Service Desk			✓	✓
Qualified message creation			✓	✓
Immediate forwarding of critical customer situations to SAP			✓	✓
Support applications based on customer's business processes (incl. third-party systems)			✓	✓
Services can be run in SAP Solution Manager			✓	✓

* SMP   – SAP Service Marketplace
* NP   – SAP NetWeaver Portal
* Sol. Man – SAP Solution Manager

Figure 7.11 Comparison of Functions for Different Scenarios—Additional Functions Are Available Only if SAP Solution Manager Is Implemented (2)

8   Cost Transparency with SAP TCO Framework

IT costs are a top priority for every CEO. But reducing costs while increasing IT flexibility can sometimes seem like an insurmountable hurdle. SAP's ESA strategy provides the requisite flexibility, while SAP TCO Framework now provides a basis for keeping costs transparent and identifying cost savers.

The economic situation in recent years has intensified the need in many companies for a detailed and comprehensive cost analysis procedure. Only this kind of procedure provides the level of transparency that enables companies to effectively tackle problem areas in a targeted way. They are looking for methods and tools to measure and evaluate cost structures and for ways to make results usable and, ultimately, to reduce costs.

In 2003, SAP decided to make the subject of total cost of ownership (TCO) a central factor in all strategic development decisions. The TCO of future products is now a focal point during development. SAP also included existing products in the new strategy to identify and leverage cost-saving potential for these products; however, SAP wanted to do much more to exploit the potential for reducing customers' IT costs. To do this, SAP needed to get an accurate picture of customers' IT structures, to correlate this to the costs, and then to check this data using key figures.

TCO as a central strategic factor

The problem at the time was twofold. First, customers' IT environments had become highly complex and highly specific. Second, previous TCO analyses were very specialized and could be compared to each other only if the same party had carried them out. Even then, they didn't necessarily determine SAP-specific circumstances, which are highly relevant and important to SAP customers. Neither of these factors did anything to help create far-reaching and comprehensive transparency. To surpass these limitations, in June 2004, SAP decided to create its own TCO framework as a way to establish its own TCO standards within its customer base.

The idea of SAP TCO Framework is to enable customers to collect data about their own IT landscape in a standardized manner. Customers themselves can compare the current data with data from previous years. A still more appealing option is to forward the data to SAP for analysis and evaluation. SAP can use the data to develop benchmarks for the customer.

Idea of SAP TCO Framework

The data can then be compared with other customers' data to give a better impression of the current cost distribution. Besides the ability to compare data, another definitive advantage of the analysis is that it links potential savings to viable cost-cutting measures.

8.1 SAP TCO Framework

IT cost blocks

Today's IT costs are made up of many different cost blocks, as shown in Figure 8.1. Not only do costs arise from the day-to-day operation of systems and hardware; the purchase and initial implementation of software and hardware, and any upgrades and expansion projects also incur costs. All these costs must be considered. If we analyze IT costs more closely, we see that they can be influenced by two factors:

▶ IT practices
All IT processes are regarded as applied IT practices—whether they are work processes used by administrators of databases, operating systems, or software, or processes within a support structure. Particularly interesting is the degree to which IT processes are automated or standardized.

▶ Company environment
A company's environment can include the number of end users, the data volume, the scope of the software in use, system availability requirements, and even the size of the company and the industry in which it operates.

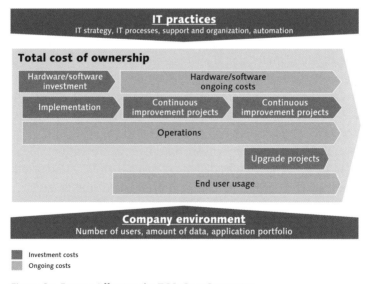

Figure 8.1 Factors Affecting the TCO Cost Categories

It's clear that the company environment has less potential for cost savings—which SAP can influence—than the IT methods it employs. Many company parameters, such as system availability requirements and industry, are fixed. Of course, this doesn't mean that we should completely disregard the company environment when looking at cost-saving potential. There are always individual areas in which SAP can provide immediate, direct help. The data volume accumulated over the years and its associated costs, for example, can be reduced considerably by services such as SAP Data Volume Management. Complex system landscapes can be simplified by judiciously exploiting new products and techniques, using the System Landscape Optimization (SLO) services for example, which, in turn, can help to minimize costs.

Potential for cost savings

Overall, the IT practices area is the principal focus of SAP's attention. In many cases, this area contains much untapped potential for cost cutting, particularly in small and midsize companies. SAP TCO Framework, however, takes a holistic approach to IT costs, identifying potential in both the IT practices area and the company environment.

8.2 Building Blocks of SAP TCO Framework

If we look at current approaches to analyzing TCO, we see that two things are indispensable for a TCO concept. One is cost categories according to which the data is organized, and the other is a list of questions that are used to classify the analyzed data and to assign it to the correct cost category. The cost categories are set up in accordance with a TCO model. Rather than being regarded as a separate aspect, reference data is collected together with the cost data via a clearly laid-out questionnaire. An example of this kind of approach is the one used by Gartner.

In SAP TCO Framework, reference data and cost categories are defined separately as individual building blocks. This facilitates information gathering because the questions are answered by people in different departments in the customer's company. The questions relating to costs are best answered by management or controlling staff, while the IT staff is usually the best source for reference information and details about the IT methods used. The separation of data within SAP TCO Framework is intended to reflect this situation by allowing staff to answer the questions in their area of expertise. Once the data has been collected, the next concerns are, of course, data storage, data analysis, and conclusions.

Reference data and cost categories

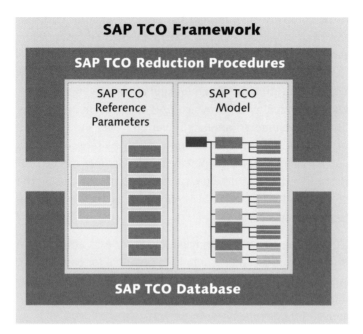

SAP TCO Framework

SAP TCO Reduction Procedures

SAP TCO Reference Parameters

SAP TCO Model

SAP TCO Database

Figure 8.2 SAP TCO Framework

SAP TCO Database

SAP TCO Framework (see Figure 8.2) is the basis for SAP TCO Database, in which the collected TCO data is stored, as well as for data analysis by SAP. SAP TCO Database enables SAP customers to identify cost-intensive areas and allows SAP to respond appropriately to these analyses, either with additional services, tools, or even new products.

Customers expect a TCO analysis to provide concrete suggestions on how to reduce costs. In some cases, a customer-specific cost reduction program is required. However, in the majority of cases, existing cost-cutting measures can be used as a basis and then adapted as needed. These SAP TCO Reduction Procedures are another building block in SAP TCO Framework. Essentially, they analyze existing services, tools, and products in terms of cost in order to show SAP customers where real savings can be made. The following section explains the building blocks of SAP TCO Framework in greater detail.

8.2.1 SAP TCO Model

SAP TCO Model records and represents all cost areas (cost categories) that are relevant for analyzing a software solution. It has a tree structure (see Figure 8.3), so the information given for each cost factor becomes more detailed at each subsequent level. The customer can obtain an overview of the costs at a higher level of the tree, or, if required, view the costs in greater detail at the lower levels of the tree (provided this detailed information is available).

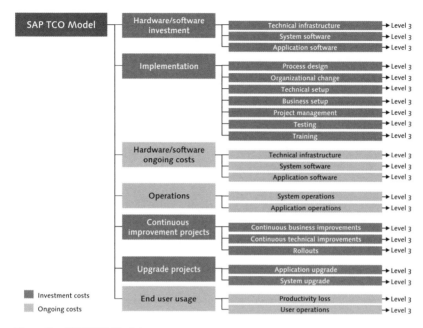

Figure 8.3 SAP TCO Model

The benefits of SAP TCO Model can be summarized as follows:

▶ A standardized procedure for identifying costs

▶ A basis for cost analyses

▶ An overall view of the entire lifecycle of a software solution

The following discussion is an in-depth look at the model.

Standardized procedure for identifying costs

SAP TCO Model contains all cost categories that are relevant to the use of a software solution, especially to an SAP solution. To facilitate the creation of a non-SAP-specific, generic cost analysis, however, the highest levels of the TCO Model are completely neutral and not specific to SAP software. SAP-specific costs are included only at the lower levels. Detailed data should be collected only in cases where there is a realistic expectation that it can be determined correctly, or that a complete set of data is available.

Basis for cost analysis

For data analysis, it is essential to base the analysis on a body of high quality data that is consistent enough to be useful for comparison purposes. The standardized procedure from SAP of using a questionnaire guarantees this high quality. Moreover, it is also important that the cost data is recorded clearly and in accordance with its source. Specifically, this means taking the different cost types into account. SAP TCO Model differentiates between investment costs and ongoing costs, as well as direct and indirect costs. Investment costs are one-off costs, and come under the headings of hardware/software investment, implementation, continuous improvement projects, and upgrade projects in the model (see Figure 8.3). Ongoing costs, on the other hand, come under ongoing hardware/software costs, operations, and end user usage. Direct costs are those costs that can be recorded within the normal financial accounting processes, while indirect costs are initially difficult to quantify. Examples of indirect costs are process costs caused by inefficiency, and unplanned costs that arise due to malfunctions such as system failures.

Overall view of the entire lifecycle of a software solution

When we refer to operating costs over the entire lifecycle of software, we assume that the software is not just purchased (investment costs), but is also run (operations). It may be extended (continuous improvement projects), and it may be upgraded to new versions, possibly in components (upgrade). We form an accurate picture of the total cost of ownership of the software in question only when all these costs are considered. However, flexibility is also extremely important here. For this reason, the cost categories have been structured to allow individual costs to be analyzed. For example, it may be necessary to analyze costs in the operations area separately. Note at this point that SAP TCO Model conforms to IT Infrastructure Library (ITIL) best practices and, therefore, is based on standards that are already established in many customers' environments.

8.2.2 SAP TCO Reference Parameters

Collecting and recording costs are only one part of the TCO analysis. The other essential step is to classify the cost data. SAP TCO Reference Parameters ensure that this is carried out in a structured manner. The parameters are divided into two areas—company environment and IT practices (see Section 8.1)—and describe what a customer actually gets in return for the costs defined in SAP TCO Model. It is the interplay of the model and the reference parameters in SAP TCO Framework that make it possible to carry out the subsequent costs analysis.

The following points summarize the properties of SAP TCO Reference Parameters.

▶ **Structured design**
Like SAP TCO Model, the reference parameters have a structured design, which guides the customer through the questionnaire. As with the TCO model, there are general as well as SAP-specific questions. Most of the SAP-specific questions are in the IT practices area.

▶ **Context-sensitive data collection**
SAP TCO Model gives the customer the opportunity to focus on individual cost categories, such as operations or upgrades. This is why the reference parameters have to reflect this division of categories. The IT practices parameters are intended to record exact processes and procedures and depend on the scope of the analysis. They have been adapted to the cost categories in SAP TCO Model and contain a block of parameters for each category.

The company environment parameters are not affected. These are more general, and all the questions regarding the company environment are always asked, because the parameters represent the minimum amount of information that is necessary for the analysis.

▶ **Data comparability**
The comparability of the data in the SAP TCO Model is an important aspect of the data analysis procedure. Data can be used for comparison purposes only if the reference parameters are used. This is why the reference parameters are a central building block in SAP TCO Framework. The higher the level of detail in the reference data from the customer, the more precise the subsequent comparison can be.

8.2.3 SAP TCO Database

Another building block of SAP TCO Framework is the SAP TCO Database. This database functions as the central repository for the completed questionnaires. In other words, reference parameters and the collected cost data are stored here. The customer uses the questionnaire provided by SAP to collect data. Once a completed questionnaire is sent back to SAP, it is imported to the database, a process that is performed completely automatically. To ensure that the data is of sufficient quality, a validation check is carried out during the import process. If any inconsistencies are detected, the questionnaire is rejected and SAP asks the customer to validate the correctness of the data.

Data analysis Once the data has been imported to the database, it is subject to a number of procedures. First, a basic, multistep data analysis is carried out and made available to the customer. It provides a preliminary overview of how the company's costs compare to similar data from other customers.

All data is anonymous. A customer cannot determine which customer "owns" which data, and data protection regulations forbid this disclosure in any case. The storage of data in SAP TCO Database is handled like all other customer data, which is described in contracts between the customer and SAP.

Next, the data in the TCO database is extracted in condensed form. This extracted data is then used to present the findings of the questionnaire to the customer in an easy-to-read and easy-to-use format.

The customer is also advised about specific SAP services, tools, or products that have helped other customers to reduce costs. These recommendations are called SAP TCO Reduction Procedures (see Section 8.2.4).

Providing the data in a condensed form helps customers to realize how the TCO Reduction Procedures can be applied to everyday situations, which helps them to envision the benefits to their company.

In some cases, SAP may not be able to recommend suitable SAP TCO Reduction Procedures. If similar cost-intensive areas are identified across a wide range of customers during the analysis, it's a strong indicator that SAP needs to create new reduction procedures, services, or tools.

8.2.4   SAP TCO Reduction Procedures

SAP TCO Reduction Procedures are the fourth block in SAP TCO Framework. The basic objective of these procedures is to pass on good experiences and results from one customer to another. In other words, they take a new look at SAP services, tools, and products in terms of costs and recommend them in accordance with a customer's specific situation.

Assignment to cost categories Once again, the basis is the SAP TCO Model. SAP TCO Reduction Procedures are assigned to the cost categories in the model so that they can be compared. This enables us to see the area in which every single procedure reduces costs. Each SAP TCO Reduction Procedure also provides an overview of potential cost reductions. Finally, a list of reference customers is compiled to show which customers have cut costs using the relevant measure.

The next step involves describing which target group directly benefits in terms of cost optimization. If customers see themselves and their requirements reflected here, it indicates that the described SAP TCO Reduction Procedure could be relevant to them. A subsequent step highlights which specific areas could cut costs and why.

Where appropriate, SAP indicates the potential savings. This information is usually based on other customers' experiences, although it may also be obtained from analyses and measurements carried out by SAP.

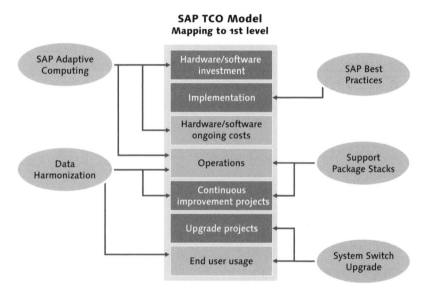

Figure 8.4 Ways in Which SAP Can Help Reduce TCO

When considering SAP services, products, and tools in terms of cost, we have to understand the cost areas in which SAP TCO Reduction Procedures can play a role. This is why they are always assigned to the SAP TCO Model. At present, SAP TCO Reduction Procedures are assigned to the first level in the SAP TCO Model. The goal is to map them to lower levels as soon as more detailed analyses become available. This assignment also shows at a glance the area in which cost reductions can be expected if the method in question is used.

Figure 8.4 gives five examples to illustrate how the assignment to SAP TCO Model is made. SAP Adaptive Computing, for instance, primarily helps reduce hardware/software costs, but also operations costs. SAP

Assignment to SAP TCO Model

Best Practices exclusively support the optimization of implementation projects. Support Package Stacks are Support Packages that SAP tests in special combinations and then makes available. The stacks enable you to obtain the current patch level much faster, which is often a prerequisite for expanding an application. When the stacks are implemented, they naturally have a positive impact on operations, which is why there is also an assignment to operations.

Upgrade　SAP System Switch Upgrade, a technology implemented using the SAP Web Application Server (SAP Web AS) application platform, shows that even upgrade projects offer considerable cost-saving potential. This technology can significantly reduce the downtime required for an upgrade. Of course, this advantage is reflected mainly in the indirect costs, because users become productive again much faster. Another example can be found in the SAP Data Harmonization services, which help customers to standardize data from different areas or systems. They primarily result in indirect cost savings—for example, caused by higher productivity due to harmonized data—but also reduce operating costs and the costs for extending the software.

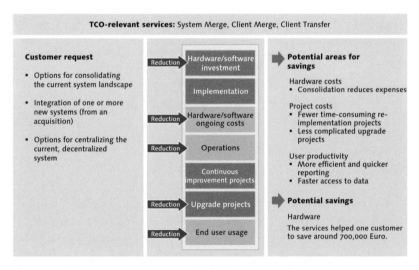

Figure 8.5 TCO-Relevant Services and SAP TCO Reduction Procedures—an Example

With reference to the System Merge, Client Merge, and Client Transfer services, Figure 8.5 illustrates how the TCO-relevant services and SAP TCO Reduction Procedures interact. The figure cited for potential hardware savings pertains to a real case, where the services helped one company save 700,000 Euro (approx. 840,000 USD).

8.3   Reducing Costs with SAP TCO Framework

Today's IT landscapes differ considerably in terms of company requirements and the IT processes applied. This makes the task of identifying the
potential for optimization more challenging, but not impossible. The
ongoing standardization of IT processes, by ITIL for instance, will surely
make the task easier in the future.

SAP TCO Framework gives companies a means of achieving transparent
and comparable IT costs. SAP TCO Database helps to identify potentials
for reducing costs and to take appropriate measures. Analyzing such measures using SAP TCO Reduction Procedures makes it easier to set priorities for implementation. Not all the examples described in SAP TCO
Reduction Procedures will be relevant and useful for every customer. It is
therefore vital that the customer can determine which examples are relevant for his or her system landscape to figure out the potential for optimization. This is precisely what SAP TCO Framework aims to do.

Identify
potential—take
measures

A Quick Links for SAP Service Marketplace and the Portals

Application management	/application-management
Best Practices for Solution Management	/solutionmanagerbp
Communities	/communities
Company data	/cusdata
Connection to SAP	/access-support
Consulting	/consulting
Customer messages, creating	/message
Development requests	/rollin
Education	/education
Fiscal year change	/fyc
Hosting	/hosting
Installation and upgrade documentation	/instguides
Internet connection to SAP	/internetconnection
License auditing services	/licenseauditing
License keys	/licensekeys
Maintenance	/maintenance
Namespaces	/namespaces
Note Assistant	/noteassistant
OS/DB migration, migration keys	/migrationkey
Partners of SAP	/partners
Release notes	/releasenotes
Release strategy	/releasestrategy
Remote connection to SAP	/remoteconnection
Roadmaps	/roadmaps
SAP Best Practices	/bestpractices
SAP Books	/sapbooks
SAP Business Process Management	/bpm
SAP Business Process Performance Optimization	/bppo
SAP Channel Partner Portal	http://channel.sap.com

SAP Codepage Conversion Check	/codepageconversion
SAP Consultant Education	/ce
SAP Custom Development	/customdev
SAP Customer Competence Center Net	/cccnet
SAP Data Archiving Optimization	/dao
SAP Data Management	/dma
SAP EarlyWatch Alert	/ewa
SAP EarlyWatch Check	/earlywatch
SAP Education	/education
SAP Empowering	/empowering
SAP Empowering workshops	/empoweringworkshops
SAP Euro Information Portal	/euro
SAP Expertise on Demand	/eod
SAP GoingLive Check	/goinglivecheck
SAP GoingLive Functional Upgrade Check	/goinglive-fu
SAP Hosting	/hosting
SAP HotNews	/hotnews
SAP Interface Management	/ifm
SAP Knowledge Shop	/knowledgecat
SAP Legacy System Migration Workbench (LSMW)	/lsmw
SAP MaxAttention	/maxattention
SAP NetWeaver	/netweaver
SAP Notes	/notes
SAP Online Knowledge Products	/okp
SAP Operations Competence Assessment	/soca
SAP OS/DB Migration Check	/osdbmigration
SAP Ramp-Up Knowledge Transfer	/rkt
SAP Remote Performance Optimization	/rpo
SAProuter, remote connection	/saprouter
SAP Safeguarding	/safeguarding
SAP Security Optimization	/sos
SAP Service Catalog	/servicecat

SAP Service Marketplace, information	/smp
SAP Software Distribution Center	/swdc
SAP Software Shop	/softwarecatalog
SAP Solution Management Assessment	/sma
SAP Solution Management Optimization	/smo
SAP Solution Manager	/solutionmanager
SAP Solution Maps/Business Maps	/solutionmaps
SAP Standard Support	/standardsupport
SAP Storage Subsystem Optimization	/stso
SAP Support Academy	/supportacademy
SAP System Administration	/sysadmin
SAP TCO Framework	/tco
SAP Test Management Optimization	/tmo
SAP TopNotes	/topnotes
SAP Volume Test Optimization	/vto
Sizing of mySAP Business Suite	/sizing
Solution Manager Diagnostics	/diagnostics
Support	/support
Support center addresses worldwide	/supportcenters /local-support
Support infrastructure	/support-infrastructure
Support services	/supportservices
System data, display and maintain	/system-data
System Landscape Optimization (SLO)	/slo
Training	/education
Training Self Services	/trainingcatalog
Upgrade	/upgrade
Upgrade services	/upgradeservices
Upgrade to mySAP ERP	/upgrade-erp
User data maintenance	/user-admin

B Glossary

Analysis of the Total Cost of Operation An analysis of the cost structure of a support organization to identify cost drivers and potential for optimizing costs.

Best Practices for Solution Management Documents that help you in the technical implementation and operation of your SAP solution.

Business Configuration Set A technology for grouping together Customizing settings flexibly so that they can be reused.

Client Consolidation The consolidation of two or more clients with a new or existing client. The source clients can be located in the same system as the target client or in a different system. The elements on the lower levels, such as company codes and controlling areas, either all remain as they are, or are consolidated in special subprojects using the conversion technology.

Client Migration Server (CMIS) A tool that helps to create multiclient environments. It helps to analyze planned client transfers to identify conflicts before performing the actual transfer. It can migrate a client to a different release and manage conversions from EBCDIC to ASCII and MDMP to Unicode.

Community A group of people or companies with common interests who actively communicate or collaborate to achieve their goals. Communities that leverage the web as their communication infrastructure are also called *virtual communities*.

Computing Center Management System (CCMS) An integrated suite of tools for monitoring and managing SAP R/3 systems and other SAP components, with which operations such as resource distribution and managing SAP databases can be automated.

Continuous Change (as Part of SAP Application Management) The implementation of new functions, components, and processes, for instance, a release upgrade.

Continuous Improvement A process of ongoing improvement for SAP solutions that involves optimizing processes, performance, application components, and Basis components.

Continuous Maintenance (as Part of SAP Application Management) Ongoing activities to monitor and optimize production SAP solutions, including the implementation of SAP Notes and service packages, data archiving, and monitoring for batch jobs.

Conversion Technology A technology developed by SAP for changing certain information (such as a specific company code), which has been determined automatically using a domain-based search in an SAP system. The search factors taken into account are master and transaction data, as well as Customizing settings. The SAP conversion services in System Landscape Optimization (SLO) are based on this conversion technology. The conversion technology can also be used in projects to optimize the system landscape, for example, if clients, company codes, or controlling areas are also expected to be merged when systems are consolidated.

Conversion Workbench (CWB) A tool for converting data, primarily within one SAP system. It can be used for changes to organizational structures, harmonizing data, and all kinds of data change. Similar technology is used to convert currencies.

Custom Development The act of creating unique, customer-specific solutions.

Customer Service Management A service that provides application-management customers with a designated contact person to support live SAP systems. It entails coordination and monitoring for all application-management services and ensures that the services are of a high standard and comply with Service Level Agreements.

Development Support These are support services provided by New Application Development (NAD) for new software components, by Installed Base Development (IBD) following volume shipment, and by Installed Base Maintenance and Support (IMS) for older releases.

eCATT (Extended Computer-Aided Test Tool) An enhancement of the Computer-Aided Test Tool (CATT), an SAP test tool that can be used universally. eCATT allows you to combine and automate business processes as repeatable test procedures.

IDoc A standard SAP format for exchanging data electronically between systems. Different message types, known as *IDoc types* (such as delivery note or purchase order), usually correspond to the different specific formats.

Internet Transaction Server (ITS) An interface between SAP R/3 and the Internet. The ITS allows Internet and intranet users to communicate directly with the SAP R/3 system by running business transactions, function

modules, and reports as Internet Application Components (IACs).

IT Infrastructure Library (ITIL) The de facto global standard in the area of IT Service Management. Developed for the British government, it contains comprehensive, publicly accessible, specialist documentation on the planning, provision, and support of IT services. The publications provide best practice guidelines for IT Service Management.

J2EE Java 2 Enterprise Edition (J2EE) is a platform from Sun Microsystems for developing and running web-based business applications.

Knowledge Management An integrated environment for creating, translating, presenting, distributing, and managing content, particularly for the areas of training, documentation, and quality manuals. It provides extensive tools and functions to support knowledge management and transfer.

Knowledge Productization Services (KPS) A service area that provides innovative products and services for transferring knowledge to SAP employees and customers.

Maintenance There are three maintenance phases:
→ Maintenance, mainstream →
Maintenance, extended →
Maintenance, customer-specific.

Maintenance, customer-specific The third maintenance phase. Customer-specific maintenance begins when mainstream or extended maintenance ends, or if the customer decides not to take advantage of the extended maintenance package. This phase is covered by the standard maintenance fee and does not have a fixed validity period. The services available are similar to those in mainstream maintenance, but with some restrictions.

Maintenance, extended The second, optional maintenance phase. Extended maintenance is offered, for an additional fee, when the mainstream maintenance period expires. It is usually offered for three years. The maintenance services available with mainstream maintenance continue to be provided.

Maintenance, mainstream The first maintenance phase. Mainstream maintenance usually lasts several years (under the new 5–1–2 maintenance strategy, five years of mainstream maintenance are offered). SAP charges the standard maintenance fee during this phase and provides all the features of → SAP Standard Support.

Migration Technology A technology for transferring data within SAP systems when system landscapes are consolidated:
(a) Data transfer using standard SAP tools, such as BAPIs or batch input, for consolidating SAP organizational units: In contrast to the conversion technology, the organizational units are consolidated on key dates, which means that the dataset that existed before the key date remains unchanged. Only the required master data and incomplete transactions are transferred to the target structure. The target structure's Customizing settings must be adapted as appropriate.
(b) Data transfer using the → Migration Workbench (MWB) or → SAP Legacy System Migration Workbench (LSMW).

Migration Workbench (MWB) A tool for migrating data between SAP systems. In the future, the MWB will be shipped with templates for specific scenarios and business objects.

mySAP Business Suite A suite of adaptive business solutions that networks all involved parties, information, and processes in order to boost the effectiveness of your business relationships. It is based on SAP NetWeaver. The applications always provide users throughout the corporate network with consistent results, thereby affording your company with the flexibility it needs to successfully adapt to changing market conditions.

Note Assistant A tool for implementing SAP Notes.

On-site service A service that is performed at the customer's site.

Primary Support Responsible for maintaining released SAP products and supporting customers if they encounter problems when using such products.

Remote Function Call (RFC) An SAP interface protocol that simplifies the programming of communication processes between systems and manages communication processes, parameter transfer, and error handling. The protocol calls and executes predefined functions in a remote system.

Remote service A service that is delivered via a remote connection rather than on site.

Roadmap An SAP methodology that includes a collection of documents with a structured list of activities and tasks, which are to be carried out in a specific sequence to ensure the success of a project. Examples: Implementation Roadmap, SAP Upgrade Road Map.

SAP Active Global Support SAP's support organization.

SAP Application Hosting Sets up systems, installs system components, provides a complete infrastructure, and operates customer systems in SAP's high-performance data centers.

SAP Application Integration A package of services that provides support and consulting services for developing and integrating customer-specific interfaces between SAP solutions and third-party applications.

SAP Best Practices A combined sales, training, demonstration, and implementation instrument that includes detailed documentation, a preconfigured system, and a comprehensible, reusable methodology.

SAP Business and Value Assessment A service that helps customers evaluate the business benefits they can achieve by implementing or enhancing IT solutions. They can quantify potential business value and use business value as the guiding principle throughout design and deployment.

SAP Business Applications Upgrade Consulting A service that helps customers take advantage of functional and technical enhancements and new SAP software releases. Customers can benefit quickly from new functions and run their business more efficiently.

SAP Business One Customer Portal The central source of information and the platform for web-based support for SAP Business One customers.

SAP Business Process Improvement A service that uses a proven methodology to improve business processes and fine-tune operations. The service enables customers to leverage SAP's industry-specific knowledge and support for Best Practices and to obtain additional benefit and value from their SAP solutions.

SAP Business Process Management A service that supports the monitoring and running of SAP customers' core business processes.

SAP Business Process Optimization A service that helps customers improve their business processes in support of their strategy. They can obtain more value from their business processes and their enabling technology, and they can gain value faster as a result of this service.

SAP Business Process Performance Optimization A service for improving the performance and throughput of SAP customers' core business processes.

SAP Business Strategy A service that assists customers in defining and setting the overall direction of their organizations to secure lasting success in highly competitive markets.

SAP Channel Partner Portal A central e-collaboration platform enabling SAP Channel Partners to exchange information and expertise and to conduct business transactions with SAP.

SAP Configuration A service that provides guidance and support in tailoring SAP solutions. SAP consultants analyze the customer's business processes and offer recommendations on how SAP solutions can best support and enhance them.

SAP Custom Development Part of SAP Services. Develops custom solutions that address customers' unique and competitive business requirements.

SAP Customer Competence Center (SAP CCC) Ensures the stable operations and continued development of SAP solutions. SAP CCCs focus primarily on central functions such as operations, support, training, information management, and contract processing. An SAP CCC is a company's central point of contact for all queries pertaining to SAP; it also provides a link to SAP, especially to Service and Support.

SAP Data Volume Management A service package for optimizing a company's data volume and archiving strategy.

SAP Developer Network (SDN) An SAP NetWeaver-based portal providing information specifically for developers and consultants, with a focus on current and future technology.

SAP Development Consulting A service that offers support and consulting for developing and integrating customer-specific applications for SAP solutions. It provides the knowledge and experience to successfully plan and execute high quality custom developments to meet the customer's specific needs.

SAP Development Maintenance Services An SAP service offering that provides maintenance options for customer-specific developments.

SAP Development/Prototype Hosting Sets up and runs a tailor-made prototype with customer data to evaluate SAP solutions. The prototype can be integrated easily in the actual system landscape at a later date.

SAP Development Review A service that determines whether the application design meets the customer's business needs. SAP

consultants focus on the status and thoroughness of the development of interfaces, conversions, reports, forms, and enhancements.

SAP Development Services An SAP service offering that provides development services to deliver customer-specific solutions.

SAP EarlyWatch Alert A proactive service for analyzing systems. It runs regularly and automatically in the background in the customer system and gathers performance data. It is used as a basis for service level reporting in → SAP Solution Manager.

SAP EarlyWatch Check A proactive service for analyzing systems. It is more in-depth than → SAP EarlyWatch Alert and provides more detailed results.

SAP Ecosystem A community of SAP customers, partners, and SAP that exchanges information and collaborates closely. For this purpose, SAP provides a high-performance service and support infrastructure that comprises → SAP Service Marketplace and → SAP Solution Manager.

SAP Empowering A portfolio of services, training, mentoring, and Best Practices. It provides organizations with the knowledge and skills needed to support and enhance an SAP solution optimally.

SAP Empowering workshops Special training courses that communicate specialized information for running and continually optimizing SAP solutions, and that complement SAP's standard training offering.

SAP Evaluation Hosting Provides and operates a suitable temporary system environment for solutions from mySAP Business Suite to accelerate the process of selecting software in the evaluation phase.

SAP Expertise on Demand A service providing additional SAP expertise to resolve problems that are not within the scope of → SAP Standard Support.

SAP Feasibility Check A Safeguarding service that analyzes business processes and the relevant components of the system landscape on the basis of an implementation blueprint. The service identifies risks and provides a plan for risk management.

SAP Feasibility Study A service that helps customers achieve their business objectives. SAP consultants understand the executive management's vision of the future, review the business goals, determine a high-level approach and the scope, cost, and timeline for the solution, and provide support to managers to help them make decisions easier and faster.

SAP Globalization and Language Consulting A globally available service that covers all aspects of globalization. SAP consultants assist customers with system architectures to support multiple countries, country-specific versions of SAP solutions, multiple time zones, multiple languages, translation tools, and code pages, including Unicode.

SAP GoingLive Check A service that minimizes technical risks that can arise during implementation projects.

SAP GoingLive Functional Upgrade Check An SAP Safeguarding service for preparing and carrying out upgrades.

SAP Help Desk A user help desk (customer service center) where problem messages are recorded, dispatched, and monitored centrally (incident management).

SAP Help Portal A web-based portal providing access to all the documentation for all SAP solutions and products.

SAP Hosted E-Learning Provides support for setting up and maintaining the technical infrastructure required for using e-learning concepts and the SAP Learning Solutions run by SAP Hosting.

SAP Hosting A 100 % subsidiary of SAP AG that provides comprehensive services allowing companies to access the latest solutions from mySAP Business Suite quickly and effectively. See also: → SAP Managed Services.

SAP HotNews SAP Notes with very high priority.

SAP Implementation Hosting Provides a tailored implementation environment for SAP solutions on a short-term basis and runs it reliably to ensure that projects start promptly.

SAP Interface Management A service for analyzing and optimizing interfaces that are required for core business processes.

SAP IT Assessment A service that enables customers to identify areas for IT and process improvement. It helps to reduce inefficiencies and costs that are associated with the IT infrastructure.

SAP IT Planning A service that enables the customer to create a feasible and efficient plan for developing an effective IT architecture. It builds on the results of the SAP IT Assessment service to help customers transition from an initial IT framework to a comprehensive IT strategy that supports their business goals.

SAP IT Risk Management A service that makes IT risks visible to the customer at an early stage in the project. SAP consultants define measures to mitigate the risks, which helps the customer achieve the project goals within budget.

SAP IT Service & Application Management An end-to-end description of the main operating and management processes that are to be applied in the lifecycle of a software application. It supplies operating standards and implementation methods that are based on the IT Infrastructure Library (ITIL) and have been enhanced by SAP.

SAP IT Strategy A service that helps customers design a global business-application landscape. Based on the customer's future business map, SAP Consulting defines a framework of all application systems, their relationships, and the technical architecture, as well as the appropriate IT management model.

SAP Knowledge Shop A catalog of knowledge products, such as books, brochures, and self-learning units that can be ordered online on SAP Service Marketplace.

SAP Legacy System Migration Workbench (LSMW) A tool for transferring data from any systems. The LSMW is not shipped with any predefined transfer procedures.

SAP List Viewer Conversion An SAP service that converts customer-specific ABAP list reports to SAP List Viewer.

SAP Managed Services Skills provided jointly by SAP Hosting AG & Co. KG and the Application Management & Hosting business area of SAP Systems Integration AG since January 1, 2005. The SAP subsidiaries offer globally scalable services for operations and support for all aspects of SAP and SAP-related systems over the IT lifecycle.

SAP Master Data and Content Management Consulting SAP Consulting offers a value-driven set of services to help customers define and implement enterprise data and content-management strategies. The services range from strategic to technical in nature and focus on enabling strategic sourcing, better customer relationship management, and operational excellence in manufacturing, logistics, and financial reporting and analysis.

SAP MaxAttention A special offering tailored to customer needs that provides support from SAP experts, as well as a comprehensive portfolio of support services. These services can be implemented throughout the course of the application management lifecycle according to the particular customer's situation.

SAP Modification Clearing An SAP service that identifies, analyzes, and, depending on the results, eliminates existing modifications, enhancements, and custom code.

SAP NetWeaver Development Services A group of customer-specific development services specializing in the SAP NetWeaver platform. Examples include creating custom composite applications and transferring business solutions to mobile devices.

SAP Notes Descriptions of solutions to known problems.

SAP Online Knowledge Products The most up-to-date information for implementing and running new SAP solutions or upgrades that are not yet available to all customers.

SAP Operations Competence Assessment A service for analyzing the support processes used by SAP

Customer Competence Centers or SAP customers.

SAP OS/DB Migration Check A service to safeguard the migration of operating systems or databases.

SAP Partner Directory A directory that lists all the SAP partners worldwide. It is located on SAP Service Marketplace.

SAP Partner Portal A portal that provides access to information and online services for SAP partners, excluding SAP Channel Partners, for whom a separate portal is available.

SAP Premium Support A new support offering that includes the following services in addition to those provided with SAP Standard Support: Service Level Agreements, regular analyses of the SAP solution, and a Support Advisor to act as a named contact person.

SAP Program Management A service that helps customers to achieve and optimize their program goals. SAP Program Management serves as a strategic enabler for large, complex programs involving SAP solutions. It addresses budget, time, resource, and quality constraints across multiple SAP projects or within a large, complex implementation project that has multiple components.

SAP Project Management A service that helps customers to reach their project goals on time and within budget and to meet or exceed their quality requirements. The result is a solution capable of achieving targeted business improvements. This service increases ROI by reducing implementation costs and allowing the customer to obtain business benefits sooner.

SAP Project Organizational Change A service that helps people to move away from their current way of thinking and working and to engage in new processes and systems. This service focuses on the effects that a new initiative has on managers and employees, and helps the organization respond in a timely manner.

SAP Project Review A service that determines whether the project scope meets the customer's business needs, ensures that appropriate goals, timelines, and milestones have been set, examines the project plans, and verifies that the plans are monitored. It also checks for sufficient management support for the project and determines whether the overall project and technical design is appropriate.

SAP Ramp-Up The process of introducing new releases to the market and therefore an integral part in the lifecycle of SAP software. The key objectives of the Ramp-Up phase are: feedback from the market (customers/field), a controlled increase in the number of customers, and qualification of the supporting SAP departments.

SAP Ramp-Up Hosting An element of SAP's Ramp-Up program that enables the IT infrastructure required for participation in the SAP Ramp-Up program to be used without having to use internal resources.

SAP Ramp-Up Knowledge Transfer A program and methodology for imparting the knowledge required when launching new SAP products (Ramp-Up phase). The program promotes a holistic learning model, the practical application of new information, and support in the event of problems. It has a strong focus on scalable, online learning methods.

SAP Remote Applications Operation The 24x7 support and remote assistance provided by SAP specialists for customer systems.

SAP Remote Performance Optimization A service designed to prevent performance and throughput problems.

SAP Risk Assessment A service that helps to identify and assess significant IT-related business risk by analyzing the IT processes and IT components that support the customer's key business processes. The assessment reveals the potential impact on the business and proposes steps to mitigate the risk.

SAP Safeguarding A portfolio of services comprising proactive checks that determine risk factors and recommend appropriate solutions. Customers can use the checks as required for their individual situation, with a focus on minimizing TCO of their SAP solution.

SAP Safeguarding for Implementation A range of services designed for implementation projects with the goal of minimizing technical risks in complex and mission-critical projects or solutions.

SAP Safeguarding for Solution Improvement Services for reducing technical risks while a solution is in operation.

SAP Safeguarding for Upgrade A range of services for minimizing the risks and costs involved in upgrade projects.

SAP Security Concepts and Implementation A service that enables customers to define and implement an enterprisewide information security policy. It ensures that users can access the information and applications they need while protecting operations from security threats.

SAP Service Catalog An Internet sales application that customers can access from SAP Service Marketplace to order services.

SAP Service Marketplace An Internet platform that enables collaboration among SAP, customers, and partners. SAP Service Marketplace and its portals give customers central access, with guided navigation, to the complete portfolio of SAP's service, collaboration, and information offerings.

SAP Services SAP's service organization.

SAP Software Distribution Center An area on SAP Service Marketplace where you can download patches and Support Packages, for instance.

SAP Software Shop A catalog on SAP Service Marketplace from which you can order SAP software.

SAP Solution Expert Consulting A service that ensures the successful completion of a customer's project by providing expert support, knowledge transfer, and ongoing evaluations. Dedicated consultants with extensive experience and direct ties to SAP development are available on site or remotely to ensure that the solution meets the customer's business requirements.

SAP Solution Implementation Consulting Consultants with knowledge and extensive experience in implementations collaborate with customers during all phases of the implementation, from project planning to requirements definition, business process design and data conversion, to user training and all aspects in between, utilizing SAP tools, methodologies, and Best Practices.

SAP Solution Management Assessment A Safeguarding service for analyzing business processes and the associated components in the system landscape in production operation. The service identifies problems and the potential for optimization.

SAP Solution Manager A central platform that integrates all the content, tools, and procedures for implementing and running SAP solutions. SAP Solution Manager helps customers to manage their complete solution landscape, including interfaces to non-SAP products.

SAP Solution Manager Starter Pack A service for configuring SAP Solution Manager. It also includes training.

SAP Solution Prototyping A service that implements a fully operational, limited-scope solution in the customer's production environment. It allows customers to ensure that their SAP solution is technically feasible and can be integrated well with their existing infrastructure before final deployment.

SAP Solution Review A service that determines whether the application design meets the customer's business need, ensures that appropriate goals, timelines, and milestones have been set, and determines whether gaps are sufficiently covered. SAP consultants also assess whether the application design is complete, flexible, efficient, effective, and maintainable, and they verify that all integration issues have been explored.

SAP Solution Testing A service that provides customers with an efficient and cost-effective test plan. It confirms and tests the integration of the software for each business process and validates end-to-end process testing and integration with non-SAP systems.

SAP Standard Support SAP's standard support offering. SAP Standard Support provides 24/7, worldwide message handling for very high priority messages, updates, and integrated support for SAP and partner products. It also includes SAP Solution Manager, access to SAP Service Marketplace, as well as selected proactive services aimed at improving the availability and performance of SAP solutions.

SAP Storage Subsystem Optimization A service for optimizing the database layout and the configuration of the storage subsystems.

SAP Strategic Organizational Alignment A service that enables customers to align their IT infrastructures with their strategic initiatives. Working closely with the top executives, SAP consultants help to define success criteria, develop key performance indicators to measure progress, and strategize for organizational development.

SAP Strategic Outsourcing Consulting Provides support for SAP customers who are outsourcing SAP-relevant components, solutions, and processes: request for bids, definition of Service Level Agreements and contracts, evaluation and optimization of the customer's existing outsourcing relationships that are relevant to SAP products.

SAP Support Academy A program that provides support-specific training and certification for service and support employees, as well as partners, sales partners, and customers who use the SAP Empowering program.

SAP Support Portal A portal providing information and applications for implementing, running, and continually optimizing SAP solutions.

SAP System Administration A service for analyzing the operation of your solution regarding interface design, database administration, recovery and backup procedures, and so on.

SAP System Architecture Planning This globally available service assists customers in developing an architectural plan that encompasses all aspects of the SAP NetWeaver platform, including its interaction with non-SAP systems and the technical aspects of the implementation project.

SAP TCO Analysis A service that provides detailed information about an IT project's actual costs. This analysis makes IT cost drivers and value drivers visible, explains the cost drivers, and recommends activities to reduce TCO.

SAP TCO Framework A framework for recording and analyzing the TCO for SAP solutions and for assigning analysis findings and cost-cutting measures. It contains SAP TCO Model, SAP TCO Reference Parameters, SAP TCO Database, and SAP TCO Reduction Processes.

SAP Technical Analysis and Design A service that specifies the technical architecture needed to support the functions identified in the overall solution blueprint. The SAP Technical Analysis and Design service helps reduce TCO by aligning the technology architecture with key business drivers from the outset.

SAP Technical Installation A service that ensures that the customer's IT environment is configured properly. Ongoing interaction with hardware and software partners streamlines the installation process and ensures long-term solution stability.

SAP Technical Integration Check A Safeguarding service that analyzes

business processes and the relevant components of the system landscape once the core business processes have been implemented. The service identifies problems and risks, particularly with regard to integration in the solution landscape, and highlights the potential for optimization.

SAP Technical Migration A service that enables a cost-effective and efficient transition to a new solution or technology. It helps move data from legacy systems to a new SAP solution, migrate operating systems and databases, or upgrade from older SAP technology.

SAP Technical Program and Project Management A service that addresses all technical topics within the entire project or program lifecycle. This service focuses on strategic, long-term engagement between the customer and SAP, with a strong emphasis on making the implementation and operation of IT solutions more efficient and cost-effective.

SAP Technical Review A service that determines whether technical documentation is being maintained properly and whether the change requests and Support Packages are being monitored and used as recommended. SAP consultants assess whether the system landscape has been designed properly, ensure that the production environment will run efficiently, and verify whether the customer's sizing needs have been met properly.

SAP Technical Upgrade Consulting A service that supports SAP customers on site in all phases of a technical upgrade of their SAP R/3, SAP R/3 Enterprise, and mySAP ERP systems. It is conducted in close cooperation with the SAP Active Global Support team.

SAP Test Data Migration Server (SAP TDMS) A solution that helps to create more manageable non-production systems that contain only a representative portion of production data, enabling you to keep a stable non-production landscape and refresh the system frequently with an extract of actual data.

SAP Test Management Optimization A service for reducing the expense and effort involved with testing.

SAP TopNotes The 10 most important SAP Notes for each component. A new list is compiled every month.

SAP Tutor A tool for creating, processing, and supplying interactive, electronic self-learning units.

SAP Upgrade Hosting Provides an infrastructure, operates a test system, and conducts the actual upgrade to increase the reliability of planning in upgrade projects.

SAP Value Measurement A service that enables customers to evaluate the business results of their solution after it goes live. Using proven methodologies and best practices, experienced SAP consultants analyze the value derived from the implementation and provide recommendations that allow the customer to use the solution to achieve targeted business objectives.

SAP Volume Test Optimization (VTO) A service for optimizing volume tests.

Second-Level Support Manages problems and provides support for users; also involves product manufacturers in third-level support.

Self Services Services that customers' users perform on their own.

Service Data Control Center (SDCC) A service tool that provides SAP customers with an up-to-date overview of those service sessions that have been held, and those that are yet to be held. It also controls data transfer between the SAP system and SAP.

Service Level Agreement Management/Service Reporting Central facilities for monitoring application management requests; the processing status of each request and the information the request contains are always transparent, because they are recorded centrally, using the service desk tool.

Service Level Management A function in SAP Solution Manager that is based on the SAP EarlyWatch Alert and enables customers to monitor the availability and performance of their SAP solutions.

Service and Support Infrastructure Comprises the two platforms → SAP Solution Manager and → SAP Service Marketplace. It provides access to valuable knowledge in the form of methods, tools, documentation, and services.

Sizing The definition of the hardware requirements for an SAP system, for instance, network bandwidth, physical memory, CPU utilization, and I/O capacity.

Support SAP support safeguards the operation of SAP solutions and ensures that customers' core business processes are improved continuously. It also helps to minimize the solution's TCO throughout its lifecycle.

Support Advocate/SAP Support Alliance Manager Contact persons in SAP Active Global Support who, through special support programs, establish close, collaborative relationships with the customer's support organization.

Support Enabling/Coaching Training, coaching, and knowledge transfer aimed at working with support organizations and SAP CCCs to define and establish effective support processes and an ideal support organization.

Support Package A set of software corrections made available on SAP Service Marketplace.

Support Process Consulting A service that provides support and coaching for organizing, structuring, certifying, and optimizing support organizations (SAP CCC).

Support Strategy Consulting A service for planning and establishing cost-efficient support structures for SAP solutions and for determining how much assistance a support organization should supply, including a "make or buy" assessment.

Support Tool Consulting Advice and coaching regarding the service and support tools, such as SAP Solution Manager.

System Landscape Design & Planning A service for defining the ideal system landscape in terms of process alignment, infrastructure, and availability.

System Landscape Optimization (SLO) A portfolio of services designed to improve entire processes—from business objects and applications to the harmonization of SAP system landscapes.

System Management & Monitoring (as Part of SAP Application Management) The monitoring of processes and system landscapes—

also following go-lives, migrations, and release upgrades.

Technical Quality Manager (TQM) A person who manages SAP's special, customer-specific support offering, SAP MaxAttention, at the customer's site.

Test Workbench A tool that assists you when organizing, monitoring, and evaluating your test results.

Training Catalog A catalog on SAP Service Marketplace that features the entire training offering. Courses can be booked online.

C   The Publisher

Gerhard Oswald is a member of the Executive Board of SAP AG, where he is responsible for global service and support. He is also a member of the Field Leadership Team, which oversees SAP's global sales, consulting, and indirect channels.

In 1981, Oswald joined SAP and immediately participated in the development of the SAP R/2 sales support network, where he was responsible for quality assurance. He then assumed management responsibilities for quality control in the critical SAP R/3 enterprise software development project. From 1987 until 1993, he was a member of the project management team responsible for the design, development, and delivery of SAP R/3.

In 1993, following the completion of this project, Oswald was named a member of SAP's Extended Management Board. In 1994, he assumed responsibility for the SAP R/3 Services division. Two years later, in 1996, he was appointed a member of the Executive Board.

After studying business administration, Oswald began his career at Siemens AG as an applications consultant for SAP R/2 business processes, a position he held from 1977 to 1980.

D   Acknowledgements

This book was made possible by the active participation and dedication of many contributors. Thanks are owed to each and every one of them for the time and commitment they somehow managed to find for this project, in addition to their daily activities. Below is an alphabetical list of all the participants, along with each chapter (or chapters) that they worked on.

▶ **Bauer, Kurt**, SVP, Knowledge Productization Services, Chapter 4

▶ **Eckert, Harald**, VP, Solution Ramp-Up, Chapter 6

▶ **Erhardt, Michael**, Product Management, SAP Active Global Support, Chapter 6

▶ **Fieres, Helmut**, Director of Programs and Infrastructure, SAP Active Global Support, Chapter 7

▶ **Frauenfeld, Dirk**, Project Manager, Service Solution Management, Chapter 5

▶ **Frey, Heiko**, Graphic Designer, Graphic Design

▶ **Gautier, Stéphane**, Service Solution Management, Chapter 7

▶ **Gerwing, Hans**, Project Director, SAP Custom Development, Chapter 6

▶ **Graf, Peter**, Executive Vice President, SAP Solution Marketing, Chapter 1

▶ **Grein, Birgit**, Project Manager, SAP Active Global Support, Chapter 5

▶ **Haller, Ulrich**, Knowledge Management Expert, Knowledge Productization Services, Chapter 4

▶ **Harder, Gerrit**, CCC Program Manager, Chapters 4 and 6

▶ **Hertwig, Hagen**, Service Portfolio Management Consulting, Chapters 4 and 6

▶ **Horak, Christian**, VP, Product Marketing, Chapters 1, 2, and 3

▶ **Huschke, Oliver**, Business Development Director, Chapters 4 and 6

▶ **Ippich, Sigrid**, Director, SMB Channel Operations, Chapter 7

▶ **Jakowski, Jürgen**, Product Manager, SAP TCO Framework, Chapter 8

▶ **Janitz, Lars**, Vice President, Application Management, SAP Managed Services, Chapters 4 and 6

▶ **Kähny, Falk**, Program Director, Service Solution Management, Chapters 2, 4, and 6

▶ **Kern, Luzian**, Portfolio Manager, Education, Chapter 4

- **Kochendörfer, Ulrich**, Marketing & Communications Manager, SAP Managed Services, Chapters 4 and 6

- **Koesegi, Armin**, Platinum Support Consultant, SAP Active Global Support, Chapter 6

- **Kravets, Jewgeni**, Business Development Manager, SAP SI AG, Chapter 6

- **Krückendorf, Andreas**, Chief Support Architect, Chapter 6

- **Lau, Oliver**, Service Architect, Chapter 4

- **Leja, Christian**, Service Business Development Consultant, Chapter 5

- **Luechau-de la Roche, Vivian**, Support Architect, Chapter 4

- **Luschtinetz, Bernd**, Product Manager, SAP Active Global Support, Chapter 7

- **Marschollek, Anja**, Marketing Specialist, SAP Custom Development, Chapters 4 und 6

- **Mattern, Thomas**, Solution Marketing Manager for ESA, Solution Marketing Platform ESA, Chapter 1

- **Melich, Matthias**, Director of Product Management, SAP Solution Manager, Service Solution Management, Chapters 2 and 7

- **Moeschwitzer, Georg**, Director of Product & Program Management, SAP Managed Services, Chapters 4 and 6

- **Mohr, Andreas**, Online Marketing Specialist, Global Partner Management, Chapter 7

- **Odabashian, Mary**, Director of Marketing and Communications, SAP Custom Development, Chapters 4 and 6

- **Plattner, Bernhard**, Solution Specialist, Service Solution Management, Chapters 1, 3, and 6

- **Preidl, Gregor**, SAP CCC Program Director, Chapters 4 and 6

- **Purkart, Thiemo**, Service Business Development Consultant, Chapter 3

- **Rademann, Cay**, Senior Product Manager, SAP Solution Manager, Chapter 7

- **Rasig, Holger**, Vice President, Global Partner Engagement, SAP Managed Services, Chapter 4

- **Reimesch, Jörg**, Program Manager, Solution Ramp-Up, Chapter 6

- **Ress, Anthony**, Field Services Program Director, Chapter 6

- ▶ **Rink, Martin**, Product Manager, SAP Active Global Support, Chapter 7

- ▶ **Rückert-Daschakowsky, Ute**, Shared Services, SAP Active Global Support, Project Lead and Editor

- ▶ **Schatz, Wolfgang**, Support Architect, Chapters 4 and 6

- ▶ **Schepanek, Dirk**, Program Director, Service Business Development, Chapters 4 and 6

- ▶ **Schöler, Sabine**, Program Director, Service Solution Management, Chapters 4 and 6

- ▶ **Schulze, Sabrina**, Knowledge Management Expert, Knowledge Productization Services, Chapter 4

- ▶ **Schulzki, Bernhard**, Vice President, Business Systems Services, SAP Managed Services, Chapter 4

- ▶ **Schwandt, Michael**, Program Director, SAP Developer Network, Chapter 7

- ▶ **Speicher, Susanne**, Platinum Support Consultant, SAP Active Global Support, Chapter 4

- ▶ **Thier, Marc**, VP, Technology Support, Chapter 4

- ▶ **Timm, Axel**, SAP Empowering Program Manager, Chapters 4 and 6

- ▶ **Wachter, Sabine**, SLO Product Manager, Chapters 4 and 6

- ▶ **Wagner, Thomas**, Expert Technical Support Consultant, Chapter 7

- ▶ **Wegener, Heinrich**, Product Manager, Chapter 7

- ▶ **Weitzel, Jens**, Director of Market Development, Business Process Outsourcing, Chapter 4

- ▶ **Wuennemann, Jürgen**, Principle Consultant, SAP SI AG, Chapter 6

- ▶ **Welz, Bernd**, SVP Service Solution Management, Chapters 1, 2, and 3, book concept and review

- ▶ **Willumeit, Andreas**, Director of Strategic Field Enablement, SAP Education, Chapter 4

- ▶ **Wittern, Svend**, Director of Strategic Field Enablement, SAP Consulting, Chapters 4 and 6

- ▶ **Wittig, Thomas**, SVP, SMEA & Partner Services, Chapter 3

- ▶ **Zeier, Frederike**, Product Management, SAP Active Global Support, Chapter 6

- ▶ **Ziemen, Thomas**, VP, Service Solution Management, book concept and review

Index

Comprehensive details on the new capabilities of mySAP ERP

Expert insights and best practices to ensure a successful upgrade

In-depth analysis of the technical infrastructure of SAP NetWeaver and ESA

293 pp., 2006, US$ 59,95
ISBN 1-59229-071-X

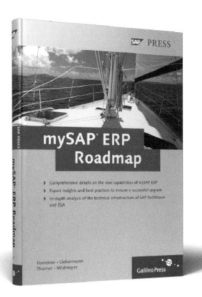

mySAP ERP Roadmap

www.sap-press.com

F. Forndron, T. Liebermann, M. Thurner,
P. Widmayer

mySAP ERP Roadmap

Business Processes, Capabilities, and Complete
Upgrade Strategy

Finally, a book that delivers detailed coverage of the
functionality and technology of mySAP ERP, and
provides you with a clear, simple and comprehensive
path to your upgrade. This book introduces you to
the business processes supported by mySAP ERP and
helps you understand the evolution from SAP R/3 to
mySAP ERP. You get exclusive insights into the
technical infrastructure of SAP NetWeaver and the
Enterprise Services Architecture, all designed to help
you hit the ground running. Through clear decision
criteria, practical examples, and Transition Roadmaps, readers will uncover the optimal path from
SAP R/3 to mySAP ERP. This book is an invaluable
resource to support your upgrade decision.

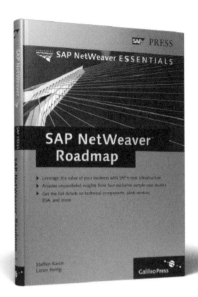

SAP NetWeaver Roadmap

S. Karch, L. Heilig, C. Bernhardt, A. Hardt, F. Heidfeld, R. Pfennig

SAP NetWeaver Roadmap

This book helps you understand each of SAP NetWeaver's components and illustrates, using practical examples, how SAP NetWeaver, and its levels of integration, can be leveraged by a wide range of organizations.
Readers benefit from in-depth analysis featuring four actual case studies from various industries, which describe in detail how integration with SAP Net-Weaver can contribute to the optimization of a variety of essential business processes and how the implementation works. Finally, detailed coverage of SAP NetWeaver technology gives you the complete picture in terms of architecture and functionality of each component.

Sizing and Availability of
Platform, Storage, Memory,
and Network Infrastructure

Adaptive Infrastructures
and SAP Adaptive
Computing Controller

Service Level Agreements,
IT Service Management,
and TCO

534 pp., 2005, US$ 79,95
ISBN 1-59229-035-3

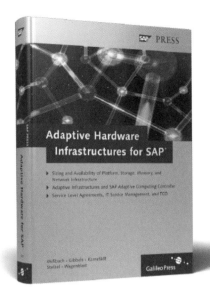

Adaptive Hardware Infrastructures for SAP

www.sap-press.com

M. Missbach, P. Gibbels, J. Karnstädt, J. Stelzel,
T. Wagenblast

Adaptive Hardware Infrastructures for SAP

Constantly changing business processes pose a
critical challenge for today's hardware. In order to
conquer this challenge, companies must respond
quickly and in a cost-effective manner, without
risking the future safety of their infrastructure. This
unique new book helps you to understand the most
important factors for determining what hardware you
'll need to support flexible software systems in the
months and years ahead. Plus, discover the ins and
outs of exactly how SAP systems support your
business processes. In addition, you'll benefit from
highly-detailed insights, essential for helping you
calculate your true Total Cost of Ownership (TCO).

Rapid ROI by use
of efficient systems

Optimization of architecture,
business processes and support

Including first-hand
information on NetWeaver
system landscapes

220 pp., 2004, US$ 79,95
ISBN 1-59229-026-4

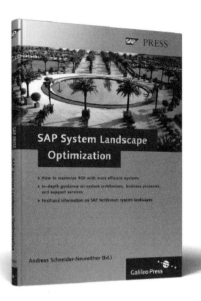

SAP System Landscape Optimization

www.sap-press.com

A. Schneider-Neureither (Ed.)

SAP System Landscape Optimization

This reference book serves as an essential collection
of insights, procedures, processes and tools that help
you unlock the full potential of your SAP systems.
First, hit the ground running with a detailed introduction to SAP NetWeaver and the mySAP Business
Suite. Then, elevate your mastery of key concepts
such as system architecture, security, Change and
Transport Management, to name just a few. All of
the practical advice and detailed information
provided is with a clear focus on helping you guide
your team to achieve a faster return on investment.

Practical Solutions to streamline 24/7 operations

Advice to conquer your biggest change management challenges

Service Level Agreements, disaster recovery, security, and more

355 pp., 2004, US$ 79,95
ISBN 1-59229-025-8

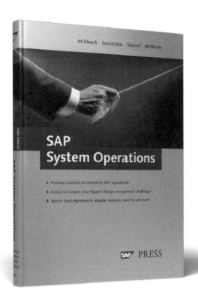

SAP System Operations

www.sap-press.com

M. Missbach, R. Sosnitzka, J. Stelzel, M. Wilhelm

SAP System Operations

With system landscapes becoming increasingly more complex, administering them efficiently is proving equally difficult. This unique new book provides you with concepts and practical solutions that will enable you to optimize your SAP operations. Get in-depth information to set up a viable Standard Operation Environment (SOE) for SAP systems, as well as time-saving tips for certification and validation of your system landscape. Plus, benefit from and customize the numerous examples and case studies extracted from the worldwide operations of many large SAP customers.

Interested in reading more?

Please visit our Web site for all
new book releases from SAP PRESS.

www.sap-press.com